MAP
ADDICT
MIKE PARKER

912

A TALE of OBSESSION, FUDGE & THE ORDNANCE SURVEY

Collins

Collins
An imprint of HarperCollins*Publishers*
77–85 Fulham Palace Road,
Hammersmith, London W6 8JB

www.harpercollins.co.uk

First published by Collins 2009
This edition published 2010

1 3 5 7 9 10 8 6 4 2

Text © Mike Parker 2009

Mike Parker asserts the moral right to
be identified as the author of this work

A catalogue record for this book
is available from the British Library

ISBN: 978-0-00-735157-2

Designed and typeset by seagulls.net
Printed and bound in Great Britain by
Clays Ltd, St Ives plc

Mixed Sources
Product group from well-managed
forests and other controlled sources
www.fsc.org   Cert no. SW-COC-001806
© 1996 Forest Stewardship Council

FSC is a non-profit international organisation established to promote the
responsible management of the world's forests. Products carrying the FSC
label are independently certified to assure consumers that they come
from forests that are managed to meet the social, economic and
ecological needs of present and future generations.

Find out more about HarperCollins and the environment at
www.harpercollins.co.uk/green

CONTENTS

To Rachel.
At last.

INTRODUCTION

Recently, some new neighbours moved in. They'd trekked halfway across the country, from the fringes of Manchester to their new life in our small village in the mountains of mid-Wales. One night, I was showing them a good local walk, using my well-worn Ordnance Survey Explorer Map (OL23 *Cadair Idris & Llyn Tegid*, for aficionados). 'Oh, yes,' one of them mused. 'That reminds me, I must get a map of the area.'

I swear the world stood still. What I wanted to say was, 'You mean, you moved here from over a hundred miles away *without buying a map first?* Without taking it out on a nightly basis, stroking its contours, gently murmuring the unfamiliar names, idly following with your finger footpaths and streams, back lanes and bridleways, feeling faintly, randomly intimidated by the angular blocks of plantation forestry and sumps of squelchy moorland, excited by the wide beaches, towering peaks, nestled lakes and market towns, all spread beguilingly across the paper? Without enjoying the thrill of anticipation of your impending move to a whole new world? Without checking out that whole new world, as captured by the gods of the Ordnance Survey? *Are you mad? What the hell is the matter with you?*'

What I actually said was, 'Oh, right. They sell them in the bookshop in town.'

If my cowardly internalised rant had you mentally nodding in agreement; if you like to check the map before a trip to B&Q; if you can sit and read a good map like others read *Hello!* or *Heat*, then this book is for you. You are a fellow-mappie, we are of one flesh. If, on the other hand, it's got you thinking, 'What a ridiculous over-reaction: what's his problem, then?' I'd advise you to put the book down now and walk away from it before it begins seriously to annoy you.

△

Many children have imaginary friends to help offset a lonely world. I had imaginary towns instead, and they were all intricately mapped. Hours would dribble by as I sat, tongue slightly protruding, drawing detailed plans of these fictional fiefdoms, giggling quietly to myself as I named the streets, threw in a ring road or bypass – this was the 1970s, after all – and methodically placing schools, stations and hospitals into the growing grid.

Any careers psychologist, observing this habit (especially the relish with which I'd drive a new dual carriageway through anything), would have predicted with utmost confidence that I was destined to become a town planner. But it wasn't the towns or the buildings or the streets themselves that interested me – just the maps. It didn't matter that they were imaginary; any map, any reduction of a complex landscape into two clean, clear dimensions, somehow thrilled and comforted me. More than thirty years on, it still does.

While some people, to shut out the insistent thrum of life, slide into the well-worn addictions of drink, drugs, sex, shopping, tattoos, piercings, plastic surgery, food or slicing themselves, my route of escape has long been thrusting my head into a map and staying there until the deafening buzz recedes. When all else around you is going psychotic, you can still depend on a map, and some of us can waste happy hours lost in its calm infallibility. Even the crisp smell of an Ordnance Survey provides its own instant Rescue Remedy.

My name is Mike and I am a map addict. There, it's said. I'm the one in the car with the map in his lap, following its route with rapt concentration and a slowly moving index finger – often at the expense of seeing the actual landscape it depicts rolling past on the other side of the window. I'm the one who, on buying my first house, moved my entire map collection into it and ensured that it was perfectly shelved in its new home before bringing in anything useful, such as a kettle, toaster or teabag. I'm the one who will annoy anyone I'm sharing a flight with by repeatedly jabbing at the window and telling them which town we're flying over, just because I recognised its shape and road pattern from decades of idle map scrutiny (and by the same token, I'm now the one losing whole days on Google Earth). It's me who'll spend longer planning a walk than actually doing it, who has to get the map out to go to the shops, who actually enjoys those interminable conversations about which route we all took to reach wherever we are, who can recognise the symbol for a bridle track or lighthouse (disused) at forty paces, whose favourite childhood show was *The Wombles*, simply because the little recycling furballs took their names from Great Uncle Bulgaria's atlas. Actually, that's not quite true. My favourite childhood show was *Ivor the Engine*, which combined a distinctly mappish sensibility with its exotic setting 'in the top left-hand corner of Wales': two of my passions deliciously stirred by one antique animation.

At the age of six, I began my own map collection, kick-started by a joyous discovery. My first true love was found lurking in the cellar when we moved into a new house. Not only was it my first love, it was my first cellar, full of spiders and dusty promise. The previous owners had left various bits of tat below stairs which were pure treasure trove to me. A peeling mural of the *Sergeant Pepper* album title, painted by their adolescent son, filled one wall. I had no idea what it was or what it meant, but it oozed cool and teenage pheromones. But the true object of my affections lay hidden, covered in cobwebs, in the back of a dusty alcove. A relief map of the West Midlands and Wales, a good three foot by two, carved out in brittle plastic, its moulded hills soaring. It was love at first sneeze.

There was the sinuous line of the River Severn winding its way up through the Worcestershire towns I knew so well. The Malvern Hills, punting proudly out of the flat plains, looked like the brassiere of some

'50s Hollywood starlet, all swaggering panache and perky promise. Like a spreading ink stain, the big pink blotch of Birmingham and the Black Country seemed in danger of engulfing the little flecks of urban outposts surrounding it, my own home town included. And Wales looked so different, and so very foreign. Where the English side of the map was a mass of pink splotches and a tangle of roads ancient and modern on a landscape that barely rose to any noticeable toy height, Wales was dark, brooding and rippled with mountains that soared and plunged in mysterious plasticity. Tiny settlements, hardly any of which warranted any pink stippling, peeked out from valley floors and river confluences. The crags of Snowdonia, by far the largest and lairiest on the map, shot skywards and soon began to lose their markings, so often did I stroke their peaks in eager anticipation of the day when those little plastic bumps would become real to me.

Hours I spent in rapt contemplation of that map. I memorised the look and shape of the conurbations, of Bristol, Stoke, Chester, Coventry, Cardiff, Brum, Manchester and Liverpool, so that I could recognise them, like a psychiatrist's inkblot test, in an instant. I ran my finger appreciatively along river courses, feeling the way the Mersey, Wye or Dee bubbled down from the hills, along ever-widening valleys before disgorging into the smooth blue expanses of estuary and sea. But nothing approached the tactility of the Welsh hills, whose come-hither bumps and lumps kept inviting me back for more.

Before long, I'd started to save my pocket money in order to buy maps, the fuchsia pink Ordnance Survey 1:50 000 series in particular. My step-mum donated an old sewing box with a padded hinged lid for my burgeoning collection, and it followed me everywhere, even on day-trips to bemused relatives. But there were 204 of the bloody things to collect, and on a fairly meagre allowance, it was painfully obvious to me that it would take decades to finish the job, an unimaginable yawn of time to a youngster. As a result, maps even accounted for the modest zenith in my teenage shoplifting career. While my mates were nicking records, sweets or fags, I was making regular forays into the Midland Educational Bookshop in Worcester to fill my school bag with bright, gleaming Ordnance Survey maps.

It was way too easy. While eagle-eyed shop assistants kept close watch on the pens and pads by the till, it was as free as a supermarket trolley dash in the ill-lit, dusty corner where the maps lived. My routine seemed foolproof. Like most fourteen-year-olds of the time, my school bag was a long sports effort with a large zip going the full length. Before entering the shop, I'd unzip it and wear it over my shoulder, with my arm held around it, keeping it apparently shut. I was never so stupid as to go straight to the maps; instead, I'd weave a tortuous route under the shop assistant's eye, picking over fountain pens and ink cartridges, ostentatiously examining maths textbooks, Bibles and anything else that I thought would make me look like some useless swot or a pillar of virtue. While the shop assistant was busy serving someone, I'd dive into the far corner where a huge stand of OS maps sat beckoning. By now, my heart was thumping in my throat, school bag at the ready, unzipped, on the floor. I knew in advance which maps I wanted, and restricted myself to no more than five at a time – well, I didn't want to be greedy. With a sleight of hand that would have impressed Paul Daniels, I picked the maps in question and swept them with one movement into my bag, covering them with school files or my football shirt. Then I'd get one map off the stand and noisily open it out to examine with rapt attention. Equally ostentatiously, I'd fold it back up again and replace it in the stand. Leaning down to pick up my school bag, I'd quickly zip it up again and hurry towards the till, smiling as casually as I could. Usually, I'd buy a pencil, a biro, a rubber, a cheap book or a sheet of Letraset, just to throw the assistant off the scent, before escaping back into the street with relief and euphoria flooding through me after yet another successful cartographic heist.

As a result of my regular larceny in the Midland Educational Bookshop, my Ordnance Survey collection grew exponentially in a very short space of time. I restricted my looting trips to no more than once a week, although, in what I thought at the time was a genius stroke of alibi-building, I'd nip into the Midland Ed at other times and flagrantly avoid the map corner altogether. But once a week, the urge for more maps, of more areas, would hold me in its vice-like grip and I'd be in there and seizing the whole of Cornwall or Norfolk in one greedy swoop.

My parents and their mates benefited hugely from my map rustling. By the time I was fifteen, I was the unofficial map library to half of Kidderminster. If anyone was heading off for a weekend in Aberporth or a trip to Auntie Ethel's in Godalming, it was me they came to for ideas on planning the route and getting the appropriate maps. Little did these upstanding citizens realise that they were handling stolen goods.

Maps have punctuated every twist and turn of my life. During the mental meltdown of early teenage years, my happiest times were spent in the company of my grandmother, touring the Midlands in an aged Ford Corsair with map on my knee and no idea where we were going. I'd be given carte blanche with the navigation, and would take us off down lanes that, from the map, looked worthy of a snoop or which led to places with odd or amusing names. Without knowing it, we were early psychogeographers, conducting our *dérive* with a flask of tea and a tin of boiled travel sweets. We'd pop into churches, shops and pubs, peer over walls and fences, engage vicars and batty old ladies in conversation, throw sticks in rivers, drive down country roads that looked, from the features on the map, as if they'd afford a bit of a view. When they did, my gran would congratulate me on my map-reading skills and I'd glow with pride and satisfaction, sensations all too rare in my hormonal hothouse.

Many of those trips were anchored by the Fosse Way, the great Roman highway that shoots like an arrow from Lincoln to Exeter. My grandparents lived in Leamington Spa, a short hop away from the Fosse. For most of its course through Warwickshire, the Fosse Way was a B road at best, and unclassified for large parts, despite being fast, straight and well surfaced. With hardly anyone else on it, it was our own private highway to all points north and south, a short plunge into the Cotswolds or the red-brick huddles of Leicestershire. Just north of the village of Halford, in the south of Warwickshire, the Fosse Way changes, in the course of less than half a mile, from an unclassified road (yellow on the OS), through a lightning-brief incarnation as the B4451 (brown), to a fully fledged major road, the A429 (red). I can still recall the electricity of anticipation the first time I spotted this coming up on the map a few miles on. Would this freak three-coloured road show its differences on the ground? I proudly told my gran of my discovery and, to her eternal credit, she showed as much enthusiasm as I did, telling me to let her know when we were crossing the invisible lines. 'We're going on to the B road ... NOW!' I hollered, finger almost through the map in excitement. Thirty seconds later, we were at the roundabout where the Fosse transforms once again, this time into a main road, and I was sated. The anomaly has, of course, been ironed out since. No longer is that Warwickshire stretch of the Fosse a gloriously underachieving, knock-kneed road only for those in the know. It's all B and A now, and doubtless to be heard on every satnav's monotonous recommendation.

Thirty years on, I find it faintly odd that I have far clearer memories of the way the map looked than practically any other part of those glorious days out, rambling purposelessly but fired with adventure. Even if I only go back twenty years, there's a bit of a theme emerging: a month's InterRailing with a college mate has almost all been excised from my memory save for total recall of the Thomas Cook *Rail Map of Europe* circa 1988. A decade further yet, I've got a sneaking suspicion that I moved to mid-Wales in part response to a map I'd been given as a present a year or two earlier, of *The Railways, Telegraphs, &c of Great Britain Engraved Expressly For The A. B. C. Railway Guide* from 1859. Black threads squirm their way across the country in lavish loops and race-for-the-line competition. Around London, Manchester and the coal seams of south Wales and Yorkshire, the knot of rails threatens to choke the living daylight out of the cities and towns. It's called a map of Great Britain, but Scotland is sliced off at Aberdeen, so that the one patch of virgin purity, unblemished by angry lines, is the interior of Wales. There's not one track between Brecon and the Nantlle quarries at Snowdon, nothing west of Oswestry or Leominster. A dotted line of vague intent ambles to Llanidloes, but that's it. The gaping maw on the map pulled me in as I stared at it above my desk, and way before I really knew why, I had upped sticks to the sticks, a tiny mountain village on the edge of the Snowdonia National Park. It was either that map or a delayed reaction to *Ivor the Engine*.

My obsession with maps has even given me a strange sort of career. After leaving university, I lasted less than two years in proper jobs, before the urge to take to the open road with an Ordnance Survey took hold and launched me as a travel writer, producing guide books to the West Midlands, Greater Manchester, Greater Glasgow and Bristol/Bath, and then into the stable of Rough Guide authors. My main work for them was as co-author of the brand new Wales book, though I also wrote various chapters of the early editions of the books on Scotland and England. Most people, on discovering that I was a travel writer, would look insanely jealous, up to the point where I told them that I was writing about Barmouth and Birmingham, rather than Bermuda and Barbados. 'Couldn't you get anywhere decent?' was the stock response. But for me, it was the dream job, and remains so to this day: I love travelling abroad, but, as a writer, have only ever wanted to specialise in the amazingly diverse landscapes and culture of our own islands. Helped, of course, by the maps: my devotion to British mapping, the Ordnance Survey in particular, is so unyielding that exposure to foreign maps leaves me feeling disoriented and slightly perturbed by their inexactitude, harsh colours and inappropriate symbols.

For six years now, I've been writing and presenting offbeat travelogues for Welsh television that have allowed me to be as pedantic, opinionated and map-obsessed as I like. Gratifyingly, it's been the more finicky features on maps, their nomenclature, borders and often strange history that have culled the biggest reaction and audience figures. And not just from gentlemen with fussy little moustaches, either (although there have been a fair few of them, truth be told). There's a lot of us out there, moustachioed or otherwise.

Maps not only show the world, they lubricate its easy movement. On an average day, we will consult them dozens of times, often almost unconsciously: checking the A–Z, the road atlas or the satnav, scanning the tube or bus map, doing a quick Google online, flying over a virtual Earth, navigating around some retail behemoth on the hunt for a branch of Boots, watching the weather forecast, planning a walk or a trip, visiting a theme park or stately home, conference centre or industrial estate, catching up on the news, booking a holiday or hotel. Maps pepper books, brochures, advertisements, web pages and newspaper and magazine articles: we barely notice them because they do their job so well. They represent practically every area of human existence, conveying, at a stroke, precise information, not just about layout and topography, but history, politics, priorities, attitudes and power. They are the unsung heroes of life, and I want to sing their song.

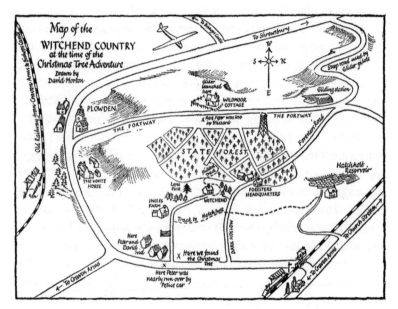

Malcolm Saville's frontispiece map for Wings Over Witchend

1. TREASURE ISLAND

'Very well,' said Uncle George. 'But before you set out we must discover if you can really find your way by the map. You can have a great deal of fun from a map, you know,' he added. 'Especially when it comes to life!'

Joanna seemed quite startled to hear this.

~ H. J. Deverson and Ronald Lampitt,
The Map that Came to Life (children's book from 1948)

Not for us British the wilderness, the outback or the week-long journey on the wide open road. Although folk have gamely tried it, there's not much of a heroic tale to be told or heart-wrenching ballad to be wrung out of getting your kicks on the A66. The American or Australian relationship with their landscape is a world away from ours. They grab their beers and their buddies, before heading out into the gaping yonder for adventurous rites of passage, laced with deadly wildlife and treacherous topography, under skies that scorch the red earth by day and, by night, fill with fire-sparks twirling lazily into a canopy of stars. How many books, movies, TV series and songs have we all sat through that have ploughed that well-worn furrow? And what's our equivalent? We go for a nice drive or a bit of a walk on a Sunday afternoon, through a landscape as tame as a tortoise, perhaps take in a stately home or a mouldering ruin, a country pub if we're feeling rakish. If we really want to push ourselves to the limits of desolation, we might pop on our walking boots, pack some sandwiches and a thermos, and tackle ten miles, and a bit of a stiff climb, in the Peak

District or the Lakes – sometimes going so far off the beaten track that we could be as much as half an hour from the nearest cream tea. A landscape that has been so thoroughly explored, so comprehensively mapped and so exhaustively written about just isn't going to throw up any life-threatening challenges. This is not Marlboro Country; it's Lambert & Butler Land. And that's exactly how we like it.

The map, spread lovingly over our knees, is the key to unlocking our interaction with what we nobly like to think of as our Great Outdoors. We set out, secure in the certainty that we are using the finest maps in the world: an index of all things possible, albeit all things measured, calibrated and recorded in painstaking detail. There may be no beasts to grapple with and precious little wilderness to explore, but we are quite happy to take our pleasures in far less sensational, less melodramatic ways. Nothing compares with the joy of setting off, not quite knowing where you're heading, with just a map and a faintly heady sense of adventure to guide you. Sometimes, a nearby name, a shape or a symbol will leap off your Ordnance Survey and demand closer inspection.

On those lovely long childhood explorations in my grandparents' Ford Corsair, where I'd be sat in the back precociously barking out navigation orders from behind a map, I can still recall the frisson of excitement that coursed through me on spotting, just outside the Warwickshire village of Long Itchington, a thrilling label on the OS: *Model Village*. These worlds-in-miniature, one of the many idiosyncratic gifts from the British to the rest of humanity, are a near-religious experience for the budding young map addict, and we can all remember our childhood visits to Babbacombe, Tucktonia and Bekonscot, or the much less impressive examples often found wedged between the crazy golf course and a candy floss stall in almost every seaside resort. Off we careered in that Ford Corsair in pursuit of the Long Itchington Model Village, even if none of us had ever heard of it before, which should perhaps have tinkled a distant alarm bell. As we got nearer, my excitement rocketed. 'Next left!' I hollered eagerly from the back seat.

My gran obediently swung into – oh – a cul-de-sac of drab semis, with a distinctly ordinary county council street sign telling us that this was, indeed, named THE MODEL VILLAGE. It was a small estate built to house workers in the adjacent concrete works. Not a toy train or a miniature town hall in sight. I was deeply disappointed, quite cross and ever so slightly ashamed.

It's no coincidence that the model village is an almost entirely British phenomenon. Bekonscot, the first and still the finest, has been bewitching its visitors since the 1920s, and still pulls in tens of thousands a year even now, despite being utterly devoid of things that bleep or flash. In fact, that's its main draw these days: the perfect encapsulation of a long-vanished Enid Blyton England, all stout ladies cycling and butchers in aprons (Blyton was one of Bekonscot's biggest fans, and even produced a book, *The Enchanted Village*, about it). It's not just the miniaturised characters that appeal; it's the whole experience, even that of arriving. You have to park up in an adjoining car park shared by a small supermarket and a church, then walk down a leafy path to find Bekonscot rooted in a residential side street. As you amble contentedly around the model village in what was once a suburban rockery garden, the stout precincts of Beaconsfield peer over the sensible fences. This Tom Thumb Albion seems so perfectly at home here, steadily, reliably plodding on with the minimum of fuss and the maximum of quiet pleasure.

Mapping and model villages are very British bedfellows. The gentle enthusiasts who created these places, and the generations that keep them going, have all spent long hours mapping their pretend worlds, giving every wood, road, cove, islet and cluster of tiny buildings a name and a whole back history. There's a curiously devout idealism at work, a desire to create a better, brighter world, even if it's only for characters just a couple of inches high. Bekonscot's founder, Roland Callingham, approached his creation with much the same zeal as his contemporary Clough Williams-Ellis. To Callingham, the fact that his kingdom was miniature and Clough's, at Portmeirion, was (almost) life-sized and for real people made little difference. It was, as Clough put it, a 'light operatic' approach to town planning and design, but there are deadly serious principles at work here too: that humour and grace have a central role to play in our built environment, and will bring out the best in its inhabitants if employed well.

A growing map addiction dictated my juvenile reading habits too. I was inescapably drawn to children's literature that set itself in places that I could find on the map, places that were unambiguously British, whether it was a real Britain or a parallel, fictional one. The appeal of the books soared even higher if they started with a map of the part of the country in which they were set, and there was no shortage of these. At the local library, I scythed through the Malcolm Savilles and Arthur Ransomes, devouring each one in just a day or so, despite the hours spent flicking back and forth between whichever part of the story I was in and the frontispiece map that glued it all together. I'd find the real maps of the areas concerned, and thrill at what the author had included from the actual topography, and what had been a figment of his imagination.

I wish I could say that it was the Arthur Ransome books – *Swallows and Amazons* et al. – that I loved the most, but no. They were too gung-ho for my rather prissy tastes, with way too much boat-building, pirate-dodging and nautical heartiness. Wild water was a largely absent element in the life of a Midlands schoolboy of the 1970s and '80s: even the most vivid of imaginations would have had trouble conjuring up Lake Windermere, Coniston or the Norfolk Broads, let alone the high seas, out of our local oil-slicked canals, where you were infinitely more likely to see a dead dog floating by than a home-made raft. I wish I'd taken more to his books because, for starters, they are far better written than anything by Malcolm Saville, and because Ransome himself was such a fascinating character. Recent papers released by the National Archives reveal that he was a spy and possibly a double agent during the Russian Revolution, that he wrote passionately pro-Bolshevik articles for liberal newspapers and managed to get a divorce in the 1920s in order to marry Trotsky's private secretary, whom he later brought back to the Lake District; they are buried together in the little churchyard at Rusland, near Windermere. Before his hurrah-for-the-Empire children's books, he'd written a biography of Oscar Wilde and numerous articles that revealed his proud Bohemianism. Unless I was missing some deeply buried subtext, you really wouldn't know any of this from the simple tales of youthful derring-do that later made him famous.

Sadly, I was much more of a Malcolm Saville kind of boy. By comparison, Saville led a life of unyielding rectitude, informed by a muscular Christianity, a towering snobbery and unquestioning acceptance of the need to obey authority in whatever guise it came. His books were relentless in promulgating these attitudes: policemen, teachers and vicars were always honest and right; anyone who wore a camel coat or dropped their aitches was guaranteed to be a no-good 'un. I lapped them up: although it was partly that I preferred mystery-solving capers to high-seas adventure, the main reason for my choice was, as ever, the maps. Arthur Ransome's were lavish and lovely, but they were of parts of the country that I neither knew at all nor cared much about. Worse, they seemed ineffably childish, transforming real places into pretend River Amazons, Pirate Islands and Rio Grande Bays, even placing an imaginary Arctic and Antarctic on a plan of what I knew to be a small part of the Lake District. Malcolm Saville, on the other hand, set his stories in some of my favourite places and mapped them with far more appealing realism: those I knew well, like the Long Mynd in Shropshire or the area around Whitby and the North Yorkshire Moors, as well as those I was fascinated by and aching to see, such as the East Anglian coast or Rye and Dungeness on the border of Kent and Sussex. The stories were entirely secondary to their locations and the maps that showed them.

Enid Blyton was a gateway drug to the works of Malcolm Saville, for her books were full of the same jolly adventures in the boarding school hols, the same cast of picaresque ne'er-do-wells, the same crashing morality and class system carved in granite. Mallory Towers was a guilty, girly secret; I could take or leave the Faraway Tree and the Secret Seven, but I devoured the Famous Five books time and again. Saville's Lone Pine Club members and the Famous Five seemed entirely interchangeable: they were led by identikit sensible boys with side partings, and each had an Amazonian sidekick who hated her girl's name and insisted on a male equivalent – Peter (Petronella) of the Lone Piners, and every lesbian friend's first pin-up, George (Georgina) of the Famous Five, with her licky dog, Timmy.

At the age of seven, I worshipped the Famous Five, even if their books suffered from one huge omission. There were no maps, no official sanction of the geography of Kirrin Island, Mystery Moor and all the other places I wanted desperately to believe in. I even resorted to drawing my own, but I knew that they would never feel like the real deal. Where were these places? There was a vague feeling and a few hints that the Famous Five's romping ground was somewhere in the West Country, but Blyton managed to be sufficiently coy when pressed on the matter. That, though, hasn't stopped the congenial Isle of Purbeck in Dorset from staking its claim as her muse and setting, and, to be fair, it has a good case. Blyton and her husband had many connections to the district, holidaying three times every year in Swanage's Grand Hotel and swimming every day in the sea, doing a circuit around the town's two piers before dinner. They became honorary residents of the district, Enid making it to president of the Swanage Carnival committee, while her husband, Kenneth, bought the Purbeck Golf Club in 1950. The impossibly cute – and congested – village of Corfe Castle, sheltering beneath its famous ruin (Kirrin Castle, apparently), promotes itself as the capital of Blyton country, with the Ginger Pop shop in the main square full of memorabilia, her books, old-fashioned sweets in jars, toys that no modern child would countenance playing with and the inevitable ginger beer. It is said that the PC Plod character in her Noddy stories was based on the village bobby at Studland, which, even in her day, was famous for its nudist beach; Blyton herself is reputed to have gone *au naturel* there. Thank God the Famous Five never stumbled across it.

In every Saville and Blyton, the format, like the countryside, was reassuringly constant. Everyone would converge for the hols, with aunties that only ever baked or knitted hoping that their charges weren't going to get into any scrapes this time, before some funny-looking, funny-sounding strangers arrived in the area to cause mayhem and a minor crime wave that only a gang of hoity-toity children could possibly solve. I, and millions of other small children cooped up in suburban bedrooms, longed for a life as action-packed and exciting, but it never came. Not for want of trying: I went through a phase of combing our local weekly paper, the *Kidderminster Shuttle*, for crimes to which I could turn my well-read investigative powers. (The *Shuttle*'s fine name, by the way, comes from the moving part of a carpet loom, in honour of the local industry. The acrid tang of carpet dye hung over the town for most of the year, beaten only in the winter months by the sickly smell from the sugar-beet refinery. It was a long way from breezy Dorset, or even the gloomy heights of the Long Mynd, just thirty-five miles down the road.)

One week, the *Shuttle* reported a break-in at a coach depot a few streets away. I persuaded my step-brother to join me on a nocturnal raid on the place, to look for 'clues'. It was only when we hoiked ourselves over the gate and landed in the depot yard that it dawned on me that I wasn't too sure what a 'clue' actually looked like, so we picked up everything, just in case. Weeks later, I found the soggy ball of old bus tickets and fag ends in my coat pocket and realised that we hadn't managed to solve the crime, despite the bundle of crucial evidence. But at least we'd given the depot yard a nice tidy.

Malcolm Saville's frontispiece maps were always purportedly drawn by David Morton, the leader of the Lone Piners. Sixteen-year-old David didn't speak much, but when he did, everyone listened and invariably agreed with him. He was strong of jaw and firm of friendship – and he could draw a great map. Whether I was aching to be him, or be with him, I'm not quite sure, but I took to drawing my own maps that, like David's, were a hybrid of the real and the imaginary. It was fun improving upon landscapes that I knew, adding in a haunted mansion to replace the golf club, putting in a new railway line, upgrading the parish church to a cathedral, spitefully taking out streets that I found depressing or ugly: there was plenty of choice in 1970s Kiddy.

Logically, I should have ended up as a dorkish (or perhaps Orcish) devotee of J. R. R. Tolkien, for the maps of his vast fantasy landscapes were an essential part of their appeal. Furthermore, Tolkien was a fellow Midlander who'd loved his maps, drawn his own and become fascinated by the otherness of nearby Wales: it was seeing the coal trains, emblazoned with the names of Welsh mines, rumbling through his Birmingham suburb that had first inspired him to enter the world of linguistics, and, to this day, there are those who are convinced that the ethereal gobbledegook of Elvish was based on the Welsh language. Some claim too that his maps of Middle Earth were inspired by the topography of mid- and north Wales, fuelling a popular insinuation, best expressed by A. A. Gill, arch-cynic about all things Welsh, that 'everything [in Wales] that wasn't designed by God looks as if it was built by a hobbit'. But Tolkien left me colder than a Mordor winter: why invent such elaborate landscapes with such daft names when there were so many fine ones to be had in the real world?

This peculiarly British habit of drawing elaborate maps of fantasy landscapes is perhaps one element of our colonial hangover, for it's not dissimilar to the way in which we first mapped the real world. Almost all advances in cartography in the eighteenth and early nineteenth centuries came as a result of our imperial adventures, when British ships plied the four oceans and brought back news – and beautiful new maps – of far-off lands to a wide-eyed population. Although many of the voyages were for trade or for battle, the public interest was more sensationally stoked by the expeditions that set out to fill in the blank parts of the globe, a globe over which Britons were becoming ever more confident of their supremacy. So much of the world was known by now, and it was the bits that remained a mystery – particularly the polar regions and the 'dark heart' of Africa – that inspired most fervour, among the public as much as the participants.

It was all done in a joyously British way: with bags of enthusiasm, a smattering of snobbery, a conviction that we knew best and a healthy dose of hit-and-hope optimism. There were many notable victories, but rather more ignoble defeats, to punishing climates, unheard-of diseases and locals who were not as pleased to see the explorers as the latter rather thought they should be. Along the way, the explorers would draw their charts and maps, loyally naming rivers, mountains, creeks and even delirium-induced optical illusions after minor royalty and government officials back home. It wasn't so far in spirit from those of us who mapped and named our imaginary towns a century and a half later.

Public hunger for news of these expeditions was nigh-on insatiable, and newspaper and periodical editors swiftly realised that an accompanying map of distant conquests was worth a thousand words and produced a sizeable hike in sales. Although the Ordnance Survey had been in existence since 1791, it was run solely as a military arm of the government – quite literally, a Survey for the Board of Ordnance, an ancestor of the Ministry of Defence. Their starchy approach was of little interest to the general public and the press, who far preferred the maps of commercial cartographers. The finest ever seen in Britain were by John Bartholomew & Son of Edinburgh.

There's always a tendency to conflate British and English achievements, though it should be even more stridently avoided than usual in terms of mapping, for both Wales and, to a far greater extent, Scotland had cartographic ambition of their own. Edinburgh, especially, became one of the great centres of map-making during the eighteenth and nineteenth centuries. Bartholomew's, with its distinctive, blue-covered maps, was the ultimate traditional Edinburgh family firm. Founded by the first John Bartholomew in 1826, the baton was passed down from father to son, each one also called John, until the death of the fifth John in 2008 finally ended the distinguished line. Although the Bartholomew name continues in the mapping division of Collins Bartholomew, it is not as a company that any of the Johns would much recognise. In the 1970s, John the Fifth, together with his brothers Peter and Robert, had, for the first time in a century and a half, brought new blood from outside the family into the company's management structure. The new blood rather turned on them, forcing the sale of the company to Reader's Digest in 1985, and thence to News International. It was a terminal move. In truth, though, the end had been steaming towards Bartholomew's at great speed, for it had slightly lost its path and was in no state to survive the tidal waves of the Thatcher revolution.

It was a long way from the glory years. John the First (1805–61), like his father a jobbing engraver of exceptional ability, had begun to specialise in maps. His were quite gorgeous: the precision of his engraving on the copper sheets created maps of unprecedented accuracy and detail, far better than anything the Ordnance Survey were producing at the time. His first published map, the 1826 *Directory Plan of Edinburgh*, was lavish and lovely. Looking at it now, what is most remarkable is how little this monumental city has changed in nearly two centuries; aside from the markets and narrow closes cleared for the building of Waverley station, you could easily use it to steer yourself around today.

John the First's Edinburgh was a cauldron of high artistic and scientific specialism, producing the best reference materials in the world. Out of it came not just Bartholomew's, but the *Encyclopaedia Britannica*, *Blackwood's Edinburgh Magazine*, *The Scotsman* and the publishing houses of Constable and A. & C. Black. Just around the corner from John's first works was the printing shop of brothers William and Robert (W. & R.) Chambers, later to become mighty publishers of dictionaries and other reference works. Edinburgh was a hotbed of all kinds: the Chambers brothers habitually slept under the counter of the shop, in order to fight off the regular nocturnal raiders.

The firm grew in a typically modest, rather Scottish way: modestly yet steadily. In his first year of business, John earned a total of £78 16s 6d, and by the time of his death in 1861, when John Junior took over the reins, they had about twenty employees and an annual wage bill of over a thousand pounds. John Junior, and his son, John George, combined cartographic excellence with canny business acumen; Bartholomew's boomed. In that, it had considerable assistance from the mood of the times: maps were the hottest new property and the public had a seemingly insatiable appetite for them. The explosion of the railways was chiefly responsible, from the need for lavish plans and prospectuses to be presented to government and as an incentive for investors, right through to their completion, and the public's desire to see where these new steam beasts could take them. Each copper sheet would have to have the appropriate parts beaten out on an anvil and re-engraved with the new railway, but it was worth every bit of trouble to the map-makers, for the results flew off the shelf.

Then there was the steam revolution on the seas too, necessitating maps of the growing number of commercial and military liners ploughing the oceans, as well as maps of the mystery lands now reachable from the ports of Southampton and Liverpool. The growing Empire needed mapping, while in Britain itself there was the rapidly changing electoral map of a country that was grudgingly allowing more and more people to participate, and, before long, the first leisure maps for those who wanted to pedal into the countryside of a Sunday on their

trusty boneshaker. Bart's also created new markets, particularly of world atlases, for both adults and children. As Rudyard Kipling commented in an address to the Royal Geographical Society in 1928, 'as soon as men begin to talk about anything that really matters, someone has to go and get the Atlas'. Bartholomew's reacted to each opportunity with relish and speed, and considerable aesthetic élan.

For the firm's trump card was not its tight-knit family fortress and sensitive ear to the ground, but the sheer poetic beauty of the maps. As can be seen in the fine Scottish example in the colour section, Barts' maps were simple, yet packed with information but never too crowded: everything *just so* (in a Morningside accent). Its most famous original feature was the use of colour shading between contours, through a spectrum of greens for the lower ground, browns for the middle, purple and finally white for the snowy peaks. Bartholomew's did the same in the areas of sea, with bathymetric contours of ever-darker shades of blue to indicate the deepening fathoms. Although this became a common cartographic tick, no one ever did it better than the company that first introduced it in 1880, and it remained Bartholomew's signature until the final maps limped out just over a century later. This was thanks to perhaps the greatest John, number three, John George (1860–1920), who was utterly obsessive about colour harmony, and not just on his maps. When postage rates rose from a penny to a penny halfpenny, he despised the shade of brown adopted for the new 1½d stamp, and insisted on using a penny red and a halfpenny green instead.

In the nineteenth century, the cartographic establishment was a fearsome beast, and it didn't take well to the rather dour, shy Scotsmen and their surprisingly flash commercial ways. The firm resisted takeovers and mergers, even from John George's relative by marriage, map-maker George Philip of Liverpool. The first great map mavericks, they refused to countenance the business leaving the family, or even leaving Edinburgh. They were also notoriously poor of health, and often ascribed some of their business success to this very fact, for they believed that disabled people made the finest cartographers, if only because they were less likely to move around so much, and were thus able to maintain the extreme concentration demanded by the job.

Bartholomew's most celebrated map – the *Times Atlas* excluded – was its Half Inch series, originally marketed as the Reduced Ordnance Survey, before the government's own map-makers forced them to drop the practice and later the Copyright Act of 1911 outlawed it. God-fearing, sober and unable to come up with any name more exciting than John they may have been, but they weren't averse to some fierce self-promotion, if it sold one more map. When, in the early 1890s, John George moved the company into a splendid new building by Holy-rood Park, he grandly christened it the Edinburgh Geographical Institute. Less impressively, it was located on a street called the Gibbet Loan, which John George felt detracted from its address. No problem if you're the city's most revered map-maker, however. He simply changed it on the next map of Edinburgh to the altogether more elegant, if anodyne, Park Road, the name by which it is still known, and mapped, today.

It was through the blue Half Inch series that I was first introduced to Bartholomew's as my map addiction flourished through the 1970s. They had a striking but slightly old-fashioned quality to them, and I quickly came to associate them with the bookshelves of elderly relatives and the smell of beeswax. I was Mr Now in my map choices, an enthusiastic consumer of the brand new metric OS sheets in their dazzling pinky-purple covers. Thanks to the soft poison of nostalgia, now that they're no longer produced, I find Bart's maps absolutely charming, and can admire their clarity, precision and use of colour for hours. In their heyday just prior to the First World War, they outsold the Ordnance Survey's own Half Inch by at least ten to one, so far eclipsing them that the OS eventually killed their own series and focused instead on the one-inch scale. Bartholomew's was outshone in its turn too, eventually. Sales started to dip badly throughout the 1970s: after all, why buy a host of separate maps, when each one costs nearly as much as a road atlas of the entire country at a scale that is only slightly less? The Bartholomew list was trimmed extensively in the 1980s, with only popular tourist areas such as the Lake District and the south-west peninsula getting updated. Even that wasn't enough to staunch the haemorrhage of sales, however, and the whole series was quietly pensioned off at the turn of the final decade of the twentieth century.

On the international stage, Bartholomew's finest hour came in its production of the mighty *Times Atlas of the World*, still regularly cited everywhere as the finest atlas available. There had been two previous editions, in 1895 and 1900, published by *The Times* newspaper in London, before Bartholomew's came on board in 1920 and transformed the book into the beautiful ogre we now know and love. Even in these days of such intricate online mapping, the *Times Atlas*, with its enormous pages and crystal-clear cartography, is more than maintaining its value, and is likely to do so long after other paper maps have been blown away.

If the *Times Atlas* has shouldered all global opposition out of the way by dint of its sheer heft, Britain's other great cartographic icon is a world-beater thanks to its skin-and-bone sparseness. Harry Beck's 1933 plan of the London Underground is admired and emulated across the globe as a masterstroke of simplicity, a map stripped of all surplus information, conveying only the necessary, and with great efficiency and elegance. Beck realised that, once you were on the tube, your real geographical position was of no great consequence; all you needed to know were the names and orders of the stations and where the lines intersected. To that end, all surface features, save for the River Thames, were cleared from the map. There was uproar in September 2009 when the river too was deleted; populist city mayor Boris Johnson harrumphed his demand for its re-instatement. The episode, and particularly the ill-informed and sometimes bad-tempered debate that it sparked off, rather demonstrated that the myth of Beck's map has overtaken its reality.

In fact, as a nation, we're obsessed with this map, more so than it perhaps deserves. Don't get me wrong; it's good, very good indeed, even if it's not been quite right ever since 1991, when they dropped Bank station down a bit to merge with Monument and the new Docklands Light Railway extension. Not only did this consign to the bin the legendary ⌐ 'escalator link' between Bank and Monument, it committed the unpardonable sin of kinking the hitherto ruler-straight Central Line, which used to shoot from Ealing to Mile End, right along Oxford Street, like a bright red harpoon, before veering sharply north into Essex – see what we've lost in the colour section. At least, I suppose, it's saved generations of inquisitive twelve-year-olds from the crushing anti-climax that I experienced when, on a family trip to London, I peeled off to go and investigate the 'escalator link' at Bank–Monument, something that had long intrigued me on the map. Imagining some futuristic subterranean world of travelators and quite possibly a teleportation pod or two, I was cruelly disappointed to find instead a long, dank corridor and a small, clanking escalator.

Woe betide anyone whose adoration of Harry Beck's tube map encourages them to attempt any kind of homage to it. In 2006, a self-confessed tube geek produced a quite inspired version of his own, each station faithfully rendered into an accurate anagram. Some were strangely apposite: Crux For Disco (Oxford Circus), Sad Empath (Hampstead), Written Mess (Westminster), Swearword & Ethanol (Harrow & Wealdstone) and the faintly creepy Shown Kitten (Kentish Town). Some were plain daft or bawdily Chaucerian: A Retard Cottonmouth (Tottenham Court Road), Pelmet (Temple), Burst Racoon (Barons Court), This Hungry & Boiling (Highbury & Islington), Wifely

Stench (East Finchley) and Queer Spank (Queens Park). His map lit up the internet, getting over 30,000 hits in the first few days. And then the lawyers muscled in. If you Google it, you will find it, but only after coming across numerous pages telling you: 'Content removed at the request of Healeys Solicitors acting on behalf of Transport for London and Transport Trading Ltd.'

Transport for London, whose predecessors paid Harry Beck just ten guineas for his original work, have been more than happy to license the tube map for an unholy array of tacky souvenirs. The anagram map's creator has publicly stated that he doesn't want any payment for it, but he wants it to be freely distributed. The idea has been picked up by artists the world over for their own transport systems. But still TfL are attempting to excise the map from cyberspace, a task only marginally less futile, and impossible, than trying to push toothpaste back into the tube. The map is a wonderful work of art: humorous, striking, colourful, beautiful. It makes Simon Patterson's much-lauded, Turner Prize-nominated *Great Bear*, a Beck map where the stations are replaced with the names of artists, writers and composers, look very limp indeed. Patterson's original was bought by the Tate, and limited prints have been snapped up for tens of thousands, by Charles Saatchi among others. It has made an awful lot of money, with full support from TfL. But then they do get 50 per cent of the proceeds, which – on the bright side – at least means that not all of their lawyers' fees to pursue pointless causes have to come from the money you paid for your Travelcard.

It's no coincidence that the two most lionised British maps, each dripping with myth and adoration, subjects of a glut of books, blogs and websites, are Harry Beck's tube map and Phyllis Pearsall's London *A–Z* (on which, more later). Despite the shrill claims of cities like Birmingham and Manchester, London remains our only true metropolis, effortlessly swatting away the pretensions of its minions. These two iconic maps are the fine line that separates experiencing the capital as either a cosmopolitan labyrinth of untold possibility or a coruscating pit of hell. Their overblown status in the story of our national cartography corresponds to the status of the city itself: if it happened in London, even if *only* in London, it is per se of nationwide significance. Although such self-regard drives us all mad in 'the provinces', we wouldn't have it any other way, for who wants a capital city without a cocky swagger in its step?

There are many rather quieter examples of the best of British mapping. Harry Beck might be the patron saint of Hoxton bedsit bloggers, but for the cagoule crowd further north, the great god is Alfred Wainwright and his hand-drawn guides to the Lake District. To his legion of devotees, Wainwright represents all that is best about the stoic determination of the English fell-walker, and his precise Indian ink drawings, maps and text written in a hand that never wavered are possibly the finest an amateur has ever produced. In 1952, he decided to embark upon a series of books, carving the Lakes into seven distinct areas that encompassed all 214 fells (hills), and worked out, with pinpoint precision, that it would take him fourteen years. The last book was duly published, bang on time, in 1966. To achieve his goal, he spent every single weekend, come hell or – more often – high water, walking alone, drawing and note-taking in the mountains in collar, tie and his third-best tweed suit. On Monday morning he would return to work as the Borough Treasurer of Kendal Council, coming home to spend every evening shut away in his study, painstakingly writing up his notes of the previous weekend's hikes. Small wonder that his wife Ruth walked out on him just three weeks before his retirement in 1967.

Wainwright became something of a reluctant celebrity in the 1970s and '80s, playing up to his curmudgeonly image by rarely granting an interview unless the would-be interviewer trekked north to see him. Sue Lawley, for *Desert Island Discs*, perhaps wished she hadn't bothered, for Wainwright was sullenly taciturn throughout the programme. The tone was set right at the outset, when she asked him, 'And what is your favourite kind of music, Mr Wainwright?' To which he gruffly answered, 'I much prefer silence.'

He had started so well: his first book, *The Eastern Fells*, published in 1955, was dedicated to 'The Men of the Ordnance Survey, whose maps of Lakeland have given me much pleasure both on the fells and by my fireside'. Those first seven books bristle with dry humour and an encyclopaedic eye for the crags, lakes and wildlife of his adored, adopted Cumbria (he was raised in Blackburn). In later years – and, as we'll see, in something of an all-too-common pattern for map addicts – the dry humour evaporated into brittle bigotry. In his final book, a 1987 autobiography called *Ex-Fellwanderer*, he let rip with his loathing of women and how he advocated public executions, birching, a bread and water diet for all prisoners and the castration of petty criminals and trespassers. As ever, such miserly chauvinism was underpinned by a blind, blanket nostalgia. 'These were the bad old days we so often hear about,' he wrote. 'But were they so bad? There were no muggings, no kidnaps, no hi-jacks, no football hooligans, no militants, no rapes, no permissiveness, no drug addicts, no demonstrations, no rent-a-mobs, no terrorism, no nuclear threats, no break-ins, no vandalism, no State handouts, no sense of outrage, no envy of others ... Bad old days? No, I don't agree.' Strangely enough, at the other end of England, Harry Beck was descending into similarly obsessive and reactionary views in his latter years.

Like most egomaniacs, I can hardly listen to *Desert Island Discs* without mentally working on my own list for the programme. Save for a few dead certs, my choice of eight pieces of music is forever changing, but the candidate for my eternal book (aside from the Bible and *Complete Works* of Shakespeare) is blissfully simple and steady. Well, I've got it down to the final two, both map-related: the *Reader's Digest*

Complete Atlas of the British Isles from 1965, and, pre-dating it by a year or so, the AA's *Illustrated Road Book of England and Wales*. Map addicts often reveal themselves on *Desert Island Discs*: plenty, including Joanna Lumley, Matthew Pinsent and explorer Robert Swan, have chosen a world atlas as their book; David Frost picked a London *A–Z*. Best choice, though, was that of Dame Judi Dench, who confirmed her place in the pantheon of National Treasures when she chose 'an Ordnance Survey map of the world' as her book in 1998.

Both of my choices are beautiful works, but I love them mainly for being such remarkable snapshots of a very specific moment in time. They are graphic, lavishly detailed pictures of the world into which I was born at the tail end of 1966. No one knew it then, but they represent a world on the cusp of fundamental cataclysm. Our industrialised island, crammed full of mines and quarries and factories and railways, was shortly to become a post-industrial place of shopping centres, theme parks, light industrial estates and speedy roads. Nineteen-sixty-six was the border between those two worlds, the year that saw both the last, gruesome gasp of the old order at Aberfan, and the sapling stirrings of our future economy, a leisure industry kick-started by the English victory in the football World Cup. It was the beginning of the era when the future ceased to be the national fetish, to be replaced, ultimately and ominously, by a slavish obsession with the past.

The battle between the future and the past raged through the late 1960s and the entire 1970s, through psychedelia, sexual liberation, student uprisings, strikes, power cuts and punk, but by the time the 1980s dawned, the past had won. Margaret Thatcher, the Grantham grocer's daughter, invoked the Britain of a bygone age to anaesthetise us to everything, from small colonial wars to her battle to destroy organised labour. Nostalgia became a driving force of the economy: the backdrop to the breakneck changes that we choose to remember is 'Ghost Town' and Orgreave, but it could just as easily have been the multi-million selling *Country Diary of an Edwardian Lady* or the spin-off frills and frou-frou by the likes of Laura Ashley. The landscape, and hence maps, began to change too: town centres, the mercantile heart of the nation for over a thousand years, wilted in the heat of the new retail parks that were mushrooming alongside new bypasses and motorways. Heritage centres, heritage railways, industrial heritage, history denuded of its scandal and gore, erupted all over the country like a pox rash.

Just how much Britain has changed in a couple of generations is witheringly evident from these two books. The *Reader's Digest Complete Atlas of the British Isles* is a huge tome: 230 A3-sized pages of maps, charts, diagrams, illustrations and tiny text showing the geography of these islands in every imaginable detail, social, cultural, industrial and political, a generation on from the end of the Second World War. The book was a mammoth undertaking: the committee of consultants, listed on the second page, comprises 118 individuals and organisations, from the Ministry of Power to L. P. Lefkovitch, BSc, of the Pest Infestation Laboratory in Slough; Professor H. C. Darby, OBE, MA, PhD, LittD, to Éamonn de hÓir (a mere MA) of the Ordnance Survey, Ireland. It includes a loose-leaf insert designed to promote the book, a document that oozes 1960s paternalism at its most lordly. On one side, three experts (two of whom sport florid Edwardian moustaches) sing the volume's praises; on the other is a long list of questions, the answers to which can be found on pinpointed pages of the atlas.

'Do you know ...' it asks, as if peering beadily at the reader over its half-moon glasses, 'how long a Queen Ant lives? (page 110)'. Hurry to page 110, and there's your response: 'ten years'. 'Where the Moscow-Washington "Hot Line" enters Britain? (page 151)'; 'Which was the first stretch of motorway to be built in Britain? (page 147)'; 'Where the first known human in Britain dwelt? (page 77)'; 'The rate of air traffic at London Airport? (page 144)'; and 'On what date the Earth is farthest from the Sun? (page 90)'. The answers being: Oban; the eight and a half miles of the Preston bypass in 1958; Swanscombe in Kent; every two and a half minutes in summer, three and a half in winter; and July 2–4.

Another section headed 'Where in the British Isles ...' continues with such questions as: '... did dinosaurs live? (page 74)', '... are there oil wells? (page 153)', '... are the most crimes committed? (page 134)' and '... do they say "mash the tea"? (page 123)'. That'll be Dorset, Nottinghamshire, Greater London and (oddly) Flintshire, and finally, most of the Midlands and north of England.

The book is a pub quiz of gargantuan proportions. Every page has you tutting in surprise and oohing in wonder, and occasionally laughing at the chest-puffed earnestness of it all, the world as seen from the gentlemen's clubs of SW1. According to the atlas, not only do we 'mash the tea' where I grew up, we say 'I be ...' rather than 'I am ...', drop our aitches, call a funnel a 'tundish' and get as pissed as an askel, rather than a newt, all of which was news to me. The most wildly diverse regional expressions seem to be for the concept of left-handedness, or keck-handedness as we had it in Worcestershire (that I do remember). Just be grateful you're not left-handed in the Pennines (dollock- or bollock-fisted), Durham (cuddy-wifted), Galloway (corrieflug) or Angus (kippie-klookit).

The Britain of 1965 was a nation still toiling and grafting and knowing its place. A double-page map of 'Birthplaces of Notable Men and Women of the Past' indicates that most of our Notable People seem strangely to have originated in the south of England: there are as many given for Somerset as for the whole of Wales (the Welsh notables, of course, do not include anyone successful only in a Welsh capacity; to warrant inclusion, they must have made it big in London or the Empire, such as Lloyd George, T. E. Lawrence 'of Arabia' and H. M. Stanley). And absolutely no one of worth, at least to a Reader's Digest editor, has *ever* emerged from Westmorland (the only English county in this ignominious list), Anglesey, Merionethshire, Cardiganshire, Carmarthenshire, Radnorshire, Flintshire, or the old Scottish counties of Wigtown, Kirkcudbright, Berwick, Peebles, West Lothian, Argyll, Bute, Kinross, Stirling, Kincardine, Banff, Nairn,

Inverness, Ross and Cromarty, Sutherland, Caithness, Orkney or Shetland.

Of all the things that have most changed in the forty years since the atlas's publication, the transport routes it portrays are the most pronounced. The infant motorway network comprised only four open routes (the M1 from Watford to Nottingham, the M2 bypassing the Medway towns and Sittingbourne, the M6 from Stafford to Preston and the reverse L of the M5/M50 from Bromsgrove to Ross-on-Wye); an optimistic map of the network to come fills in the gaps. The fact that the M5 and M6 were tarmac reality before the M3 and M4 harks back – as the map so prettily demonstrates – to the original numbering system for British A roads, where the country was divided by spokes radiating out from London. The A1 went straight up to Edinburgh, the A2 to Dover, so that all main roads between the two were numbered A1x or A1xx. The A2s were between Dover and Portsmouth, the A3s a long tranche right to the far end of the West Country, the A4s a giant wedge that took in most of the Midlands and Wales, the A5s everything between the lines from London to Holyhead and Carlisle, and the A6s the remaining backbone of England, back round to the A1. The last three numbers – A7, A8 and A9 – are Scottish-only roads that were similarly centred on Edinburgh. I'm half expecting to hear from some indignant Welsh radical demanding a couple of the numbers to be re-apportioned to Cardiff.

On the opposite page of this plan for the future is a rather starker image of the past, in the shape of the railway network that, by the mid-1960s, was contracting fast. Much as I squirm at the admission, I know that if I could magically transport myself into another age for a week, it wouldn't be for a bystander's view of the Battle of Hastings or the Last Supper, but seven glorious days, probably in May, trundling around Britain's pre-Beeching railway network. From the very first day of my infatuation with the Ordnance Survey maps of the 1970s, it was the text reading 'Course of old railway' that most caught my eye, next to those spectral dashed lines tiptoeing their way across the country-side like the slug trails of history.

Sumptuous though the atlas is, for sheer page-turning wonder to pass the time under my palm tree, the AA's *Illustrated Road Book* would probably have the edge as my final desert island choice (spending the rest of my days with a product, however good, of the Reader's Digest couldn't possibly be cosmically healthy). The key word is 'Illustrated', for the England and Wales book, and its companion tome to Scotland, are dotted with the cutest little pen-and-ink drawings of interesting things to see. Every double-page spread has a gazetteer of towns and villages on one side, and five or six drawings from these places on the other. The England and Wales volume is more than five hundred pages long; there are well over two thousand illustrations. As if that wasn't enough, the whole country and scores of towns and cities are exquisitely mapped by Bartholomew's.

In the mid-1960s, 'places of interest' were not, for the most part, the things that brown tourist signs point to these days. After all, back then there were no theme parks, designer-outlet shopping malls or fully interactive heritage experiences. Instead, the book presents a dizzying array of interesting houses, churches, memorials, ruins, wind-mills, stones, bridges, carvings, gargoyles, inns, follies, tollbooths, plaques, graves, wells, even trees, topiary, maypoles and mazes. The illustrators had a particular fondness for unusual signposts, whether pointing down country lanes to oddly named hamlets like Pity Me, Come To Good, Bully Hole Bottom, Pennypot, Wide Open, Cold Christ-mas, Fryup, Wigwig, Land of Nod, Make Em Rich, New York (Lincolnshire), Paradise, Underriver, Tiptoe and The Wallops, or city street signs such as Leicester's Holy Bones, Hull's Land of Green Ginger, and Whip-ma-whop-ma-gate in York. Other unusual signs illustrated in the book include a warning of a 1 in 2 gradient on a road outside Ravenscar, one declaring 'Road Impassable to Vehicles of the Queen Mary Type' at Bampton in Oxfordshire, and one on the A35 near the kennels of the East Devon Hunt stating 'Hounds Gentlemen Please'.

It all sounds wonderfully archaic, a feast of nostalgia, but in fact the vast majority of the things featured and illustrated in this substantial book are still there. They may sometimes be a little overgrown or hard to find, but that's part of the joy in searching them out. I've not found any more up-to-date book that is so comprehensive in its sweep through the weird and wondrous features of the British landscape, and it's still the first guide book into my camper van when I head off to amble around part of the country, particularly if it's an area I don't know too well. It has steered me to many memorable encounters with places and objects that represent the soul of this country, introduced me to some fascinating people and given me countless shivers down my spine as I come face to face with things I half expected to have vanished. That's the crux of it: this book makes me feel part of a long, unbroken continuum of travellers, pilgrims and folk who just love poking their noses into their own – and others' – back yards to root around for the truffles of our national identity. Many of these pilgrims are long gone, but the spirit of their modest adventure lives on, and it will outlive any of us. I've known this book for decades, for my grandparents, both also gone, had a copy that I spent many quiet hours contemplating, and I was overjoyed to find my own in a second-hand bookshop in Presteigne. It still has the price – £8 – pencilled on the first page; truly the finest eight quid I've ever spent. If I could calculate the number of hours I've spent combing its pages, it would easily run into several hundred, yet every time I open it, I still find something brand new that I want to go and see immediately.

Alone on my desert island, the maps, descriptions and little sketches of the country I'd loved and lost would be a terrific condolence. The British landscape, a patchwork of astonishing variety spread over a comparatively small area, is the perfect antidote to any malaise of the spirit; I am sure that for almost any condition of the heart or

Bampton, Oxon. Unusual road
sign on the Faringdon road,
A4095
[For BANBURY see following plate

Balsham, Cambs. A quaint thatched house, with a projecting gable

PLATE 15 (facing page 168)

Bampton, Devon. Tablet on the outside wall of the Church

Baldock, Herts. The Wynn almshouses (1621) the
original endowment of which was to the
'World's End'

Bainbridge, Yorks. A Wensleydale village, with an extensive green

Bakewell, Derbys. The carved Saxon cross
in the churchyard

The country as captured by the artists of the 1960s AA Illustrated Road Book of
England & Wales

head, there is a landscape to soothe and calm, or invigorate and inspire. We have a bit of everything, but not too much of anything.

A map reminds us constantly of what is possible, of how much we have seen, and how much we have still to see. This therapeutic longing for place and rootedness has its own word in Welsh, *hiraeth*, for it is central to the Welsh condition. Homesickness doesn't quite cover it in English, but what cannot be readily expressed in one word has found ample expression over the centuries in art, literature and music. In the mud and madness of the First World War, it was the poetry of A. E. Housman, invoking an England of foursquare permanence and bucolic tenderness that filled the pockets of the poor bastards in the trenches. From the same war, Cotswold composer-poet Ivor Gurney was invalided back to Britain, eventually cracking under the strain of his own imagination and the horrors that he'd witnessed, and committed to an asylum in Kent. There, he would respond to nothing except an Ordnance Survey map of the Gloucestershire countryside that he adored, had explored so freely, and had written about with such vivid *hiraeth*. The map was a cipher for all that he loved, the last thread that connected him with life.

Our eternal love affair with our own topography is one of the defining features of being British. Of course, every country has this to some extent, but we have long honed it into an art form and an obsession. It's the 'sceptr'd isle' thing, for even the frankly weird shape of our country is enough to get the juices flowing. The island of Britain is the oddest of the lot: a long, thin, slightly cadaverous outline, yet prone to sudden bulges and protuberances that hint at a fleshy softness and yielding giggle. There are the satisfying semi-symmetries of East Anglia and Wales, Kent and the West Country and the jaws of Cardigan Bay, the raw geology of Scotland's unmistakeably bony knuckles, the little Italy of Devon and Cornwall. The island of Ireland, that 'dull picture in a wonderful frame', with its smooth east and shattered west, sits there knowing all too well that its larger neighbour, entirely shielding it from the European mainland, is going to be trouble.

I used to have a huge map of Great Britain and Ireland on my wall, and invite any visitors to place a pin in it where they felt that they most belonged. Some people plunged in their pins with relish, while others hovered for ages: 'D'you mean, where I live?' 'No, where you feel you belong – it can be where you live if you like, but it doesn't have to be.' I loved to watch the mental process going on, the look of wide-eyed wonder as even people who'd never much thought about maps stared hard at the familiar shapes and let themselves mentally patrol the landscape. How differently people perceive the same place is a never-ending source of fascination to me. We all have our own prejudices – justified or not – against certain locations, and we'll go to the grave with them. There is institutional snobbery at work too, for there are, and have been for centuries, two very different maps of the country that reinforce almost every aspect of our history and identity. I call them the A-list and B-list maps of Britain.

The A-list map presents all the places that don't need to be preceded by an apology: the high and mighty locations that know themselves to be the chosen ones. The map of B-list Britain – where I was born, raised and far prefer to live – covers everywhere else. When I've written travel features for the national press, it has always been about places that are firmly on the B-list: Birmingham, the Black Country, the East Midlands, Hull, Glasgow, various parts of Wales and Limerick in Ireland. The pattern has been the same every time. I submit my copy, and get a phone call or email a couple of days later suggesting that the feature needs a new introduction; something along the lines of 'Well, you thought it was all a bit grim and rubbish, but – surprise! – there's more to Blah than that these days.' Sometimes they don't even bother with the phone call or email, just add it as their own introduction, the generic view of B-list Britain as seen from the desk of a London hack. You see it even more graphically in the newspapers' property pages: it's cheap, but – oh dear – it's *Humberside*.

Every country has its split, its Mason–Dixon Line; the British equivalent was always held to be one that connected the River Severn south of Gloucester with the Wash on the east coast. South of this diagonal lay the comparatively wealthy, Conservative-voting, white-collar, Church of England part of the land; to the north, the poorer, Labour-voting, manual-working, Nonconformist tribes. The line rippled in places, so that the southern tranche extended to Malvern and Worcester, around Warwick and Leamington Spa, and included the hunting country of Leicestershire, Northamptonshire and Rutland.

Growing up, it was a border I was acutely aware of, for I crossed it every day on the way to school. It was only a 25-minute train journey from Kidderminster to Worcester, but they were in different worlds. Worcestershire is an England-in-miniature in this regard: the county's favoured images of orchards, cricket and Elgar belong entirely to its more upholstered, southern half. We in the northern triumvirate of Kidderminster, Bromsgrove and Redditch clung to the coat tails of the West Midlands and felt like scruffy gatecrashers in our own county. It was painfully evident at school, which drew its pupils from right across Worcestershire. The kids from Malvern and the Vale of Evesham had dads in Jags and strutted around the place as if they owned it, which they quite possibly do by now. There was never any doubt that they were several cuts above the far fewer of us who spilled off the train every day from Kidderminster, Stourbridge and the Black Country, with accents to prove it.

We even name our goods and companies keeping to the strict rules of the A- and B-list maps. This was something that hit me with a slap years ago in an airless undertaker's parlour, where my mother and I were trying to sort out the arrangements for my grandfather's funeral. With that sickly, faux-somnolent air they wear while thinking gleefully of all the noughts on your bill, the undertaker slid the catalogue of available coffins under our noses. They were all called the Windsor, the Oxford, the Canterbury, the Westminster and so on. Where, I wondered, were the Wolverhampton, the Barnsley or the Wisbech? Were Scots offered a Stirling or a Brechin in which to cart away their dearly departed?

A-list names conjure up the solid, dependable image that companies are desperate to tap into. Men's products, in particular, mine the same seam repeatedly, whether in colognes called Wellington and Marlborough (but not, definitely not, Wellingborough), or the Crockett & Jones range of fine footwear – pick from, among others, Tetbury, Chepstow, Coniston, Brecon, Welbeck, Bedford, Chalfont, Pembroke or Grasmere. We buy insurance from Hastings Direct, rather than Bexhill Direct, where the company's actually based, and smoke smooth Richmonds, not dog-rough Rotherhithes.

We map addicts are the oddest patriots. Maps bring out a curious British nationalism even in those of us normally allergic to displays of flag-waving. Wherever we go in the world, we pick up a local map and our very first thought is, 'Hmmm, not as good as an Ordnance Survey.' We feel sure, we *know*, that our maps are the finest the world has ever seen. Sneaking in there, too, is the certainty that the landscape they portray is also up there with the very best. We have neither very high mountains, nor very deep ravines nor very wild wildernesses, but the scale – like our climate – is modest and comforting, and the scenery often extremely lovely. And all of it so beautifully mapped.

It's a force that mystifies me, while still it engulfs me: in absolutely no other aspect of life do I feel so resolutely, determinedly, proudly British. I've never voted Conservative (or, God help us, UKIP), bought the *Daily Mail*, sung 'Rule Britannia', stood in a crowd to wave at royalty, watched the Last Night of the Proms with anything other than incredulity or so much as cracked a smile at *Last of the Summer Wine*. Nearly a decade of living in Welsh-speaking Wales has brought me to the view that the UK as a nation-state might well have had its day, and the sooner we realise it, the better all round. And yet, open up an OS, a Bartholomew, a Collins or even – if nothing else is available – an AA road atlas that cost £2.99 from the all-night garage, and something deep within me trembles. That familiar layout and colouring, those tantalising names and the histories they hint at, the shape of those cherished coasts, the twisting tracks and roads, the juxtaposition of the great conurbations and the wild, empty spaces: a few minutes staring, once again, at the map of this island, or any part of it, and I'm stoked up with a love and a loyalty that knows no reason and no limit.

You have to be careful, though. Not only are there the siren warnings of the pioneers who have gone before, and ended up as wizened, cranky obsessives, but such certainty about British superiority can manifest itself in some pretty strange attitudes, if allowed to seep off the map shelf and into almost any other area of life. Britons are routinely encouraged to cling to the idea that they are, inherently, the best at anything, and if not the best, then at least the most worthy, noble or underrated. And if we can't be that, we'd rather be the absolute worst: cosmically hopeless, the Eddie the Eagle among nations, usually coupled with a graceless sneer when we lose: 'Pfft, well, we never wanted it, anyway.' Rarely are we either the best or the worst, but it's our actual position of mid-table mediocrity that we struggle hardest to cope with.

Though not when it comes to our maps: even Johnny Foreigner grudgingly admits that we're still world-beaters in cartography. There is no other patch of land on the planet that has been as comprehensively, and so stylishly, measured, surveyed, plotted and mapped as the 80,823 square miles of Great Britain. We might have been late starters in the game, but we've more than made up for it subsequently, especially over the past four hundred years – ever since, in fact, we started needing maps in order to go and rough up bits of the rest of the world and declare them to be ours. Again, this is the perverse predicament of the British map aficionado: were it not for the Empire and our military bravado, we would be a great deal further down the cartographic rank-ings. It's a dilemma to wrestle with, for sure, but boy, are we grateful for the maps.

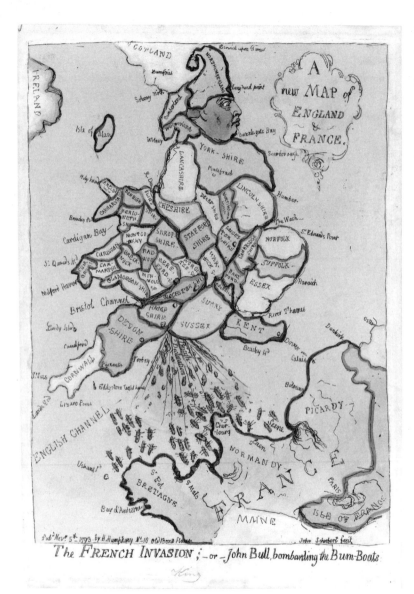

James Gillray's map of England as King George III, crapping 'bum boats' into France's mouth

2. L'ENTENTE CARTIALE

> We always have been, we are, and I hope that we always shall be, detested in France.
>
> ~ The Duke of Wellington

That our cartography is transparently the best in the world is the battle cry of every British map addict. We wave our OS Landrangers in the same spirit that the English longbowmen at Crécy flourished their state-of-the-art weaponry at the French, confident that we are holding the latest, the most accurate, the loveliest maps known to man. And one single fact underpins this whole fabrication, the slender basis for our patriotic fantasy. We must have mapped the world better than anyone, because every measurement, in all its precision, and the whole grid on which every map depends are taken from a base that passes through – and is named after – an otherwise unremarkable suburb of London. Greenwich Mean Time, and the Greenwich Meridian, the world's cartographic backbone, is ours.

And we don't have to put our country's name on our stamps. Same principle. We were first, therefore we were the best and got special privileges.

Take that *République Française*, with your overly wordy *timbres-postes* and your redundant meridian, left abandoned and overgrown like a Norfolk branch line closed in the 1960s. And take that USA, for that matter. You may have superseded us in just about every possible aspect of superpower status, but we've still got the maps, the clocks and the meridian. It's a small victory, granted, but it'll have to do.

To a junior map addict, who gazes at a British map with the fondness of Rod Stewart at a brand new blonde, the certainty that our maps are the best is buried deep within, but occasionally breaks out in pustules of xenophobic acne. In the 1970s, watching the TV news, I was genuinely and repeatedly surprised to see how developed the rest of the world seemed to be when it flashed past on a nightly basis. Surely, these places couldn't be as sophisticated as the Land of Hope, Glory and the Ordnance Survey? When, at the age of six, I first visited my mother after she'd moved to France, I couldn't quite believe that Paris had traffic lights, zebra crossings, decent shops, well-dressed people – people even fully dressed at all. It was Not England; therefore it was supposed to be dusty and primitive. It looked – whisper it quietly – just like home. Only – whisper it even more quietly – rather better.

Ah, *la belle France*. Our nearest neighbour, archest rival, flirtiest paramour, oldest, *bestest* friend and bitterest foe, all rolled into one. We and the French are like an ancient, brackish couple locked into what looks from the outside like the stalest of wedlock, but which, behind firmly locked doors, is as doe-eyed as a Charles Aznavour chorus. We sneer at them, but around eleven million of us make our way over the Channel every year to wallow in their wine, cheese and meats of dubious provenance. They sneer at us, but can't get enough of our culture, either high, in the ample shape of royalty and aristocracy, or low, from punk to getting pissed properly. We look down on them for their pomposity, their flagrantly over-inflated sense of their own importance, their rudeness, their insularity, their ponderous bureaucracy, their clinging to a long-vanished past, their dodgy new best friends, their fiercely centripetal politics, their all-round unwarranted, swaggering arrogance. They look down on us for precisely the same reasons.

It is this intense neighbourly rivalry between Britain and France that has driven most of the advances in mapping over the past four hundred years – or, more specifically, it is the ever-watchful competitiveness between their two capital cities, London and Paris. These city-states in all but name have been peering haughtily at each other across that slender ribbon of water for the past two thousand years. Both are convinced that they are the epitome of all that is civilised and progressive in this world, and both have so much in common – not least their terribly high opinion of themselves.

It's a rivalry that endures, even constantly reinvents itself, like a family feud that passes down the generations long, long after the original protagonists are cold in the sod. Some of the finest mapping of its age was the by-product, such as the forensically detailed eighteenth-century invasion plans that each side drew up of the other's nearest coastline during that hundred years or more of semi-permanent war that existed between the two nations until the 1815 full stop – or rather, semicolon – of the Battle of Waterloo. As the nineteenth century progressed, the arena for mutual Anglo-French antagonism was widened, each side having already flexed its muscles in competing for territories in north America. Now, no part of the globe was immune from the colonisers, with each side racing to capture – and, for the first time, map – lands in Africa, Asia, the Middle East and the Caribbean. The tectonic plates of power were shifting in Europe too, and lavish maps, often with home territories boldly exaggerated or shown as definite possessions when they were little more than statements of ambition, were produced by British and French cartographers in each nation's struggle to be perceived as the continent's top dog. France and Britain took the idea of the map as one of the boldest, and most swiftly absorbed, tools of political indoctrination and launched it into the modern era.

Even in today's much reduced times, the snippiness between London and Paris continues to fuel outbreaks of hubristic condescension on both sides, wind-assisted by maps. Londoners will glower over the maps, drawn up by London County Council, of sobering Second World War bomb-damage, showing the city utterly blitzed and razed in hard-won victory, and could be forgiven for comparing them with their Parisian equivalents, depicting only the lightest of grazes to the city's elegant face, thanks to its people's early capitulation to the losing side. Parisians in the 1980s and '90s loved to brandish their metro map in the faces of any passing Brits, showing as it did the splendid new RER (Réseau Express Régional) lines that scorched across the city like high-velocity darts, while muttering darkly about their last visit to London and memories of chaos on the Northern and Central Lines. And how fitting was it that, once the extravagant French plans and maps had been compared with the more down-to-earth British ones, London squeaked its victory to host the 2012 Olympics over Paris, the long-time front runner and bookies' favourite?

When it comes to comparing the current standard of our respective national maps, it's a shockingly one-sided contest, and I'm really trying to be impartial. The French equivalent of the Ordnance Survey is the Institut Géographique National (IGN), and its maps are awful. Leaden, lumpy, flimsy and downright ugly, they are often hard to find, and not worth the bother of trying. The 1:25 000 series, the equivalent of the OS Explorer maps, is an assault on the eyes, with its harsh colours, grim typefaces and lousy printing; they look plain cheap and you'd be hard pressed to work out a decent walk from any of them. Don't just take my word for it though – compare the two maps in the colour section. The 1:50 000 orange series, the equivalent of our OS Landrangers, somehow manages to be even worse. France is larger than Britain, granted, about two and a half times the size, but they've carved up the country so ineptly that you'd have to buy 1,146 of these dreadful maps, at a cost of nearly €10,000, to cover the whole country – *nearly six times* the number of OS Landrangers (204, costing less than £1,500), which would get you the whole of Britain at exactly the same scale and in far greater style. IGN maps at 1:100 000 are not quite as bad, but really, at any scale, you'd be better off in France with the Michelin series, for they are always far more elegant than the government jobs. But still nowhere near as good as You-Know-Who.

At least there's one area of life where you can always rely on the French, and that's managing to squeeze a bit of soft porn into the most unlikely topic, even cartography. Back in those innocent pre-internet days, when you had to rely on a late BBC2 or Channel 4 film for a glimpse of flesh, I remember catching one night an early 1970s movie by the name of *La Vallée*. In English, it was called *Obscured by Clouds*, after the intriguing caption written over a huge blank space on the map of Papua New Guinea. This, they stated in the film, was an unknown mountainous region, the last place on Earth that had yet to be mapped. A gorgeous young French consul's wife, Viviane, is in the country to find exotic feathers for export to Paris; she joins an expedition into the unmapped mountains, which soon turns into a phantasmagoria of mind-expanding substances, writhing bodies and an accompanying soundtrack by Pink Floyd. Even at the age of seventeen, I found the idea of the map a far bigger turn-on than a few soft-focus French hippies in the buff.

When it comes to mapping Paris, the 'us versus them' contest is a little more equal. Despite endless redesigns, they've never managed a metro map with quite the same panache and clarity of the equivalent one of the London Underground. Even when they tried to mimic Harry Beck's design directly, the result was the proverbial *dîner du chien* and it was quickly scrapped. With the street maps of the city, however, the French have long since hit on a winner. While the London *A–Z* and its myriad of near equivalents do the job with postman-whistling efficiency, the little red book that can be found in the handbag of any Parisian (except perhaps for the ones that house small dogs) combine utility with élan. Considering how much the French love to make of their superior sense of style, it's just as well they've got at least one map to prove it.

The little red book – by Cartes Taride, Éditions André Leconte and others – fits Paris perfectly: it's lightly stylish, full of fascinating detail, slightly bewildering and extremely easy just to lose yourself in. Its art deco titling on the cover, like the classic *Métropolitain* signs, and its format have been pretty constant since the end of the nineteenth century. The main mapping – colourful, cheerful and crowded – is done arrondissement by arrondissement, with the spill-over of the suburbs to follow. There are fine fold-out maps of the metro and the RER, but the fun is only just beginning. Every street in the index – which has those handy A–Z dividers you find in address books – is given its nearest metro station, every bus route is represented by a scaled-down version of the classy linear map that you find on board the bus, with each stop clearly marked, and there are map references, addresses, phone numbers and nearest metro stations given for every police and fire station, government office, embassy, hospital, monument, museum, cinema, theatre, cabaret, railway terminus, place of worship and even cemetery. All contained within something measuring just three and half by five and a half inches.

I may well be biased, for the Paris street atlas is something I've known intimately and loved unconditionally for over thirty-five years, ever since my mum moved there. Although it was no fun being the first in class to have his parents divorce, there were definite benefits, regular trips to Paris being a pretty obvious one, especially when the other parent is in a Midlands town that can only be called a capital within the very tight confines of carpet manufacturing. The first time my sister and I went over there to visit Mum, I was terrified; convinced that the law in France demanded that everyone speak French all the time, and that I wouldn't be able to say a word to her, nor understand anything she said to me. Mum would let me go off to get breakfast from the local boulangerie, sending me out with a ten-franc note and the phrase *une baguette et trois croissants, s'il vous plaît* drilled into my brain. On the second visit, I'd walk a little further to another boulangerie, then a little further still, until, by the time I was about nine, I'd hotfoot it into the nearest metro station (Porte de Champerret, ligne 3), ride a train or two and collect some bread from whichever random part of the city I surfaced in. Fortunately, my mum and my sister weren't averse to having breakfast at about eleven o'clock.

My hunter-gathering for bread was beyond excitement: armed with my little red book, I felt such an integral part of this sophisticated city, a tiny corpuscle pelting through the arteries of this statuesque *grande dame*. It was an intoxicating buzz, one which encapsulated so many of the things that I've most come to value: freedom, travel, spontaneity, humanity. For I never felt in any danger – quite the opposite, people couldn't have done more to help. I was reminded of those happy days when, in April 2008, 'America's Worst Mom' (as she was dubbed by Fox News and the shock-jocks), a newspaper columnist, wrote about letting her nine-year-old son ride the New York subway on his own. America divided down the middle, many cheering her for taking on the media-fuelled paranoia of modern parenthood. They didn't generate quite as much noise, however, as the half of the country who screamed cyber-abuse at her from within their fortress compounds, while their inert, incarcerated children fantasised about the day they'd go beserk in a shopping mall with a handgun. What about the murderers, they ranted, the muggers, the paedophiles, the gropers, the platform-shovers, the terrorists lurking round every corner? Are you out of your mind, lady? But have they been to New York lately? You're more at risk walking through Ashby-de-la-Zouch on a Saturday night.

So many years of getting to know Paris made me support her instinctively in the eternal duel with London. Our capital seemed angry and chaotic by contrast, a sensation that only deepened when I lived there for four years at the end of the 1980s, initially at university and then trying to commute every day right across the city for my first job. London during that period *was* a mess: the glistening towers of Dock-lands rising fast out of the debris around them, a glassy two fingers to the squalor and poverty, the doorway-sleepers and the disenfranchised. It suited me well, though. Being angry and chaotic myself, London couldn't have matched me more perfectly. From the lofty heights of my college in leafy Hampstead, I joined every campaign, protest and march, finding myself applauding Tony Benn most weekends at some rally or other in Trafalgar Square. *What do we want?* Er, student grants, no poll tax, freedom for Nicaragua, Nelson Mandela, Thatcher's head on a pole ... what was it this time? *When do we want it? NOW!*

Two days before the dawn of the 1990s, I left London, smug and thankful that I was quitting this seething metropolis for a return to the safety of the Midlands. Paris was still on its elegant little pedestal in my mind, and I ranted at anyone who'd listen about its vast superiority, and that of France as a whole, over our mean-spirited little Tory island and its yuppie capital. Gradually, though, I fell in love with London all over again, seduced by its energy, its caprice, its sheer balls. One up, one down: the lustre of Paris was peeling, its Mitterand-era chutzpah shrivelled into a matronly conservatism.

↓

So many of the advances in cartography, as well as practically every other discipline, have stemmed from the ancient grudge and eternal competitiveness between these two great cities; it is a theme that reappears as the steadiest leitmotif through any analysis of modern maps and mapping. The victory in securing the world's prime meridian for Greenwich was perhaps our literal high noon in the battle, which came at the 1884 International Meridian Conference in Washington, DC. Delegates from twenty-five nations gathered on the first of October, charged with finally settling the question that was dogging the world's governments, and its transport and export industries.

Up until then, anyone anywhere could, and did, work to their own meridian. While the Equator is a fixed line of latitude – determined by its position at the centre of an oblate (i.e. polar-flattened) spheroid, its particular climate and the fact that its days and nights are of equal length the whole year round – the defining line of longitude, namely a full circle around the globe that connects the two poles vertically, can

be placed anywhere. Establishing longitude was essential for navigation, especially at sea, but also for working out relative time zones.
When the sun is overhead at noon in one place, 15° (i.e. $\frac{1}{24}$ of 360°)
west or east it is an hour different. Time was delineated in what might
be called the way of the sundial, so that it was noon in any particular
place when the sun was highest in the sky. Even in a country as tiny as
Britain, this meant that there were numerous different local times in
operation. With the advent of the railways, this had to change on a
national basis, and soon, thanks to the massive upsurge in ocean-
going trade, the need to standardise time zones between countries
became acute, especially as there was a plethora of meridian lines
being used by different countries.

The 1884 Washington conference came exactly a year after the 7th
General Conference of the European Arc Measurement, held in Rome.
It was at this geodetic gathering that the French had secured international agreement to use their metre as the global standard unit for
measuring length. Their definition of a metre – one ten-millionth of the
section of the Paris meridian between the North Pole and the equator
– had been achieved by impeccably scientific means that demonstrated
to all the advanced nature of their geodetic powers. Using the line that
passed through the Paris Observatory to calculate the metre also subtly
cemented that meridian in the world's consciousness, at a time when
calls were becoming ever louder to create one super-meridian, from
which all else would be calculated. To decide where that should be was
the raison d'être of the Washington conference, twelve short months
later. The French must have arrived in America feeling that the prevail-
ing wind was well and truly in their sails.

Not for long, though. There had evidently been some anglophonic
stitch-up going on behind the scenes between the host Americans and
their British cousins. Use of the Paris Meridian to establish the world's
measuring stick was employed not in advocacy of its adoption as the
Prime Meridian, but as a sly argument by the English-speakers against

such an eventuality. After all, they cried, it's *someone else's turn*! You got the metre, now be a jolly chap and leave go the damned meridian, won't you? Of course, the irony should not escape us that this Anglo-American pincer movement, so much of which depended on their reminding delegates of the recent French victory in measuring the world, came from two countries who have had as little to do as possible with the metric system ever since. Even today, the USA remains one of only four countries on Earth officially using imperial weights and measures (it's an unlikely foursome: the others being Burma/Myanmar, Yemen and Brunei), and with its ever-growing ranks of metric martyrs, save-the-pint campaigners and kilometre refuseniks, it can hardly be said either that Britain has embraced the New (well, 1883) World Order.

At Washington, the French swiftly realised that no one else was going to support the Paris Observatory as the proposed site of the Prime Meridian, so they set about plan B, namely the standard fallback position that, if they weren't to have the prize, they must do all they could to scupper the chances of the British. We would doubtless have done exactly the same in their tiny shoes. It wasn't just the French performing beautifully to their own national stereotype: the conference minutes are a quite hilarious catalogue of every nationality living up to its most dastardly clichés. The Americans, swaggering into their role as world-leaders-in-waiting, were bullish, yet smarmy, and masters of manipulation, particularly of the easily flattered British. To that end, the Americans played the good guy, genial hosts with absolutely no self-interest in the process, while shooting across everyone's bows at the very first session with a clear reminder of their latent muscle. The chairman of the US delegation, Admiral C. R. P. Rodgers, was elected President of the Conference. In his opening address, he declared:

Broad as is the area of the United States, covering a hundred degrees of longitude, extending from 66° 52' west from Green-wich to 166° 13' at our extreme limit in Alaska, not including the Aleutian Islands; traversed, as it is, by railway and telegraph lines, and dotted with observatories; long as is its sea coast, of more than twelve thousand miles; vast as must be its foreign and domestic commerce, its delegation to this Congress has no desire to urge that a prime meridian shall be found within its confines.

The minutes do not record if he expounded this while stroking a white cat in his lap.

Rodgers' statement made clear where the host delegation were to place their support when it came to deciding the location of the Prime Meridian: Greenwich. Indeed, it was only on the second day of the conference that American delegate Naval Commander W. T. Sampson jumped the gun and formally proposed it, stating:

As a matter of economy as well as convenience, that meridian should be selected which is now in most general use. This additional consideration of economy would limit our choice to the meridian of Greenwich, for it may fairly be stated upon the authority of the distinguished Delegate from Canada that more than 70 per cent of all the shipping of the world uses this meridian for purposes of navigation.

The French delegation were horrified, and filibustered the proposal off the table, with a speech by their prime delegate, M. Janssen, the Director of the Paris Observatory, that culminated in his demanding more time to consider the question but which, to reach that point, took well over an hour as he pondered the enormity of the matter in hand. He voiced their opposition to Greenwich in the most tremulously righteous terms:

This meridian, instead of being chosen with reference to the configuration of the continents, is borrowed from an observatory;

that is to say, it is placed on the globe in a hap-hazard manner, and is very inconveniently situated for the function that it is to perform ... Instead of profiting by the lessons of the past, national rivalries are introduced in a question that should rally the good-will of all ... Since the report considers us of so little weight in the scales, allow me, gentlemen, to recall briefly the past and the present of our hydrography, and for that purpose I can do no better than to quote from a work that has been communicated to me, and which emanates from one of our most learned hydrographers. 'France,' he says, 'created more than two centuries ago the most ancient nautical ephemerides [tables showing coordinates of celes-tial bodies at particular times] in existence. She was the first to conceive and execute the great geodetic operations which had for their object the construction of civil and military maps and the measurement of arcs of the meridian in Europe, America and Africa. All these operations were and are based on the Paris meridian'. If another initial meridian had to be adopted, it would be necessary to change the graduation of our 2,600 hydrographic plates; it would be necessary to do the same thing for our nauti-cal instructions, which exceed 600 in number.

Although happy to have a good sulk about how much more inconven-ient a change of meridian would be for the French than anyone else, Janssen knew well that there was little mileage in further banging the drum for the Paris Meridian, whose cause was already lost. He seized instead on a more nebulous point that, he hoped, would sink the cause of the British, demanding of the conference that 'the initial meridian should have a character of absolute neutrality ... and in particular espe-cially should cut no great continent – neither Europe nor America'. While Britain pretended to be above such squalid argument, their attack-dogs, the American delegation, weighed in with ready answers: 'The adoption of the meridian of Greenwich has not been sought after by Great Britain,' Commander Sampson boomed back. 'It was not her proposition, but that she consented to it after it had been proposed by other portions of the civilised world.' How very gracious of us: we can only imagine the holier-than-thou expressions adopted by the British delegation at this point. In his opening address, the American Admiral Rodgers had presaged this question of neutrality:

Should any of us now hesitate in the adoption of a particular meridian, or should any nation covet the honor of having the selected meridian within its own borders, it is to be remembered that when the prime meridian is once adopted by all it loses its specific name and nationality, and becomes simply the Prime Meridian.

Absolute horse-shit of course, but high-minded horse-shit of the finest grade. The Americans were really getting the hang of this diplomacy lark.

M. Janssen was the undoubted star of the event, able to turn in grandiloquent speeches, on any topic, that lasted an hour or two. Realising that the neutrality argument was all that lay in the way of the adoption of Greenwich, he worried at it like a starving poodle:

An immense majority of the navies of the world navigate with English charts; that is true, and it is a practical compliment to the great maritime activity of that nation. When this freely admitted supremacy shall be transformed into an official and compulsory supremacy, it will suffer the vicissitudes of all human power, and that institution [the meridian], which by its nature is of a purely scientific nature, and to which we would assure a long and certain future, will become the object of burning competition and jealousy among nations.

Anyone particular in mind, Monsieur?

Professor J. C. Adams, of the British delegation, waspishly replied that Janssen's 'eloquent address, in so far as I could follow that discourse, seemed to me to turn almost entirely upon sentimental considerations', and reiterated the point of practicality, that the most 'convenient', i.e. widely used, meridian would make the most sense. He didn't sully his purity by naming it; he didn't need to.

In turn, Janssen rebuffed Adams in the politest way possible, while managing a few withering digs at his British counterparts ('and we are still awaiting the honour of seeing the metrical system for common use in England'). He protested – rather too much – that the French objection was nothing whatsoever to do with 'national pride' and questioned the idea of the 'convenience' of the Greenwich Meridian. To whom exactly, he postulated, was it convenient? Ah, the Brits and the Yanks: the 'advantage is to yourselves, and those you represent, of having nothing to change, either in your maps, customs or traditions – such a solution, I say, can have no future before it, and we refuse to take part in it'. He persevered in even darker tones: 'You see, gentlemen, how dangerous it is to awaken national susceptibilities on a subject of a purely scientific nature.' Ratcheting up his rhetorical powers, he concluded one particularly long speech with a flourish: 'Whatever we may do, the common prime meridian will always be a crown to which there will be a hundred pretenders. Let us place the crown on the brow of science, and all will bow before it.'

Janssen's sterling verbosity was only delaying the inevitable, so, realising that they were backed into a corner, the French hit their nuclear button, issuing veiled threats that they might walk out of the conference and then, when that went almost unnoticed, strident complaints about the standard of translation into their language at the conference. They demanded a recess in order to find a better French stenographer, a process that kept the conference from reconvening for a full further week. When all the delegates reassembled on Monday 13 October, everyone's positions, after seven days of backstage back-stabbing, had coagulated into immutability.

The French kicked off proceedings by playing what was their only remaining decent card, the demand for the 'absolute neutrality' of any chosen meridian. It was put to the vote and heavily defeated by 21 to 3. As a faintly placatory gesture, Sandford Fleming, one of the British delegation, invoked the idea of placing the Prime Meridian 180° from Greenwich, thus, he said, giving it some political neutrality and positioning it largely in the uninhabited Pacific Ocean. The idea didn't mollify the French at all, who sneered that even if the Prime Meridian was 180° from Greenwich, it was still the Greenwich Meridian in all but name, only in reverse.

This proposal from the British delegation was typical of our faux-humble demeanour at this stage in the proceedings: it's easy to be magnanimous when you're clearly winning, especially in a contest in which you are feigning absolute disinterest. The British vat of oil to pour on troubled waters was soon generously employed again, as the French and Spanish reminded delegates that their governments fully expected Britain and the USA to join the metric system, if not in a quid pro quo for the adoption of Greenwich, then certainly in the same spirit of global good manners and scientific unity. One of the British delegation, General Strachey, smoothly replied:

> *I am authorised to state that Great Britain, after considering the opinions which were expressed at Rome, has desired that it may be allowed to join the Convention du mètre … [and] that there is a strong feeling on the part of the scientific men of England that, sooner or later, she will be likely to join in the use of that system, which, no doubt, is an extremely good one.*

In other words, we'll get home and do precisely nothing about it for a century, but thank you *so* much for your concern. Stuff you with a smile, Monsieur.

The definitive vote on adopting Greenwich loomed, and the French made one last desperate bid to prevent it. The loquacious M. Janssen deferred to his colleague M. Lefaivre to make their final plea. 'The meridian of Greenwich is not a scientific one,' piped Lefaivre, 'and its adoption implies no progress for astronomy, geodesy or navigation.' It was only 'convenient', not scientific, a fact that

> our colleague from Great Britain just now reminded us of by enumerating with complacency the tonnage of British and American shipping ... Science appears here only as the humble vassal of the powers of the day to consecrate and crown their success. But, gentlemen, nothing is so transitory and fugitive as power and riches. All the great empires of the world, all financial, industrial and commercial prosperities of the world have given us a proof of it, each in turn.

This was the sound of grand nobility in defeat, for the vote was then taken and Greenwich confirmed as the world's Prime Meridian by 22 votes to 1, with two abstentions. Only San Domingo (the island of Hispaniola) voted against, with Brazil and France abstaining. They didn't want to look like sore losers. Or rather, they were saving that for later.

After further lengthy arguments about how to calibrate degrees from Greenwich, and how to calculate time zones, the French asked for another deferment of the conference. They returned six days later with a small bombshell of a proposition: that the metric system – which, they reminded delegates, everyone had spoken so voluminously in favour of – should be extended from the measurement of length, volume and weight and into the realms of degrees, angles and time. Greenwich might be getting the line through it, but at least the grid of longitude and the calibration of the day that spun off it might be expressed in a French way – or, at the very least, in a way that was designed to piss off the Anglo-American alliance. The British and the Americans cried foul, that such a decision was beyond the remit of the

Style over substance: the Paris meridian

conference. For the first time in weeks, the French smelled English-speaking blood and pressed home their slender advantage, demanding a vote on whether or not a vote could be taken on the topic. It was close. Thirteen countries agreed that the issue of metricising time and angles could be considered; nine, Britain and the US included, voted against. Two abstained. So, as eager not to appear bad losers as had the French been on the Greenwich vote, the Americans and British then ostentatiously supported the metric system in the subsequent vote. In fact, no one voted against it – not that that made the faintest bit of difference in actually making it happen.

Flushed with their pyrrhic victory, the French demanded a further adjournment to the conference, which briefly reconvened two days later before its final adjournment, for nine days, in order that the conference protocols could be drawn up, in English and, of course, in French. On the first of November, a month to the day since the delegates had first gathered, the conference closed in a mutual orgy of back-slapping and vainglorious speeches about how the international community was united as never before and that they had made history. Thankfully, the sagging balloon of hot air was peremptorily pricked by the very last contribution noted in the conference minutes: the ever-vocal M. Janssen of the French delegation complaining about the standard of French used in their translations.

As expected, the French reaction to the conference's decision was to ignore it for as long as they possibly could. The Paris Meridian was still marked as 0° on French maps until 1911, and even beyond that, they continually refused to refer to the notion of Greenwich Mean Time, preferring instead to name the concept the altogether snappier 'Paris Mean Time diminished by 9 minutes 21 seconds'. It's a shame it didn't catch on: PMT has such an appropriate ring to it for matters of timekeeping. Even though the Paris Meridian has long been shunted into the sidings, the French still keep polishing it and showing it off to the world like a priceless relic. One of their main millennium projects was to plant lines of trees the entire length of France along their old meridian line. It might no longer be functioning, but hey, you could see it from space, or at least if you look closely enough on Google Earth in a few decades' time. To a chippy Brit (and, when it comes to any dealings with the French, that's most of us), the project smacked of dismissive looking down the Gallic nose at the lack of presentational flair that attends our meridian line.

The world's timekeeping and cartographic staff it may be, but as the Prime Meridian enters Britain in the retirement town of Peacehaven on the Sussex coast, it's marked only by a dowdy obelisk and the Meridian Centre, a deathly 1970s shopping mall with the unmistakeable aroma of incontinence. Two hundred and three miles due north, it leaves English soil in similarly dreary fashion, on a beach just south of the Sand-le-Mere caravan park, near Tunstall on the Holderness coast of Yorkshire's East Riding. Britain's bleakest coast is also

Substance over style: where the Prime Meridian enters England at Tunstall, East Yorkshire

the fastest-receding in Europe, where houses and roads tumble regularly over the edge, leaving their forlorn traces to be washed over by a freezing sea the colour of a river in high flood. In the circumstances, the great local millennium project – placing a huge carved boulder on the cliff top to mark the point at which the global meridian arrives in its home country from the North Pole – was something of a triumph of optimism over experience. Instead of lasting the full thousand years, it managed just three, disappearing over the muddy cliff in a storm in January 2003. In between these two inauspicious gateposts, as well as the whistles and bells of Greenwich itself, the meridian is marked by a number of plaques, columns, archways and, in Cambridgeshire, a line of daffodils planted by Boy Scouts. It's either disarmingly modest or just a bit crap. Either way, it's British through and through.

↓

If – and, frankly, it's a bloody big if – we accept British pre-eminence in modern mapping owing to the adoption of the Greenwich Meridian as the gold standard for measuring lines on a map, then one event gave birth to this certainty. That was the creation of an earlier imaginary line on the landscape, the first precisely calibrated base line across a stretch of English countryside, from which all initial triangulations were taken to produce what soon became the Ordnance Survey. It took place in the summer of 1784, and for reasons that are also gloriously British: once again, a fierce spirit of one-upmanship against the French and a supremely thin-skinned paranoia that they were insulting us.

We had a lot of making up to do; by the late eighteenth century, French map-making was leagues ahead of that of its clod-hopping British cousin. Nearly a century earlier, their experiments in establishing accurate lines of longitude and latitude had proved that the world was an oblate spheroid, rather than a perfect sphere, which had tremendous impact on the precise measurement of relative distances, radically altering the shape and size of France itself as presented on a map. Coupled with advances in triangulation and surveying, the Académie Royale produced, in 1789, by far the finest and most ambitious cartography that had ever been made of one country: a complete set of 180 maps, covering all of France, at a scale of 1:86 400, just under one and a half miles to the inch. Even the detail on the maps was starkly different: while we were still delineating our upland areas with crude shading or lumpy molehills scattered over the landscape, the French were developing sophisticated systems of hachures – groups of parallel lines to indicate height – before pioneering the use of contour lines on some maps from the 1750s.

The year 1789 is better remembered in France for rather bloodier reasons than the publication of the national map, the *Carte de Cassini* as it became known, after César-François Cassini de Thury, the Director of the Paris Observatory and its principal progenitor, who had died of smallpox in 1784, leaving his son to continue the work. The new revolutionary government looked with grave suspicion on anything *royale*, the Académie included, although they were more than delighted with the maps and promptly took over all responsibility for their production and publication. The Académie Royale was closed down (to resurface a few years later as the more egalitarian Académie des Sciences), Cassini junior was imprisoned, while Académie director Antoine Lavoisier was carted off to the guillotine. It was at just this moment in history that the British were starting to get their act together, and, aided by the chaos in France, were soon able to outstrip their neighbours. Though, as ever, it took some pompous prodding by the French to sharpen us up.

That came six years before the Revolution, in the shape of a missive from Cassini de Thury to King George III, in which he loftily pointed out that the world's two principal meridians, those of Paris and London, were out of kilter in both longitude and latitude. His inference was that, thanks to the superior surveying and triangulation of the French, the mistake was almost certainly on our side of the Channel, and would His Majesty care do something about it? He further rubbed salt into the wounds by pointing out that he himself had checked the trigonometry on the French side all the way up to the Channel coast, and, using a telescope, had established many landmarks on the English side that could be useful if we could be bothered to do a proper survey. The King's principal Secretary of State, Charles James Fox, passed on the letter to Sir Joseph Banks, President of the Royal Society in London. Many of its members were outraged by the slurs it contained, the Astronomer Royal, the Reverend Doctor Nevil Maskelyne, firing off a hasty rebuttal of the French claims. But there was one Fellow of the Royal Society who received the news with equanimity, bordering on glee, for he knew that this was the chance for which he had been waiting for decades.

We know frustratingly little about Major-General William Roy (1726–90), a map addict of impeccable credentials and the father of the Ordnance Survey. No portrait survives of him, few biographical details have come our way, but, from his plans, letters and publications, we can see a man utterly driven by maps and an insatiable urge to make them ever better. He started in his native Scotland, working with the surveying crews that had been drafted in as a response to the Jacobite uprisings in the Highlands of the 1740s. The official response was the same as always: go deep into enemy turf, build roads and military outposts, move the population to where they could better be tracked, and, most importantly of all, comprehensively map it. For years, this was Roy's day job, though, as a sideline, he also worked obsessively to map the Roman remains of Scotland, for they had employed much the same techniques in suppressing the clans fifteen centuries earlier. There's not much doubting what his specialist subject would have been on *Georgian Mastermind*.

The first survey of Scotland, between 1747 and 1752, was of the troublesome Highlands, when Roy was teamed up with the young Paul Sandby (1731–1809). Sandby, who later became one of the age's most celebrated landscape painters and a founder member of the Royal Academy, provided the artistic talent for the beautiful maps that they produced, complementing Roy, the technical wizard who worried perpetually about getting the topographical detail correct. Once the Highlands had been comprehensively mapped, it was decided to survey and plot southern Scotland, but Sandby had returned to England by then and the resultant maps were nowhere near as spectacular as the earlier ones of the far north. Roy was a perfectionist, and the lack of precise measuring equipment frustrated him enormously; late in life, he wrote about these early map-making efforts in Scotland, describing them as 'rather a magnificent military sketch, than a very accurate map of a country'.

From Scotland, Roy enlisted in the army and served with distinction in the Seven Years' War with France. Once again, his map-making skills, and perfectionism, were usefully employed in his work as a special adviser on troop deployment and strategy. Roy's reports on such matters included beautifully drawn maps that he always insisted on doing himself, the army draughtsmen and his subordinate officers just not being up to his exacting standards. This lack of trust in anyone else became a growing theme as his career moved towards its apogee.

On his return, he settled in London, and continued rising through the ranks of the army, while spending more and more time on his cartographic pursuits. Central to his ambition was finding the right equipment, or rather, having the right equipment created for his needs. Much of his time was spent experimenting with measuring instruments in order to see how they could be employed to produce the greatest possible accuracy. They were never quite good enough. Nonetheless, his military experiences abroad, and his knowledge of how far advanced the Dutch and French were in such matters, had convinced him that the time was ripe for a comprehensive national survey, and he first approached the authorities about the matter in 1763. With a canny knack for telling the government what he most thought they would respond to, he emphasised Britain's vulnerability to invasion, particularly along the south coast, and the importance of conducting such a survey 'during times of peace and tranquillity', rather than waiting to do it under the chaotic cloud of war. They turned him down on grounds of expense. He re-presented his plans three years later, only to have them refused once again.

Impatient but undeterred, William Roy used every moment of his spare time to conduct his own informal triangulation experiments around London, establishing the position and distance of landmarks in the capital in relation to the Royal Observatory at Greenwich. Triangulation remained the bedrock of map-making until it was supplanted, less than thirty years ago, by satellite Global Positioning Systems (GPS) technology. The principle of triangulation is that if you know the length of one line of a triangle, and two of its angles to the other lines, the entire triangle can accurately be plotted for both distance and elevation. It's an extremely time-consuming business, depending as it does on caddying heavy equipment up to the highest vantage points: the first triangulation of Britain and Ireland, started by William Roy in 1783, took nearly seventy years to complete.

Roy regularly presented his London triangulation findings to the Royal Society, so that when the inflammatory missive came from Paris in 1783, he seemed the obvious man to restore Britain's dented honour by conducting the experiment. He was extremely well prepared, for he had used every one of his travels, both at home and abroad, to map the landscape and establish the most suitable places for triangulation. The flat expanse of Hounslow Heath, to the west of London, had long been selected as his preferred choice for the perfect base line. And although the project was nominally to establish only the precise relation of the London and Paris observatories, Roy knew well that it could, and should, be the harbinger of something far greater; that it could 'extend different serieses [sic] of Triangles ... in all directions to the remotest part of the Island'.

William Roy is an undoubted hero to any British map addict, but he is also something of a siren warning to us all. The brilliant young adventurer turned inexorably into a grumpy old man, for whom no one, and nothing, was ever quite good enough. Sounds familiar? I rather fear so. So fixated did he become by his great triangulation project that he picked fights with anyone who failed to come up to his exacting standards, most spectacularly in the case of instrument-maker Jesse Ramsden (1735–1800). Ramsden was just as much of a perfectionist as Roy, and with just as great a cause: his scientific and astronomical instruments attracted customers from across the world to his Piccadilly workshop. Roy's greatest frustration throughout his map-making career was the fact that the measuring instruments available couldn't cope with the precision that he demanded. For the great triangulation project of south-east England, Roy commissioned Ramsden to design and build the most exact theodolite ever seen.

Unfortunately, Ramsden failed to employ enough workmen on the project and thus to produce the goods soon enough for Roy, and the cartographer began to cast increasingly bellicose aspersions on the instrument-maker's professional ability. The massive theodolite – it weighed over fourteen stone and had to be hauled around on a specially designed truck – was the finest ever created, but, to Roy's continuing chagrin, it was still prone to some tiny errors and, most annoyingly, took a whole three years to build. In fairness to Roy, he was sixty years old and in failing health, so must have felt the continued delays with increasing impatience, urgently wanting to finish the project while he still could. That doesn't excuse his behaviour, however, as he repeatedly complained about Ramsden to the Royal Society in letters and papers that became ever more dyspeptic. Ramsden, also a Fellow of the Society, responded in kind, so that members found themselves piggies-in-the-middle as complaints and counter-complaints between the two men resounded throughout the Society's hallowed halls. Roy charged Ramsden with being 'remiss and dilatory' and 'very negligent';

Ramsden whined back that 'nothing could equal my surprise on hearing the charges brought against me by Major-General Roy ... I was the more affected by it as coming from a Gentleman with whom I considered myself in Friendship'. This spat reached its climax in May 1790, when Ramsden demanded that the Royal Society expunge some of Roy's more colourful slaggings of him from their records. Sadly, William Roy died a few weeks later, the matter still unresolved. It was an acrimonious – and, to us, salutary – end to a brilliant career.

Although William Roy died before the official foundation of the Ordnance Survey in 1791, he was its undoubted progenitor. The event that gave formal birth to the organisation was the re-measuring of the Hounslow Heath base line that Roy himself had first established some seven years earlier. In April 1784, following the French submission to George III, Roy had swiftly secured government backing for the survey and wasted no time in getting on with it. He had at his command twelve Army NCOs and an entire division of the 12th Foot Brigade from nearby Windsor; these he set to levelling and clearing the five-mile-plus route of his line. Having a burly crew of soldiers around was also good insurance; Hounslow Heath in the eighteenth century was the most dangerous location in Britain, and certainly not a place for gentlemen to linger. London and Bath were the two wealthiest cities in Georgian England, and the busy road connecting them ran (as it does still) along the heath's northern edge. The low-lying ground, with its unexpected fogs, suppurating ditches and numerous copses, was the ideal hiding place for highwaymen and cutpurses, who had rich pickings among the well-to-do on their way to Windsor or the West Country. Contemporary maps show a string of gibbets along the Bath Road across the heath. Many of these would have contained rotting corpses swinging in the breeze, for the policy of the authorities was to return the bodies of those hanged at Tyburn to the place of their misdemeanours, to be displayed to all as a shocking deterrent.

Jesse Ramsden – still, at this point, in Roy's good books – had made a steel chain exactly one hundred feet in length, together with wooden rods of twenty feet apiece: both were used alternately to calibrate the distance as the party progressed slowly from King's Arbour Field and across the heath, with the distant witch's hat spire of Banstead church as their guidance point on the horizon. Work progressed through a monumentally wet summer, conditions that didn't suit the wooden rods, which were found to expand and contract way too much for accurate measurement. The project ground to a brief halt. Glass rods were commissioned and produced, which required the utmost delicacy as they were hauled across the heath, particularly when it came to crossing the busy Staines Road.

Delays occurred too because the surveying team became something of an unlikely attraction, especially after King George III dropped by on 19 July to see how the work was going: unfortunately, so torrential was the rain that Roy was unable to demonstrate much of their work. The King returned on 21 August and spent two hours examining the team's work and discussing it with them. This, according to Roy, 'met with his gracious approbation'. In his wake, all manner of society notables trotted by to see what was going on, and it was left to Sir Joseph Banks, the President of the Royal Society, to erect mobile refreshment and hospitality tents in order to cope with the crowds and to keep them at a discreet distance from the work of the surveyors. The team finally reached their destination, the workhouse at Hampton, on the penultimate day of August. By now, the steel chain had been abandoned and the entire measurement had been made using the glass rods. The base line, announced William Roy, was 27,404.72 feet: just over 5.19 miles long. 'There never has been,' he declaimed, 'so great a proportion of the surface of the Earth measured with so much care and accuracy.'

Three years later, when Ramsden's theodolite was finally ready, the survey continued, using triangulation to work its way from Hampton down to Dover and the English Channel. The supposed aim of establishing the precise relation of the London and Paris observatories was never quite attained, but the process had, in Roy's eyes, been hugely successful in his main ambition of showing how poor and imprecise current British maps were and how a national survey was both urgently desirable and eminently practicable. In his final report to the Royal Society and the King in 1789, Roy egged them all on:

> *The trigonometrical operation, so successfully begun, should certainly be continued, and gradually extended over the whole Island. Compared with the greateness of the object, the annual expence to the publick would be a mere trifle not worthy of being mentioned. The honour of the Nation is concerned in having at least as good a map of This as there is of any Other country.*

Such as France, Your Majesty, he might have added. It took less than a year for the authorities to agree and to find the money, but, by then, Roy was dead.

The fogs, footpads and gibbets may be long gone from Hounslow Heath, but the land still has a melancholy tang to it, if only thanks to the fact that so much of it has been eaten alive by Heathrow Airport, located there for precisely the same reasons (vast expanse, flat as a pancake, near London) as Roy's base line. The airport has swallowed whole villages along the northern part of the line, its route south-east has been filled in with shops, factories, houses, roads and all the normal suburban detritus of the outskirts of London. The line, dotted across field and factory, and marked portentously as General Roy's Base, used to appear on OS maps up until the early twentieth century, though not since. Strangely, the northern end of it at Heathrow is labelled, on the current OS 1:25 000 Explorer map, with the supremely wordy 'Cannon: West End of General Roy's Base (site of)'; although the cannon is firmly there in precisely the spot indicated, there is nothing 'site of' about it. The other end, at Hampton – which is far easier, and more pleasurable, to find – doesn't even warrant that, and goes completely unmarked.

Trying to trace the line today, I was reminded of the late Linda Smith's immortal observation that Greater London was something of a misnomer, for 'the further you get away from the middle of it, London doesn't really get greater – it's more Lesser London'. She came from Erith ('not so much the city that never sleeps, more the town that lies awake all night staring at the ceiling'), which sits crusted on the rim of the capital in much the same way as Feltham, Bedfont and Hanworth, the sprawls that now cover William Roy's historic line. There are other invisible lines to contend with here: these undistinguished, indistinguishable towns are firmly on the other side of the tracks from leafy Hampton (as in Court), where Roy's measurement ended. This lies in that odd little corner of south-west London, the Twickenham–Richmond triangle: embarrassed Tory, so often votes LibDem, super-smug with its own greenness, yet death by bungalow and leylandii.

After Major-General Roy conducted his experiments, wooden posts were interred in the ground at either end of the recorded base line as a memorial. In 1791, eleven months after Roy's death, the party led by the Duke of Richmond, charged with re-measuring the line for the Board of Ordnance, found that the posts were rotting and so they were replaced by upended cannons. There, wondrously, they still remain. Both cannons have seen untold change unfold around them over two centuries. The southern one, at Hampton, witnessed the demolition of the borough workhouse nearby; it thence lived in an area of open ground known as Cannon Field until Twickenham Borough Council built housing estates on it in the late 1940s. At least they left the cannon intact and had the good grace to name the two nearest cul-de-sacs Roy Grove (where the cannon can be found sat in a grassy gap between two post-war semis) and Cannon Close (which, indeed, it is). This is Hampton as the acme of suburbia, so much so that the street opposite is Acacia Road.

Handily, there's a bus – the 285 Kingston-on-Thames to Heathrow – that almost precisely connects the two cannons, taking a route that's only a little over a mile longer than William Roy's 5.19-mile straight line. The good general wouldn't recognise it these days. The bus coughs its way up the Uxbridge Road and into Feltham, doing a quick detour into the Sainsbury's car park, and passing forlorn-looking light industrial estates, the Clipper Cutz hair salon, the Chirpy Chaps barbers, Cindy's Nail Bar, Fryday's chippy, a Subway or two, the A3 roundabout and parades of Metroland semis displaying either a St George's flag or a 'No To Heathrow Expansion' sticker, sometimes both (albeit quite hard to see through the triple glazing).

I broke my journey at Feltham, in order to take a look at another memorial to William Roy, an eponymous modern pub off the High Street. This, it claims, is named after him because of its position more or less halfway along his historic line, although it's stretching things slightly, as the General Roy pub is nearly a mile to the south of the route. There's nothing there to indicate its homage to Roy, save for one old map of the district on the wall, showing the Feltham area as a bucolic cluster of villages, before they were entirely obliterated by the spreading gut of the capital and its main airport. The pub is pitched at workers from the nearby industrial park, home to something glassy and chromey called the Feltham Corporate Centre – a name to strike even greater terror into the loins than the town's rather better-known Young Offenders' Institution.

From Feltham, the 285 fairly closely follows the route of the base line north-west towards Hatton Cross and Heathrow. Even without the growing taste of diesel in the air and the ear-splitting screams of the jets overhead, you'd know that there's a major airport coming up. It dominates everything, especially when the tired, tatty – and increasingly impossible to sell – houses finally give way to the dispiriting landscape of international aviation: the pavement-less roads clogged with traffic, the giant hangars, mysterious metal buildings housing anything from security firms to haulage companies, car parks galore, miles of razor wire, CCTV whirring and winking in every direction and a collection of hotels that no one, surely, has ever spent a second night in.

Heathrow Airport only came into existence thanks to government sleight-of-hand at the end of the Second World War. The site, on the richest agricultural land in the country, was commandeered under Emergency Powers in 1943, purportedly for the RAF. It was never used as such. The then Under-Secretary of State for Air, Harold Balfour, revealed in his autobiography that the requisition and construction work undertaken were entirely bogus, and that the plans had always been to turn the airfield into London's principal civil airport come the end of hostilities. Playing the national emergency card simply allowed the authorities to circumvent any normal planning procedures – and so the pattern continues.

Even Major-General William Roy fell foul of the airport zealots' economy with the truth. When the never-to-be-used RAF base was being built in 1944, the memorial cannon that marked the north-western end of his base line was removed, in a theatrical attempt to demonstrate that no impediment – even one just five feet tall – should be placed in the way of our magnificent men in their flying machines. Sense eventually prevailed, and the cannon was returned in 1968, and finally replaced in its original position four years later, where it still squats. It's not easy to locate: indeed, the irony is that you need a bloody good map to find it. Tucked away in a grassy corner nibbled out of a long-stay car park, the cannon sits alone and unloved, overlooking the airport's main police station and the northern perimeter fence. You'd hardly notice it, especially compared with the huge banner that hangs off the car park fence above it: 'Exclusive Parking: Park Today. Complimentary 15 Minute Spa Treatment' – well, who wouldn't want a rub down from a car park attendant? In Paris, you suspect that a monument this significant would have been turned into a vast pyramid, visited by coachloads of schoolchildren by day and extravagantly flood-lit by night.

I paused, gulped down a little more airborne diesel, and felt strangely proud of the British way.

Index to 1:50 000 Series

The original index map for the OS 1:50 000 series: there's Aysgarth, but no Sheffield

3. EVERY NODULE
AND BOBBLE

> Ordnance Survey maps in all their shapes and sizes are the
> most beautiful manifestation of twentieth-century British
> functional design. Ever since I can remember, I have spent
> stolen moments, wasted evenings and secret hours studying
> the mystery and beauty of the Ordnance Survey maps of these
> islands. The concrete trig points that had originally been used
> in their creation became almost as powerful in mystical prop-
> erties for me as standing stones.
>
> ~ Bill Drummond, *45*

Grimsby and Cleethorpes. Could there be a more inauspicious debut
to a lifetime's obsession? It was 1974 and the Ordnance Survey had
just published its first swathe of new 1:50 000 maps, the metric
replacement for the longstanding, much-loved one-inch system that
had divided the country since the very first map in 1801. Whether it
was their eye-catching colour (a goutish pinky-purple) or stark 1970s
visual functionality, I don't know, but as soon as I saw the new maps
in W. H. Smith, I was hooked. I wanted them, and before I discovered
how easy they were to steal, I was even prepared to save up my pocket
money to get them. The going rate in our family was 2p for every year
of your age, earning me a princely 14p every week. The maps were
65p each, so it took some saving – and some serious creeping to
grandparents.

   The 1:50 000 series (the 'Landranger' title only appeared in 1979)
is the best range of general-use maps in the world. The whole of Great

Britain is carved into 204 squares, each one a 40 x 40 km portrait of its patch of land. The variety is breathtaking: from map number 176 (*West London*), which is covered in the dense stipple of cheek-by-jowl population, covering the homes of perhaps 4–5 million people, to map number 31 (*Barra & South Uist, Vatersay & Eriskay*), where nine-tenths of the map is pale blue sea, and the rest just a few straggling islands of the Outer Hebrides, home to no more than a couple of hundred hardy souls.

I loved every aspect of these maps: the clarity and efficient good sense of their colour scheme, their neat typography and lucid symbolism, the fact that they are at precisely the right scale to include every lane, track, path and farmhouse, every nodule and bobble of the landscape, yet cover a sufficiently large area to afford us a one-glance take on the topography of a substantial part of the country. Even the 1970s cover plan, a stylised square summarising the area to be explored within, has a pleasing visual economy, the size of the settlements upon it indicated by the depth of boldness of the type: darkest for the largest towns through to ghostly light for the villages. In the early days of the new series, before the marketing men decided to plaster the cover with a tourist board shot of somewhere on the map, the cover plan filled the map's purple front: bold, clean and perfectly in keeping with the times. A lifelong OS collector-turned-dealer told me of the 'moment of conversion' that ignited his passion on unfolding a One Inch map for the very first time nearly half a century before, his captivation with the beauty and elegance of an Ordnance Survey map. Most OS aficionados can remember their own such moments of epiphany, when a lifetime's love was, in an explosive moment of clarity, mapped out before them. And so very well mapped, at that.

The modernist mania for streamlining was evident in the new 1:50 000 map series, and not just in the cool lines and clear typeface of the covers. One of the all-new features of the maps was that everything was metric. The old one-inch (to one mile) scale, itself a masterstroke of simplicity, translated in metric terms to the rather more cumbersome 1:63 360. Expanding the scale slightly meant that the maps looked less crowded, and that each grid square, an orderly 2 x 2 cm, represented one kilometre. Not that you ever heard anyone refer to them as the '2 cm to 1 km' series. It was – and is still – the 'one and a quarter inches to the mile'.

Contours had to be translated into metric measurements too, and this produced one of the series' daftest anomalies that remained obstinately in place for years, until the whole country's height differentials could be re-surveyed and re-plotted at ten-metre intervals. As the key next to the map put it: 'Contour values are given to the nearest metre. The vertical interval is, however, 50 feet.' In other words, contours were merely renumbered metrically, making the gap between them a decidedly forgettable 15.24 metres. Thus, instead of a hill rising through 50, 100, 150, 200 feet and so on, it was now growing through 15, 30, 46, 61 and 76 metres. Things got even sillier the higher you went. Then there was the potential confusion in some of these odd contour measurements: 61, 91, 168, 686, 869, 899, 991 and 1,006 metre lines could all be misread upside down. Therefore it was decreed that such figures could only be placed on contours on the south-facing slopes, so that the numbers would be the right way up. As a result, you had to follow your finger round an awfully long way on some of the hills, the higher ones in particular. That said, anyone who thought that there were contour lines of 9,001 metres to be found in Britain should have been banned from going anywhere near a map.

There were very few contours on *Grimsby & Cleethorpes*, 1:50 000 map number 113. This really was the very first map that I frittered away my pocket money on, at the tender age of seven. I took it into school, hoping to impress everyone. Unsurprisingly, the ploy failed; as I unfurled the portrait of distant Humberside to a small crowd, there was puzzled silence and then a small voice piped up, 'So where's Kiddy on that, then?' The realisation that others failed to share my enthusiasm, or even to understand the concept that there was a whole big country out there that Kidderminster wasn't a part of, was crushing, but it didn't deter me. Before long, I'd saved up for my second OS map, right down the other end of England, number 189 (*Ashford & Romney Marsh*). I wasn't especially interested in seeing close-up details of my own neck of the woods, or even any of the places that I knew. Thirty-five years later, I've still never been to Grimsby, Cleethorpes or Ashford, but they were the first places I wanted to scrutinise on the map, to wander around in my febrile imagination.

Hard though it may be to believe, those first two maps represented a glimpse of the exotic. And it was a very specific kind of exoticism that appealed to me. Even at that early age, I had become fascinated by end-of-the-world places and communities, set at the far end of bumpy tracks and sliding lethargically into the sea under lowering, leaden skies. Part of it was undoubtedly the call of the ocean. The sea holds a very specific place in the psyche of a Midlander. When you only see it once or twice a year, and that's when you're on holiday and there are endless ice creams and amusement arcades to accompany it, even the steely Scarborough briny comes to represent all that is exciting, infinite and free.

Of all the 11,073 miles of British coastline (19,491 if you include the offshore islands), the two areas that I first chose to own by proxy of a map seem strangely perverse, even now and even to me. This is not the Kiss Me Quick seaside; more the Wring Me Out and Leave Me For Dead coastline. But each of those first two maps held one feature that enthralled my besotted mind. On the *Grimsby & Cleethorpes* map, it was the long spit of land known as Spurn Head at the mouth of the River Humber, while on *Ashford & Romney Marsh*, it was the ethereal swell of marsh, bog and nuclear power station known as Dungeness. Spurn Head and Dungeness. Even the names sound vaguely suicidal.

Hours I spent poring over those obscure corners of this island. Nowadays, a precocious seven-year-old with similar tastes would merely tap the names into Google, and find himself presented almost immediately with galleries of images and reams of facts. Nothing so instant in 1974. It was left to my overheated mind to create images of these weird-looking landscapes. On the map, the lack of contours, the ruler-straight lanes and irrigation ditches, the banks of shingle and the odd names all conjured up a misty melancholy seeping over the bleak countryside like an unseen plague. Back in my Midlands bedroom, I hugged these unknown, unknowable places to my chest and swore that one day I'd get to meet them.

Spurn Head I managed to tick off my list decades ago, although it took until very recently to make it to Dungeness. My love affair with end-of-the-world landscapes has continued into adulthood, and, in my twenties, I was fortunate enough to have a good friend who shared this strange passion. Jim and I would borrow a car for the weekend and head off to places whose sole criterion for us was that they just looked weird on the map. Hours we spent poring over my OS collection, trying to find just the right balance of oddities in any one place. Hence the Isle of Thanet, the Suffolk coast, Portland, the Forest of Dean, the Wash, the Isle of Wight and the Humber estuary all came under our critical gaze at some point or other. Best were those places that not only afforded the opportunity to look out over marsh and mudflat, but also gave us the chance to hang out in its dead-end urban twin, the out-of-season British seaside resort. Thus Skegness was a great base for the Wash trip, Thanet gave us chance to be depressed by Margate long before Tracey Emin gentrified it, and Bridlington was a superbly moribund HQ for that ultimate trip to my long-awaited paramour, Spurn Head.

Spurn was no disappointment. In fact, I can recommend it as the ultimate British road-movie destination for that nowhere-to-run explosive climax. Whichever way you come at it, you will have to travel through miles of pancake-flat scenery, where the sea frets roll in and blanket out the grim farmhouses, lonely church spires and caravan parks clinging to cliff edges. Occasionally, just to heighten the surrealism of the scene, the dim shape of an ocean-going tanker will glide by in the distance, looking as if it is ploughing through the black fields.

The best route to Spurn Head is along the Holderness coast to its north. This is the fastest-eroding coastline in Europe, receding at an average of two metres per year, although single-occasion erosions of six metres and more have been recorded. Over the past few centuries, dozens of villages have fallen over the edge and been wiped from the map altogether: a roll-call includes such fine-sounding settlements as Owthorne, Auburn, Cowden Parva and the particularly appealing Hartburn. Today's Holderness villages are on Death Row. Official policy is quietly to abandon places like Kilnsea, Easington, Holmpton, Rolston, Atwick and Barmsden to the mercy of the sea. The coast's two main towns, Hornsea and Withernsea, have coastal defence systems in place, although they still face some uncertainty, and periodic pieces appear in the local press wailing about unsellable houses and plummeting property prices. Such are the forces of nature in these parts, however, that the comparative security of these two towns only heightens the misery of others: if one part of this dynamic coastline is artificially shored up, it only means that some other part, a bit further south, will be eroded all the more. You can imagine what that would do for community harmony and the length of debates in the local council chamber.

As ever, their misery is our fascination, for this is a weird, woeful and riveting place. Jim and I drove slowly down from Bridlington, taking the odd small lane that headed eastwards towards the sea and, on numerous occasions, finding it disappearing over the edge of the cliff. Shards of broken tarmac pointed out to sea, abandoned houses teetered on the brink of the drop, seabirds swooped and shrilled a maritime last post. The frailty and the melancholy only increased as we headed further south towards Spurn Head. In every sense of the phrase, it blew me away.

Over the past millennium, there have been five different Spurn Heads, each one slightly to the west of its predecessor. The cycle of the spit's growth, increasing fragility and then ultimate destruction and regrouping, tends to do a full circle about every two hundred and fifty years, meaning that the current Spurn Head is living on borrowed time. The slender neck of the four-mile-long spit is in constant danger of being breached.

Driving down this tiny thread of land is like walking a tightrope in a gale. The concrete road is poor and rutted, with drifts of sand blocking the way and sea spume whacking your windscreen like a scorned lover. At times, the road is virtually all there is between the two banks of angry, choppy sea falling away on either side. There is no safety net. At the end of the spit are a few brutal government outposts: a lifeboat station, with Britain's only permanently sited crew, a lighthouse and the Vessel Traffic Service Centre, tracking the lumbering great tankers heading up the Humber to Immingham, whose Meccano-like gas terminals can be seen blazing across the muddy estuary. All are blasted by gale-force winds for most of the time. When Jim and I pitched up, it was a fine, calm day in dear old Brid, but by the time we got to the end of the Spurn, it took every ounce of shoulder power just to get the car doors open. We stood around on the beach for a while, until our eyeballs started to pop and tears were flowing from the whipping, sand-blasting laceration of the wind – all in all, about five minutes. It is one of the ugliest, rawest places of beauty I've ever experienced. And it is quite wonderful. Twenty years it had taken from running my eager finger along my first Ordnance Survey to standing on the point itself, but it was worth every minute of the wait. We headed back to Brid, and I was a man fulfilled.

I recently bought a new version of that initial map to see how my first love had fared over the past third of a century. There's no swifter way of getting a handle on the huge changes in the layout of Britain over the last couple of generations than by comparing Ordnance Survey sheets of the same area, especially one as varied, in its rural, urban, industrial and coastal mix, as the *Grimsby & Cleethorpes* 1:50 000. Poor old Cleethorpes has got the push for starters, as the map is now titled plain *Grimsby*, with Louth and Market Rasen as the smaller sub-heads. That's despite the fact that Cleethorpes is one of the towns on the map that has ballooned the most between the 1970s and the 2000s; whole fringes of squiggly new housing estates are plugged into every available corner, including one laid across what, three decades earlier, is marked on the map as a marsh. The town's expansion has been positively slim-line, however, in comparison with some of the villages south of the Humber. Our national hunger for the pastoral life seems unstoppable, even if villages here, such as Humberston, Waltham and Holton-le-Clay, are little more than modern, steroid-packed doughnuts throttling the original settlements.

In 1974, the new Ordnance Survey series' pièce de résistance was in mapping, for the first time, the sleek new counties that had arrived in April of that year. Here, we see Humberside make its cartographic debut; born in the hope of uniting the Yorkshire and Lincolnshire banks of the Humber, despite the fact that, for the first seven years of the county's life, the only way between them was a creaky ferry or a huge diversion inland – the road journey from Grimsby to the Humber-side County Council headquarters at Beverley was almost one hundred miles. The ferry's replacement, the Humber Bridge, may well have opened as the largest single-span bridge on the planet, but it was costly to cross and did little more to gel the county together, except as a too-little, too-late symbol and one that, like the county itself, proved to be something of a white elephant. Small wonder: the bridge had only been built as one of the most blatant bribes ever served up by politicians.

The announcement of the project came in the middle of the campaign for the Hull North by-election of January 1966. The death of Labour MP Henry Solomons, who'd wrested the seat from the Conser-vatives with the tiniest majority in the general election of October 1964, had cut Harold Wilson's parliamentary majority to just one. Wilson threw everything at the by-election campaign, most startlingly the promise of the Humber Bridge. It worked; Labour upped its majority to over five thousand, enough of a swing to persuade Wilson to call another general election and secure a more comfortable majority.

Antipathy towards Humberside grew locally and, indeed, nationally: it became the Page Three girl of the We Want Our Old Counties Back movement, and was regularly cited as the most steadfast proof that the 1974 changes had been the victory of bloodless bureaucrats over local loyalty and natural identity. Many protests, reviews, commissions and changes later, we eagerly turn to the new map to see what civic pride has been restored to the area now that the county of Humberside has been so thoroughly dumped. And that's when you notice something a little odd, for the reviled county border has not shifted an inch, only the names have been changed. The ghostly shape of the despised authority is entirely intact on the map, but instead of showing the border between the counties of Humberside and Lincolnshire, it now details the split between the two-tier county of Lincolnshire (further divided into the district council divisions of East Lindsey and West Lindsey) and the unitary authorities of North Lincolnshire, North-East Lincolnshire and, across the Humber, the East Riding of Yorkshire. Glad they cleared that up so effectively.

The most startling difference between the two maps, however, is their portrait of the merciless rise of tourism as the mainstay of our economy. In 1974, there was not one museum marked on the map. Its 2006 version is awash with the blue hatching used to denote 'selected places of tourist interest', and shows four museums, three visitor centres, one theme park, two country parks, a zoo, an 'Animal Gardens' and numerous other attractions of varying degrees of dubiousness. There's also the inevitable heritage steam railway carved out of a tiny fragment of line closed in the Beeching cuts of the 1960s. It has two stations, Ludborough, re-opened in 1984, and North Thoresby, finally reached in August 2009. Your £5.50 buys you a mile-and-a-half's shuttle between the two, through a succession of pancake-flat fields, before stopping and then being gently pulled back to where you started. The middle of nowhere return, please. Even the most excitable marketing guru would have trouble turning that into a 'staycation' success story. In terms of the map, the fact that these pointless excuses for both railways and tourist attractions are shown with exactly the same symbology as a real railway, connecting real places, is something that pains me to see on a modern OS. On the 1:50 000 Landranger, the Lincolnshire Wolds Railway, with its 1.7 inches of track and solitary ‑•‑ symbol (as of December 2009, it hasn't yet caught up with the re-opening of North Thoresby), looks frankly risible. There should be a special symbol for these toy trains that doesn't confuse them with the real thing: my suggestion would be a pictogram of a grinning old man dragging a reluctant grandson along. Such an image could be misconstrued, I realise, but perhaps not entirely without justification.

It was only in 2007 that I finally made it to the location of the second OS map that I'd bought over thirty years earlier: number 189, *Ashford & Romney Marsh*, purchased in order to gaze lovingly at another mysterious coastal protuberance, Dungeness. I'd go so far as to say that it is quite possibly the most awe-inducing place I have ever visited in Britain. Dungeness plays with all five senses: the sight of the endless skies, seas and shingle, the background hum and plunk of the nuclear power stations, the slap of the wind, the sweet wafts of honey from the sea kale poking defiantly out of the pebbles, the tang of salt. Strewn around the headland are a few dozen shacks, huts and railway carriages, brought here to their graveyard after the First World War as wind-blasted homes for fishermen and rock-crushers, historically, the two sole occupations available in Dungeness. Then they cost a tenner each; today, thanks to Derek Jarman and the succession of dropouts and artists who followed in his slipstream, they go for around two hundred grand apiece.

Aside from their novelty beauty, their most startling attribute is that there is not one fence between them, just a succession of driftwood and debris gardens strewn among the shingle for anyone to amble through; as Jarman put it, 'My garden's boundaries are the horizon.' Just up the road, in the clipped little resorts of Lydd-on-Sea, Littlestone and Greatstone, normal Kentish service is resumed in the brick bungalows, security warnings and picket fences which serve only to exaggerate Dungeness's scattergun democracy. It is impossible to be ambivalent about the place: you either despise its squally shabbiness or adore it for the very same reason. I'm firmly in the latter camp – even the twin nuclear plants, with their attendant forests of pylons, failed to offend me in the slightest, so naturally did they seem to sit in this quite crazy landscape. Indeed, they provide one of the Ness's most pleasingly surreal sights in the patch of boiling sea where the outflows disgorge, attracting shoals of fish and clouds of screaming birds.

Malcolm Saville, that upright, uptight children's author that so appealed to me as a youngster thanks to the maps in his books, based some of his Lone Pine adventure stories in nearby Rye, and Dungeness featured in his 1951 book *The Elusive Grasshopper*. Saville hated the place, as was clear from his deathless prose:

> *Some days later Jon tried to describe Dungeness to his mother and found it very difficult, although it was little more than a desert of shingle which had been made even uglier by slovenly and haphazard building of bungalows, shacks and old railway coaches. ... [It was] a horrid sight and even on this sunny afternoon Jon felt that this outpost was both curious and uncanny.*

To those of a more iconoclastic bent, the place acts as a magnet. More than perhaps anywhere in England, Dungeness deserves the clichéd epithet of being 'at the end of the world', which is surely what draws so many of life's outsiders to it. This is land that was, not so long ago, sea, and it could so easily be again, its very insubstantiality a balm and a redoubt to those weary of the fortress mentality that so characterises all too much of our landscape. Dungeness is *The Last of England*, the name that Derek Jarman gave his raging cinematic riposte to the Thatcher years, some of which was shot on location here. Jarman may be gone, but anarchic playwright Snoo Wilson still has a shack there, and the late comedienne Linda Smith chose to have her ashes scattered at Dungeness, partly in honour of having located the perfect crab sandwich in the miniature railway café there a few years earlier.

That night, I lay in my camper van right up against the power station's perimeter fence, bathed in the plant's arc lights and dreaming through the constant fizz and crackle of its reactors. For an hour, I scrutinised the map that I'd bought so many years earlier and that had first ignited the urge to see this mad place. The map had hinted at all the eccentricities and delights of the area, and I was thrilled that I'd spotted them so readily and that they'd been so gloriously confirmed in reality. *Ashford & Romney Marsh* is a beautiful example of the Ordnance Survey at its finest, especially in its portrayal of the two utterly different Kents, divided by the old sea cliffs and the Royal Military Canal at their base. To the north and west, the gentle contours and rippling orchards of the Downs and the Weald; to the south and east, the shaggy flatlands, ditches and shingle of Romney Marsh and Dungeness. The marsh is a land of spectres, where nothing is quite as it seems. Villages have vanished, changed their names and moved, leaving just crumbling church ruins and stagnant pools in remote fields.

It was pleasing to discover that the area had had a significant role in the Ordnance Survey's birth. This was the very first part of Britain mapped by the OS, its inaugural Kent sheet appearing in 1801. When the Survey's double centenary was celebrated in 1991, the commemorative Royal Mail stamps nodded to this piece of OS history, showing four maps of the marshside village of Hamstreet through the ages. Even earlier, in the 1780s, the area had played a significant part in the genesis of the OS. Once William Roy had successfully plotted his base line across Hounslow Heath, a series of triangles between London and the Kent coast needed to be measured in order to secure the accurate positioning of the London and Paris meridians. The main base line for verification was across Romney Marsh, from the village of Ruckinge to High Nook on the seawall at Dymchurch, the region's flatness being its principal appeal. It was not a happy project: Roy himself writes that it was an 'operation of so delicate and difficult a nature', thanks to 'the country so much intersected by ditches, and where there were so many ponds of water to be avoided'. Furthermore, thanks to delays in the delivery of the apparatus, the measuring operation didn't begin until 17 October 1787, continuing for two months, through weather that Roy wearily described as 'tempestuous'.

To be fair, Roy was not a well man, and by the time the Ordnance Survey was officially born on 21 June 1791, he had been dead a year. The Survey's birth date is given as the day on which it was first granted expenditure from the public purse – £373 14s to pay for Jesse Ramsden's second, superior theodolite. Ramsden's original instrument, whose tardy progress had caused William Roy such apoplexy, was blown to bits in a Second World War bombing raid on the OS headquarters in Southampton, but his second one can still be seen, in all its enormous, intricate glory, in the Science Museum in London. It's a sweet apposition that the Survey was born on the summer solstice, the day of greatest daylight, for its work has so gloriously illuminated British topography, history and culture ever since.

For us map devotees, the Ordnance Survey is the high altar of our cartographic temple. No other mapping agency comes close, either at home or abroad; the maps it produces are regularly, and deservedly, cited as the finest in the world, and not just by Brits either. Such adulation is a comparatively modern phenomenon, however, for it hasn't always been that way. At certain times in its history, the OS has been hopelessly out of kilter with the needs of its many masters, be they the map-buying public, politicians, the Exchequer or, these days, those who campaign hard for the release of topographical data from the OS's tight clutches, for it's not unreasonable to say that the publicly funded Ordnance Survey has historically had a near monopoly on the lie of the land, and it's not been afraid to use or defend it. This has been a running sore since the earliest days. In 1816, Major-General William Mudge, Superintendent of the Survey, huffed that 'an idea has gone abroad among the Mapsellers of London that as a portion of the Public, at whose expense the Ordnance Survey is carried on, they have a right to reduce from and publish Copies of the Ordnance Survey on Scales to their own convenience'. As a state agency, the Survey has always been able to commandeer the ears of government, even having copyright laws bent in its favour.

One paymaster that the Ordnance Survey has never seriously fallen out with is the defence establishment. For its first hundred years, OS top brass and their modus operandi were entirely military. The maps were also available to the public from the beginning, but the right was periodically revoked at times of national emergency, particularly in withdrawing from sale maps of the south coast on those occasions when Napoleon was peering avariciously across the Channel. The bans never lasted long, however, and a growing band of civilian enthusiasts for the new maps beat a path to the door of the only two outlets for their sale: the Ordnance Survey's own headquarters in the Tower of London, and Geographer Royal William Faden's business in Charing Cross.

This unswerving loyalty to the defence of the realm has had some noticeable effects. Although the first tranche of map-making that came to result in the OS was William Roy's mid-eighteenth-century survey of the Scottish Highlands, there's been an institutional bias against the north of Britain since then that has permeated down the centuries, despite the perception among those of a certain mindset that the precise opposite was the case. In an 1883 House of Lords debate, Lord Salisbury, soon to begin his first term as Prime Minister, boomed his complaints about the Ordnance Survey's progress with its six-inches-to-the-mile survey of the entire realm:

> *They seemed to have gone on the principle of serving first those parts of the Kingdom which were the most disagreeable to the Government, and which were not in so much need of the maps as England. The most disagreeable part of the Three Kingdoms was Ireland, and, therefore, Ireland had a splendid map. Next to Ireland, Scotland was the most disagreeable part of the country to the Government, and, consequently, Scotland had a map; but poor, meek, humble, submissive England was necessarily left to the last.*

In truth, the first parts of the country that demanded maps from the OS were the coasts of southern England, those most vulnerable to invasion from the Continent. Since then, almost every new imprint of OS maps has followed suit, with plans of southern parts of Britain being published sometimes long before those of the north. This happened not just with the very first maps, but the old series of One Inch maps in the mid-nineteenth century and then with the large-scale 1:2500 series that formed the basis of all detailed mapping, in which some of the plans of rural Scotland first appeared more than forty years after their southern counterparts. Even in modern times, the trend has continued, albeit less dramatically: the 1:25 000 Explorer maps gradually covered the country from the bottom up, while the launch of the new 1:50 000 series, the flagship of the Survey, was split into two, with the southern half of Britain, below a line from Lancaster to Bridlington, being published in 1974, the remainder in 1976. Two years was a long time to wait for a seven-year-old: I was through the doors of W. H. Smith at opening time on the day the new northern maps were due to be published, and, to my delight, they'd arrived. To me, it was the Harry Potter launch of its day, even if I was the only one in the queue. I'd been frantically saving up for the big event and bought three of their

North Yorkshire sheets on the spot, racing back home to spend long hours in my bedroom scrutinising the places that we visited every year on our annual jaunt to Aunty Molly's in Scarborough.

This inherent southern bent doesn't come as any surprise in an organisation incubated within the British military establishment and firmly rooted in the south of England. The forces, from their parade grounds in Sandhurst, Horse Guards and Winchester, have long looked at the north and the west of our islands as distant, stroppy outposts of the Empire, full of tetchy natives in inhospitable terrain. All director-generals of the OS, from the very beginning and almost to the turn of the twenty-first century, came from a pool of colonels, brigadiers and major-generals. The very first DG without military training was Professor David Rhind, who took up his post only in 1992.

Inevitably, the maps have reflected such influences. Even now, and even when there is absolutely no trace to be seen on the ground, the site of a battlefield is enthusiastically marked with its striking crossed-swords motif. By contrast, as OS historian Richard Oliver has tartly put it, 'no one would guess from an OS map that there was such a thing as labour history'. Military and ecclesiastical remains are the only ones worth marking, it would seem, which speaks volumes about the Ordnance Survey's historic view of the land and the cultural influences woven into it.

From those early days, it's hard not to picture extravagantly moustachioed OS types marching over the country in pursuit of their information, bringing with them attitudes that reeked of the public school and the parade ground. Such a scenario even made it as a mediocre movie, *The Englishman Who Went Up a Hill, But Came Down a Mountain*, from 1995, which told the tale of an Edwardian map surveyor despatched to gather topographical information about a small Welsh village, whose inhabitants are horrified to find out that their beloved mountain will have to be reclassified as a hill, as it falls a few feet short of the requisite height. The comedy, such as it was, came from the misunderstandings between the terribly English officer (the inevitable Hugh Grant at his most bumbling and floppy-haired) and the conniving natives, determined to delay him long enough to enable them to shore up their hill so that it squeaked past the necessary threshold. And – wouldn't you know it – the enforced delay is just long enough for the strait-laced surveyor to fall head over heels for a local raven-haired lovely.

Victorian imperial attitudes of geographic and cultural rank permeate all aspects of the Ordnance Survey's development. Surveyors, when heading out into the field, were issued with detailed instructions on what to look for and how to present it on the maps. The names of places could prove particularly thorny, laden as they were with local custom, variant spellings, even variant languages. OS's field guide from 1905 cut through such potential pitfalls with nary a blink:

For names generally the following are the best individual authorities, and should be taken in the order given: Owners of property; estate agents; clergymen, postmasters and schoolmasters, if they have been some time in the district; rate collectors; road surveyors; borough and county surveyors; gentlemen residing in the district; Local Government Board Orders; local histories; good directories ... Respectable inhabitants of some position should be consulted. Small farmers or cottagers are not to be depended on, even for the names of the places they occupy, especially as to the spelling, but a well-educated and intelligent occupier is, of course, a good authority.

We map addicts have to forgive the Ordnance Survey its inevitable pomposity, for no one could emerge from such a deeply Establishment background entirely unscathed. The organisation has, after all, been pretty thoroughly decontaminated, the band of the Royal Engineers performing a ceremony of Beating the Retreat in the Southampton headquarters car park in October 1983, an occasion intended to symbolise the cutting of the military apron strings. The last four director-generals have all been from civilian backgrounds, the current DG, since 2000, representing a decisive change as the first woman to hold the post and from a background far more relevant to today's OS: publishing and information technology. This DG, Vanessa Lawrence, has unquestionably softened the edges of the organisation, spearheading cuddly new policies such as giving a free Ordnance Survey map to every eleven-year-old in the country. Evidently, I was just a little ahead of the times with my map larceny of the early 1980s.

Today's OS is a very different beast from its earlier incarnations, even that of only thirty years ago. The appointment of Vanessa Lawrence as Director-General is the most obvious symbol of the new, digitally oriented, more feminised OS, but it is far more than a marketing trompe l'œil. When, in 2007, after thirty-three years of collecting OS maps, I finally made it to the headquarters in Southampton, I was amazed to see the sheer quantity of women working there, many in senior roles. More than that: there was a decidedly, and unexpectedly, matronly atmosphere to the place, much augmented by the fact that many of the employees hail from 'OS families', third- and even fourth-generation workers whose roots in the organisation, and loyalty to it, delve down extremely deep.

It's partly a Southampton thing, for a large, prestigious organisation in a smallish city is far more prominent than it would have been had the Survey remained in London. As a child collector of OS maps, even their address seemed impossibly exotic – no mean feat when you remember that this was Romsey Road, Maybush, Southampton. I had absolutely no idea what sort of a place Southampton might be, but I gazed at it on the maps, spread so becomingly along the north shore of its estuary, and dreamed of seeing it one day. In my head, it was a city of swaggering sophistication, boosted by the fact that the only other time it ever flickered across my radar was as the launch pad of the *QE2* or the glamorous, doomed HMS *Titanic*. Furthermore, it was in swanky Hampshire, which, from a satellite town of the West Midlands, oozed prosperity and pony-paddock class. When I finally got there in my early twenties, I couldn't quite believe that the Coventry-with-seagulls before me could possibly be this hallowed Mecca.

A rough old bird Southampton might be, whose rivalry with Portsmouth must constitute the nastiest spat between neighbouring towns anywhere in Britain, but a pretty port is usually a dull marina these days, so long may it remain as dowdy and grumpy as it is. The city has, however, proved to be a perfect home for the Ordnance Survey: the geek and the plain lass rather fell for each other, though neither expected to. The move was forced on the young OS by a fire in its Tower of London headquarters at Hallowe'en in 1841. Southampton was proposed only because there was a big, empty government building there (the former Royal Military Asylum): the OS mandarins were horrified by the idea. A century later, the Southampton site was badly bombed as a strategic target in the Second World War and the Survey was scattered around temporary sites across the country. After the war, the government proposed that the organisation should leave such a vulnerable spot on the south coast and relocate to Northamptonshire. The OS, despite its battering, was hearing none of it, and bludgeoned successive governments until they gave in and built it a new HQ in its, by now, firmly home city. And still the love affair continues. Generations of Southampton families are woven into the fabric of the OS; the city is deeply proud of its status as the organisation's nest.

On my visit, this all came as quite a shock, especially after first seeing the HQ building (officially William Roy House). It's a vast 1960s monolith, built to house OS at a time when its payroll was approaching five thousand. Today, the building houses fewer than a third of that number; whole wings, floors and corridors lie empty and echoing. I've been in so many buildings like this: regional newspaper offices, TV studios, council and company headquarters – all constructed in the heyday of full employment and modernist chutzpah, but overtaken since by the digital revolution and slice after slice of cutbacks, the prize-winning architecture springing leaks and asbestos alerts on an almost weekly basis. They're the kind of buildings that normally guarantee a migraine within half an hour of entry, and – like the Survey's HQ – they're all gradually being abandoned and demolished. Yet despite the unprepossessing surroundings, I've never come across a massive office block with such a genuinely cheerful atmosphere as the Ordnance Survey's. People seemed to adore their jobs there and, unless the management had been slipping serotonin into the water coolers, it all seemed wholly authentic.

I might, however, be colouring the experience with my own delirium. Visiting the headquarters of the Ordnance Survey, an organisation that I'd been in love with for a third of a century, was seventh heaven. Their press office had kindly sorted me out with a day of seeing how their whole operation – from initial survey to printing and distribution of the maps – worked; it would not be an exaggeration to say that it was one of the most blissful days of my life. At last, I could have in-depth conversations with people who cared even more than I did about these beautiful maps. No cartographic subject was too pernickety for these folk, no one's eyes glazed over at detailed discussion about the symbols and colours on the maps, the cover images or the names chosen to market them.

Most illuminating was a long chat with the Product Manager, responsible for the paper-map output of the OS. Startlingly, this accounts for less than ten per cent of Ordnance Survey's income these days, and the figure is falling rapidly as the demand for digital data grows by the day. The market for the traditional OS map is ageing and shrinking, or, as she put it, 'We know exactly where we stand. There is something distinctly Enid Blyton about the Ordnance Survey. It's all very Middle England, National Trust and Radio 4.' I thought about trying to contradict her, but quickly realised that I couldn't be more firmly in that camp than if I was sat in The Bull, quaffing a ginger beer and consulting the OS Explorer, *Felpersham & the Am Valley*, for local NT properties to visit. Even the maps' names hint at the target audience: is it pure coincidence that the flagship Landranger series sounds like a hybrid of a Land Rover and a Range Rover? Are we to expect a new series called the Golden Retriever?

Ordnance Survey knows its demographic intimately, for the simple reason that it hears from them on a very regular basis. Just as any change to the Radio 4 schedule elicits howls of protest in the shires, so does any slight tinkering with the maps. In the early 2000s, OS briefly removed the borders of national parks from the 1:25 000 Explorer maps; a huge outcry soon saw that decision reversed. One of the cartographers told me that, because many of the 1:50 000 Landranger maps were in danger of becoming too cluttered, they would have liked to take the footpaths and other rights of way off them, but knew that the resultant palaver would be terrible PR and more trouble than it was worth. The most thunder-striking example came from a couple of years ago, when the tankard symbol, for a country pub, was modified on the Explorer maps. The level of beer in the glass dropped slightly in the revised version, and quite a few people actually wrote in to OS complaining that they were being short-changed of their pint. Granted, this could have been a prime example of Home Counties humour, the 'And Finally ...' of the *Telegraph* letters page, but hearing it made me feel ashamed to realise that I am but a novice in the map-addict stakes: not only had I failed to notice the change, I couldn't muster any feeling about it either way. I'd love to see the reaction if OS announced that the cheery tankard was, in fact, a half-litre, not a pint, or, even better, that it was being abolished altogether in favour of a sponsored pictogram of a Bacardi Breezer. Oxfordshire would implode.

Symbols and boundaries on the map, or lack of them, cause more trouble and indignant letters than just about anything else to the Ordnance Survey. There is constant and unremitting pressure on the organisation to add yet more features to every map, particularly from the tourism industry, which wants dedicated new symbols for every hokey craft centre and artist's studio flogging winsome watercolours of the locale. OS is mindful that the vast majority of paper maps these days are bought for leisure purposes, which is why the Landrangers and Explorers are already crammed full of blue symbols for what seems to be every conceivable tourist attraction or service. But the 1:50 000 Landranger series, in particular, is already at the point where any more symbols will begin seriously to detract from the map's utility – there really are only so many colourful dots, blobs, dashes and diamonds that the eye can take. Currency – keeping up to date with topographical changes – is the principal watchword of the map-makers, but clarity comes a close second, and that is increasingly under threat.

More and more, Ordnance Survey is finding itself under pressure to expand the repertoire of what is mapped, not from the ordinary map addict, but from the hired professionals. Tourist boards are the main culprits; they won't rest until the maps are as stuffed with blue symbols as the roads are with brown signs inviting car drivers to hurtle between one disappointing leisure experience and the next. The exponential growth in the brown-sign industry is a clear warning to map-makers not to go the same way. Twenty years ago, there was a threshold of visitor numbers to qualify for the signs, but now it's something of a free-for-all, as well as being a nice little earner for the Highways Agency and local authorities. They promote a grimly reductive experience of the country, where practically everywhere can be – and is – pared down to a meaningless catch-all, like the ubiquitous 'Historic Market Town'. Where isn't? It was back in the early 1990s that the Queen reportedly blew a fuse when she first saw the huge sign on the M4 pointing to 'Windsor: Royalty & Empire'. Things have got a whole lot worse since then, Ma'am.

The latest ruckus about what should and should not be marked on Ordnance Survey maps came in 2007, when a PR company, knowing all too well how many column inches could be crowbarred out of the credulous regional press, rounded up a handful of hungry MPs to shout about the lack of recognition for the fast-vanishing coal industry. The politicians and the snake-oil sellers combined as one to demand a new symbol on the OS maps for every site that had once been a pit, even if it had been entirely built over subsequently and there was no evidence of any mining to be found there now. They have a point: thanks to its inherently conservative heritage, the OS and industrial history make reluctant bedfellows, but it's hard to see that this is the answer. How big did the mine have to be and how long did it have to function to warrant inclusion? And after coal mines, then what? According to the PR guff of the campaign, 'It's about marking the fruits of men, children and women's labour. The injuries. The chronic illnesses. The culture. The history. The communities. The decimation. The demolition. The rejuvenation. The regeneration.' So what about the often equally deadly quarries, mills, factories, armaments depots or even harbours? Where do you stop? And how pleased would people be to find that, on the map, their housing estate is obliterated by a little blue symbol of a pithead wheel or a pickaxe, something screaming 'potential subsidence' to house-buyers and insurance companies?

❧

Although Ordnance Survey issues maps and data in a dizzying range of different scales, the most exciting publications, from a map addict's perspective, are the two principal paper-map series, the 1:50 000 Landrangers, successors to the gold standard that was the One Inch map, and the 1:25 000 Explorers, the hugely successful, and comparatively new, series at double the scale of the Landrangers. A few maps at this larger scale had been printed for the army before World War II, but it was only from 1945 that they were put on sale to the public. They were not hugely popular – indeed in 1973, Ordnance Survey proposed abandoning the scale altogether, an idea swiftly jettisoned after considerable protest, and it wasn't until 1989 that they finally came to cover the whole of Britain. Part of the reason for their lack of appeal was that most of the sheets were hopelessly small, with just a few of the popular tourist areas covered by the much handier Outdoor Leisure Maps. The 1:25 000 scale was comprehensively relaunched as the complete national series of orange-covered Explorer maps, which appeared between 1997 and 2003. That the Explorer series has been welded together out of different previous editions is obvious in their strange, and sometimes inconsistent, numbering, as well as the very many shapes and sizes of the maps themselves: some are double-sided, some not and there are some very oddly shaped areas of coverage. A few of the Outdoor Leisure maps (now officially re-branded as Explorer OLs) are vast *and* double-sided, beautiful to look at if you can spread them out on the floor or a sufficiently large table, but downright exasperating if you need to turn them round in the passenger seat of a car or, even worse, on a wet, windy mountainside.

Despite being so comparatively new, over the past decade sales of the large-scale Explorer maps have far eclipsed those of the more established Landranger series. They have become the sexy new pin-ups, OS's biggest seller – Explorer Map OL24, *The Peak District: White Peak* – shifting around 40,000 copies a year, over three times as many as the best-selling Landranger map, number 90, *Penrith & Keswick,* which covers a large tranche of the Lake District. It is the Explorers, not the Landrangers, that the OS has chosen to dole out for free to every eleven-year-old in the country, a scheme that, by its seventh year of operation in 2008, had seen 5 million maps distributed to schoolchildren as their own personal property, and which has led to a significant improvement in map literacy among the young. The Explorer maps are now the unquestioned brand leader for Ordnance Survey.

It's not hard to see why. If tourism and leisure are the driving forces for paper-map sales these days, that almost always includes our national love of rambling, and the 1:25 000 range is the perfect map for that, peerless in its coverage of footpaths and other rights of way.

This is, without doubt, the main reason for their success, amazing to consider when you remember that rights of way information has only been included on OS maps since 1960, and only patchily until very recently. The Explorers are also the smallest scale at which field boundaries are shown; this, when so much of the footpath network is badly signposted, blocked or inaccessible, is nigh on essential for a reduced-stress hike. The series was also given a huge boost by the 2000 Countryside and Rights of Way (CRoW) Act, which opened up over two million acres of England and nearly a million in Wales as Open Access land. After much consultation, many quibbles and considerable drawing and redrawing of the maps, the scheme was finally launched in September 2004, with OS hurrying out a huge number of Explorer maps updated to show the accessible land in detail. And *only* the Explorer maps; Open Access land is not marked at all on the 1:50 000 series. The new maps sold in droves.

The long-awaited right to roam over such a large part of the country was greeted with massive enthusiasm in almost every quarter. Once again, it was the maps that brought the enormity of the change home: seeing great swathes of my local area in mid-Wales suddenly marked as open to all was astounding and extremely exciting. At a stroke, the percentage of publicly accessible Welsh land had gone up from 4 to 22, almost a quarter. The map, and the countryside, would never look the same again.

Cause for celebration indeed, and not just for the generous spike in the sale of OS maps, but still sobering when compared with the situation in Scotland. You'll notice that Ordnance Survey maps of Scotland do not plot either rights of way or Open Access land in the way that their English and Welsh counterparts do. They don't have to, for Scotland has always had a far more democratic presumption of the right to roam than has ever been the case south of the border. This was augmented by the Scottish version of CRoW, the Land Reform (Scotland) Act of 2003, which enshrined in law principles of complete access to the countryside, and not just for walkers. In England and Wales, only a shade over 2 per cent of inland waterways have rights of access to them, despite the fact that no one actually 'owns' the water that flows in the rivers and streams, although they can lay claim to the riverbeds and banks. Thus canoeists or swimmers can all too readily find themselves trespassing, even if they don't touch land. In Scotland, the Land Reform Act explicitly included access to inland waterways, and even enshrined the right to responsible wild camping anywhere, following the Scandinavian model. We in Wales and England have a long way to go.

The huge success of the 1:25 000 Explorer maps has had an axiomatic consequence in the slump of sales for the 1:50 000 Landranger series. On a sentimental level, this saddens me greatly, for the bright pink maps that have enthralled me for so long are the bedrock of the Ordnance Survey, the direct descendants of its very first map, the One Inch of Kent, over two centuries ago. It is, however, inevitable. Why would anyone buy the three 1:50 000 Landranger maps for a holiday exploring Pembrokeshire, when they could examine the precise same area, at twice the scale and detail, in just two 1:25 000 Explorer OL maps? This strange anomaly is repeated across the whole of Britain: it takes two Landrangers to give you a complete picture of England's newest national park, the New Forest, but only one generously proportioned Explorer. You want a complete map of the Shetlands? Four sheets at 1:50 000 or five at twice the scale?

Despite their tumbling sales, and despite the fact that only about eighty of the 204 sheets either break even or make a profit, Ordnance Survey makes all the right noises about its commitment to the Landranger series. It promises to keep the entire series intact and updated, as befits the national map agency, even one run these days on largely commercial grounds. The government subsidy that kept the organisation in profit ended in 2006, although OS can now charge the various government departments that rely on it a market rate for data and maps, so it balances out in the end.

I do worry about the 1:50 000 series, though. Commercially, some of the more remote Scottish sheets sell only two or three copies a year – how on earth can that be sustainable in a cut-throat commercial world? As with the Royal Mail, the business and the money is all in the urban centres, but, to qualify as a truly national service, it needs to provide the same standards to the thinly populated, eternally unprofitable bits of the country too. As someone who lives in just such a place, I'll be watching carefully.

For now, though, the series remains intact and integral, a splendid portrait of our islands that can still keep a map addict quiet for hours in enthusiastic perusal. Much as I love the 1:25 000 Explorer maps, especially when out walking, they haven't yet captured my heart – and I don't think they ever will – in quite the same way as the 1:50 000 series. The Explorers' view of the country is just a bit too close up to afford you the bigger picture, leaving you a little cross-eyed with all that detail. Furthermore, if you wanted to collect the full set of England, Scotland and Wales, you'd need to buy 403 maps, rather than the far more attainable 204 that will give you a complete picture of every British road, railway, track, settlement and farm at a scale of one and a quarter inches to the mile. And although I was a reluctant convert to the idea of having to plaster every map's front cover with a photograph, the images on the covers of the Landranger series are far more beguiling – 'sculptural' was the word the OS Product Manager used – than the shots of identikit families grinning in bike helmets that are generally used on the Explorer covers, doubtless to emphasise their invaluableness in fully enjoying the splendours of Leisure Britain™.

Like Britain itself, the 1:50 000 series is often beautiful, sometimes ugly, but always revealing and forever fascinating. It portrays the very best and the very worst of our country with admirable equanimity. Some sheets work better than others, of course, and to illustrate those differences, as well as many of the facets that make this the world's finest collection of general-purpose maps, I've picked out what I consider to be the five best, and five worst, Landranger maps:

THE TOP FIVE 1:50 000 LANDRANGER MAPS

Although they are in undoubted contention for inclusion on this list, I've already wittered on enough about my first two 1:50 000 maps, numbers 113 (*Grimsby & Cleethorpes*) and 189 (*Ashford & Romney Marsh*), so shall leave them out here. Besides, there are plenty of other very strong candidates, far more than for the list of the worst maps.

123 Llŷn Peninsula

The perfect symmetry of this map, together with the fact that it details one of the most singularly self-sufficient parts of the country, more than compensates for the fact that the bluewash of sea covers two-thirds of its surface. The 40 x 40 km square encapsulates the peninsula with pin-point accuracy: the town of Cricieth, traditionally the gateway to Llŷn, is neatly bisected at the map's eastern edge; the demarcation line between the peninsula and Snowdonia, the main A487, cuts along parallel with the far right of the map.

It is, however, the peninsula's shape that fits the map so beautifully. The 'mainland' (Llŷn feels so much like an island that you do find yourself looking back at the Snowdonia mountains and thinking of them in that way) is connected only at the very top right, north-east of the map; from there, the muscular landmass of Llŷn stretches south-west like an outstretched arm that's either pointing or straining to grasp. Either way, the object of its focus, or grasp, is the peninsula's legendary full stop, Ynys Enlli (Bardsey Island), the Welsh Avalon, the shapely island of pilgrimage and sainthood that sits plumb in the map's bottom-left corner. There's a sinewy sparseness to this map, a sense of quiet perfection with nothing spare: in the area that became the bulwark and muse of R. S. Thomas, it's the cartographic equivalent of one of his poems.

131 Boston & Spalding

Had I been drawing up this list for my own consumption only (and it is exactly the kind of thing I would have happily spent a wet afternoon doing thirty years ago), the chances are most of the entries in my Top Five OS Maps would have been of the flat fringes of our country – the Spurn Head and Dungeness sheets that were, after all, the origin of my collection. Strange though it may seem for someone who has chosen to live in the mountains, I find a rare thrill in those blasted landscapes where the line blurs between sea and sky – and they make for uncommonly striking maps.

There's no flatter map than OS number 131. Uniquely among the 204 sheets of the Landranger collection, it includes not one single contour within its borders: nowhere reaches the modest height even for the preliminary ten-metre line. Well, that's the case on my original 1970s version of the map; I see that the gorgeous blankness of the sheet has now been sullied by the inclusion on the map's southern edge of a handful of zero-metre contour lines. As well as ruining the effect, I rather think that's cheating. This is a map that speaks volumes about our east coast's eternal battle with the ocean, before the ditches, dykes, canals and reclamation projects formalised the line between sea and land, or at least attempted to, for the sea will always have the last word on that. Ancient Sea Banks are delineated many miles inland, for instance around the village of Moulton Seas End, now more than six miles from the coast. I remember a school history atlas that I spent hours poring over, where I was particularly engaged by the few parts of our coastline that had substantially changed shape over the past two millennia. One of those few was the Wash, that mysterious inlet at the crook of the east coast, and best known as the place where King John lost his crown jewels to the greedy mud. And still the Wash changes. My First Series 1:50 000 version, from the late 1970s, shows an entirely different frill of coastline to the latest Second Series effort. It's not a place that we'll ever be able to pin down.

104 Leeds & Bradford

The redrawing of the map of Britain in 1974 for the new 1:50 000 series ironed out many anomalies of the old one-inch system. Crucial to the new series was the realisation that our great cities needed, wherever possible, to be set centre stage on their appropriate map, so that we could, at a glance, get a sense of Manchester, Birmingham, Glasgow, Bristol or Newcastle within the integral context of their suburbs, feeder towns and green belt. All those cities are presented beautifully and make for some of the finest maps in the series.

In the conurbations of Yorkshire's West Riding, the principal challenge was to present both Leeds and Bradford well, and this map does that exemplarily. The context to understanding the two cities is their place within the tight knot of vertiginous mill towns such as Halifax, Dewsbury and Wakefield, as well as the wild spaces of moor and mountain and the genteel cobbles of Harrogate and Haworth. It's also a riot of names that could be nowhere else but Yorkshire: villages such as Luddendon Foot, Mytholmroyd, Farsley Beck Bottom, Wibsey, Odsal, Idle, Owlet, Harden, Greetland, Rastrick, Ossett, Soothill, Scarcroft, Wike, Kirkby Overblow, Spofforth, Scriven, Blubberhouses, Stainburn, Birstwith, Thwaites Brow, Cringles, Glusburn and Goose Eye – a list that sounds more like entries in a dictionary of Dickensian ailments. Everything gets a look-in on this well-framed map. There remains an enigma, however. So particular is the terrain of West Yorkshire that proximity on a map often means very little on the ground, as towns can be isolated from each other by steep hills, strange road systems and a proudly singular history. To the untrained eye, the southern half of this map might look like an almost continuous urban rash, but that's only a fraction of the story. Like the Valleys of south Wales or the Black Country to the west of Birmingham, the area looks like a city, but is, in truth, a conglomeration of very different towns and villages, and woe betide anyone who gets them mixed up.

196 The Solent

As you'd hope from the sheet that covers Ordnance Survey's own head-quarters, this is a wonderful map: a tight frame of staggering variety and much beauty. Within the same sheet, there's the heath and woods of the New Forest, the full might of two great cities, a frantic network of motorways and dual carriageways, buxom estuaries and, capping it all, the entire Isle of Wight. It's the island that really does it, with its beguiling shape so perfectly touching the sides; the jagged chalk outcrops of the Needles demanding a little expansion at the left margin that only emphasises their prominence. Islands that so snugly fit their OS maps are always highly satisfying – such as sheets 95 (*Isle of Man*), 60 (*Islay*), 6 (*Orkney – Mainland*) and 114 (*Anglesey/Ynys Môn*) – and so it is with the Isle of Wight. It's often described as lozenge-shaped, though, to my mind, the island looks more like a crusty old pie, prob-ably a good old-fashioned steak and kidney, which is what I also imag-ine it would taste like.

They say that visiting the Isle of Wight is like going back to the 1950s, and there's a slight feel of that even on the map: the physical look of very different decades gazing at each other across the Solent. The island contains all of one mile of dual carriageway: beyond that it's mainly B roads, country lanes, villages, farms, harbours, downs and chines. On the mainland, by contrast, it's all very *now*, the numer-ous marinas and jetties snaking up the estuaries, the sly marketing (Hamble village, after acting as the set of the yachtie TV soap *Howard's Way*, is rechristened on the new map as the estate agent's far dreamier Hamble-le-Rice), the vast oil refineries, the growing guts of bitter rivals Southampton and Portsmouth.

Modern (i.e. Landranger Second Series) versions of this map also contain rare and intriguing examples of an Ordnance Survey joke. When, in the 1950s, a bored draughtsman drew some cartoon boats on the Manchester Ship Canal, he inadvertently left one on the map as it went to press. Months later, a phone call from a startled architect alerted OS to the alien presence and the maps were consequently pulped. Slipping in little visual jokes or coded messages is the challenge to any creatively minded draughtsman, and here someone has managed it – three times. Look very closely (a magnifying glass is best) at the cliffs on the Isle of Wight's south side, immediately east of the Needles. The symbol for cliffs, a rather random downward hatching, is one of the least precise on the OS and thus possibly the easiest in which to slide something hidden. Just below the label 'Warren Farm' is what looks like REV (possibly KEV), and a mile further east, below the label 'Tennyson Down', we see the word BIRSE. Who or what Rev, or Kev, Birse was, we don't know. It's a lot better hidden than Bill's effort; his name can be seen as clear as day in the cliffs a mile north-west of the island's southernmost point, just above the label 'Blackgang'. (Type SZ485766 into the Get-a-map facility on the OS website and scale down to the 1:50 000 map.)

34 Fort Augustus, Glen Roy & Glen Moriston

Among the dozen or so Landranger maps that portray the deep interior of the Scottish Highlands, there are many candidates for excellence. It's the breathtaking emptiness that impresses most, the sheer lack of anything very much save for mile upon mile of moor, forest, river and mountain. And what mountains they are: the contours are piled up in the dizziest formations, soaring in all directions, occasionally giving way to sheer cliff faces and plunging scree slopes. The emptiest of the lot is probably number 20, a map with so few settlements on it that there was nothing to name it after save for a mountain and a lake, *Beinn Dearg & Loch Broom*. My choice, however, combines nearly this level of emptiness with a portrait of the most thumping geological feature in Britain, the Great Glen, that fracture in the planet that rips through not just the geography of Scotland, but its entire history too.

This map frames the Great Glen flawlessly. The fault line begins, as the infamous Loch Ness, in the north-eastern, top-right corner, descending directly south-westwards, through Loch Oich and Loch Lochy (were they running out of names by then?), before vanishing in the bottom left of the sheet, having split it with precision symmetry. Threading between the lochs are rivers, the Caledonian Canal, the trackbed of a very short-lived railway and General Wade's Military Road, constructed as part of the well-mapped clampdown on the Highland clans in the mid-eighteenth century. There's a strange incongruity in the Highlands, in evidence on this map, between the sublime natural landscape and the suppression and brutality that it witnessed.

Even if you only consider the aesthetic splendour of the landscape, the lochs and mountains in particular, it's galling that so much of the attention hereabouts is soaked up by the existence or not of the Loch Ness Monster, for the loch itself is staggering enough with no help needed from all the hype surrounding it. Loch Ness contains 263,162,000,000 cubic feet of fresh water, more than the combined total of every single freshwater lake in England and Wales. As can be seen from the isobaths, or underwater contours, on the map, the loch is over 750 feet deep, enough to engulf the fifty-storey One Canada Square tower at Canary Wharf, leaving just the top seventeen feet of its pyramid poking out above the water. This is a land of physical superlatives, consummately encapsulated in this fascinating map.

And the Bottom Five

Even the Ordnance Survey don't always get it quite right. Here are some of the 1:50 000 Landranger maps that just don't work very well.

11 Thurso & Dunbeath

Truly, a crap map. This has to be the most pointless of all the 204 Landranger sheets; it's no surprise that it is right at the bottom of the list of sales, for there is no real reason to buy it unless you're an OS obsessive who simply has to have the full set, or one of the residents of Lybster (population 530), Latheron (51), Latheronwheel (201) or Reay (296), for these are the only villages unique to this map. Every Landranger covers 1,600 sq km, and many have inevitable overlaps with neighbouring sheets. On map number 11, however, 1,208 sq km, over three-quarters of the map's surface area, is replicated on other OS sheets, most notably number 12 which is more or less the same map, just with its coverage area shifted a few miles north-westwards. Only 392 sq km is particular to map number 11 – and a fair bit of that is sea.

So why does this map, rather than the near-duplicate number 12 (*Thurso & Wick*: even half the title is repeated), deserve the accolade of the worst OS? Well, this is the far north of mainland Scotland, remember, as declared by the inclusion in its title of mainland Britain's most northerly town, Thurso (which Victoria Wood, in a television travelogue, memorably described as 'sounding like something you'd rinse your curtains in'). What of the phenomenal coast? The seabird-swirling Dunnet Head, Britain's most northerly point? The world-famous John O'Groats? The Highland mountains? That's the problem – the map has none of these. This is Caithness, a turgid flatland of wet moor and angular forestry plantations; there are no mountains to speak of. Worse, the map slices through the upper limits of Thurso town and doesn't quite make it up far enough to include any of the spectacular northernmost coast. All of the interesting bits are on map number 12.

176 West London/177 East London

While, in many ways, the two 1:50 000 maps that cover the capital are hugely impressive, especially when placed and pasted together on a wall, there's something not entirely satisfactory about London at this scale. It looks good as a purely aesthetic rendition of a huge, sprawling city, but you'd never use a Landranger map to navigate through the streets of London, and if you did, even the finest map-reader would go wrong somewhere. There's just too much crammed into too little a space, rendering invisible all of the things that make the city such an exciting place. The Underground system, for instance, which makes unpredictable appearances only when it emerges into daylight, mostly at the city's fringes, seems to come out of thin air. So, while the great tube stations of the West End and City remain entirely unseen, every last Legoland halt on the Docklands Light Railway is painstakingly delineated, and, to make matters much worse, in the OS's garish new scheme of light-railway stations as yellow discs instead of the customary red. It looks awful, none more so than in areas of the East End with a glut of outdoor stations, overground and DLR. The tangle of black lines, together with the seemingly random blobs of yellow and red, look like some strange shrub that's sprouting poisonous berries.

We shouldn't expect a 1:50 000 map of London to be able to cope with all the demands potentially laid upon it, of course. We shouldn't expect it to show the tube stations, the passageways, the arcades, the tiny parks within squares or every building of significance, because it can't. And that's where these maps become nearly redundant, for it is those features that make London so magical, not the Westway or the North and South Circulars, all massively mapped here. Landranger London looks choked to death, an impenetrable block of no potential and no great interest. It's not as bad, however, as the picture of London on the 1:250 000 *Travel Map*. Thanks to the slavish adherence of OS to the blandishments of the tourism industry over all else, central London is obliterated by an illegible splurge of symbols for museums, churches, historic houses and a welter of those blue stars that can mean anything from a standing stone to a puppet theatre. It is utterly unusable; the scale is way too small to locate things with any accuracy, the 'attractions' aren't identified and the whole sorry mess tells you nothing more than that there are lots of things to see and do in central London. Who'd have thought it? The 1:50 000 Landrangers are not quite that bad, but the 1:25 000 Explorers are much better, and, it's got to be said, the *A–Z* better still. *That* is London's natural map.

148 Presteigne & Hay-on-Wye

How could I even appear to pick on such an idyllic stretch of Welsh–English borderland as this? I adore both Presteigne, the handsome old county town of Radnorshire, and Hay-on-Wye, the eccentric – if a little too self-consciously so – second-hand-bookshop capital of the world. As a ten-year-old, I was thrilled by the hoo-ha that attended 'King' Richard Booth's unilateral declaration of Hay's independence, complete with its own passports, border posts and stamps, on April Fool's Day 1977. These days, such pronouncements are two-a-penny (Lonely Planet has even published a guidebook to the world's *soi-disant* micro-nations), but this was the first I'd been aware of, and it enthralled me. Twenty-seven years later, I interviewed King Richard for my *Great Welsh Roads* TV series, and, although much diminished by a stroke, he was still a towering and hugely entertaining figure.

Between and around these two titular border towns are some of the most appealing villages and unhurried countryside you could find anywhere. So what is wrong with the map of such a blessed part of the world? It's a bit of a repeat of the Thurso situation, really, if not on such a dreary scale. Because Britain has the bad manners not to be exactly wide enough at this point to accommodate a neat row of Ordnance Surveys with little overlap, it's all got rather banked up and squashed here. Five other sheets overlap number 148, leaving only 395 sq km out of a possible 1,600 as unique to this one map – only a sneeze over the total of the unfortunate sheet number 11. When I was building up my collection as a youngster, I waited ages before bothering to get this map, despite the fact that it bordered the area where I lived; I just wasn't getting enough that was original for my pocket money (this was before the epiphany dawned that they could be had so easily for free). Both titular towns, Presteigne and Hay-on-Wye, make cameo appearances on neighbouring maps, though that's nothing compared with the plight of the Herefordshire villages of Orleton, Yarpole, Luston and Eyton, to the immediate north of Leominster. They sit in a 5 x 8 km rectangle that can be found on this map, and three others. The residents of this little slice of gastro-pub England are the most over-represented on Landranger maps of any in Britain; it would cost them the best part of thirty quid just to collect the sheets that they appear on. A wonderful area, but a bit of a rubbish map.

110 Sheffield & Huddersfield/111 Sheffield & Doncaster

On the back cover of any pre-millennium Landranger, take a look at their index map of Britain. To help you find the right sheet for your purpose, numerous towns and cities are marked, from LONDON (the only capitalised example), through most of the large and medium-sized conurbations and down to some surprisingly obscure choices: Helmsdale, Kingussie, Girvan, Moffat and Tongue in Scotland; Dolgellau, Pwllheli, Bala and Fishguard in Wales; and, in England, Bude, Ilfracombe, Ripon, Workington and Blyth. For the first decade of the Landranger series, Aysgarth (population 197) in the Yorkshire Dales was deemed sufficiently important to be marked on the national map, but not on the cover plan of its own sheet, number 98, *Wensleydale & Wharfdale*. There's Hereford and Gloucester, but no Worcester; Leicester and Birmingham, but not Coventry; Cambridge but not Peterborough; Southampton but not Portsmouth; Whitby but not Scarborough; and no Stoke-on-Trent, Cheltenham, Ipswich, Bath, Milton Keynes, Canterbury, Bournemouth, Reading, Newport, Bradford or Darlington. Most bizarrely of all on the index map, there's Doncaster, but no Sheffield.

That the fifth-largest city in England failed to appear on the national map gives a small hint that what worked so well in West Yorkshire, on the *Leeds & Bradford* sheet, has gone a little awry in what used to be called the People's Republic of South Yorkshire. Unlike any other major British city, Sheffield is tucked in so close to the margin that it has to appear twice, on overlapping sheets, and then spirited away at the very bottom. To get any decent idea of Sheffield's hinterland, you'd need to buy four maps. What has OS got against poor old Steel City that they snubbed it twice?

46 Coll & Tiree

It's a fairly close contest for the title of Landranger map that shows the least amount of dry land, but this is the winner, and for that reason alone, it deserves to go in the list. Map number 46 covers the two islands of Coll and Tiree, to the west of Mull (also quite badly served by the 1:50 000 series, needing three rather clumsily divided sheets to show its 338 square miles; the island of Anglesey, by contrast, at 276 square miles, needs just the one). The two islands, with the scattering of uninhabited skerries known as the Treshnish Isles, account for about 9 per cent of the map's total surface area, leaving a whopping 91 per cent as featureless pale blue sea. And featureless it surely is: had Ordnance Survey continued with its plan to map isobaths of the sea, so that we could tell at a glance the comparative depths around our shores, the map would have been far more interesting. The blank blue-wash of sea, especially on a map like this, where it is so much the dominant feature, is one of the Landranger series' least endearing features. Many of the Scottish lochs have isobaths mapped, and the old One Inch series showed them in the sea at five and ten fathoms, but it was decided to do away with those for the new series as they were seen to encourage amateur sailors to recklessness. The result makes the sea look bland and uniform, with no hint as to its thrills and dangers. This was something that a company like Bartholomew mapped so very much better; its seas a gradually darkening series of blues according to the water's depth. It wasn't a massive difference, but it was enough to allude to the mysteries below.

It would perhaps be unfair to write off a map simply for the unavoidable fact that so much of it is sea, but that's not the only problem here. With all due respect to the 850 inhabitants of Coll and Tiree, their islands do not, from the map, look like the most fascinating parts of the Hebridean archipelago. Lovely beaches, for sure, but a largely flat and watery landscape broken by precious few features. At least, that's the case on the 1:50 000 sheet. Look on the 1:25 000 Explorer (number 372, also *Coll & Tiree*) and the explosion of comparative new detail is extraordinary. And that's the final good reason for inclusion of this map in the list of shame. One Explorer map covers exactly the same amount of land as this one Landranger map. You'd be a bit of an idiot buying this, when for an extra pound, you get it all at twice the scale.

∿

Like the hard Manhattan schist that is almost entirely out of view, but which provides the bedrock for the world's most iconic skyline, the Ordnance Survey One Inch series, and its successor, the 1:50 000 Landrangers, have underpinned the explorations of generations of Britons, helping them to get to know and grow to love their own country, particularly in the last hundred years. It was just before the First World War that the OS started to take seriously the potential of selling its maps to the public, for up to that point it only really considered the needs of government and the military (though even the War Office preferred Bartholomew's Half Inch series, with its coloured layering of contours, to that of the OS). The bicycle craze was the main catalyst for the upsurge in map-buying: gone were the boneshakers and penny-farthings of the mid Victorian age, to be replaced by far more comfortable, practical and increasingly affordable machines that were enthusiastically taken up by men and, crucially, women of every social class. Commercial map-makers were quick to cash in on the craze, but the Ordnance Survey was predictably sluggish, and that was despite its name, and even its maps, being used by its competitors; most were sold under the Ordnance, Reduced Ordnance or Ordnance Survey label. Some were just shoddy copies of OS maps or were printed off redundant, worn copper plates that were many decades out of date: a map of the London environs, for example, produced for customers of *The Cycle* magazine in 1890, was printed from a John Cary plate of 1794, with the railways crudely scratched on to make it appear topical. It would be the same as trying to navigate your way around Britain now on a map from the First World War.

The first salvo in OS's battle to capture their due slice of the fast-growing market was to clamp down on the widespread abuse of their surveying data. The 1911 Copyright Act established the concept of Crown copyright on Ordnance Survey maps, a phrase that has appeared on them ever since. Other companies now found themselves unable to use the OS name, or its products, in any way that was in direct competition with the Survey. The first test case came in 1913, when OS took map-makers H. G. Rowe & Co. to court and proved that their *Rowe's New Road Map for Cyclists & Motorists* was a direct photographic reduction of the OS. Rowe's were forced to destroy all copies of the map and the plates from which they were printed; Ordnance Survey publicised the decision as widely as it could as a warning to other unscrupulous plagiarists.

The successful court case spurred OS on to establish a committee whose brief was to work out quite why its toehold in the commercial market was so precarious. They didn't need a committee; any bright twelve-year-old could have told them what the problems were. The most glaring one was the packaging of their maps. The commercial companies understood the power of an attention-grabbing cover for their products, often using charming pictures of countryside and cheery cyclists, while Ordnance Survey maps, despite the superior quality of the product within, were still packaged in utilitarian covers that looked as if they should have had 'Top Secret' stamped across them. Companies such as Philip's and Bartholomew understood their customer base intimately and could use techniques such as offering fancy marketing displays and sale-or-return to map-sellers. By contrast, OS belied its military personality with sales only through a fearsome network of approved agents and the distinctly off-putting

'Rules for Ordering Ordnance Survey Maps' pasted into every sheet. They were spectacularly misjudging the mood of the times: the rise in popularity of bicycles and then cars gave many Britons an unprecedented taste of freedom to roam the land. They wanted maps that rejoiced in that freedom, that seemed to share it, not ones that barked orders at them like an irascible colonel.

Once the war was over, the switch of emphasis from military to commercial was swift and thorough. It had to be; the war had left the country perilously broke, and no government department was immune from swingeing cuts. The first OS Tourist Map, *Snowdon*, was published in 1920, and quickly followed by others that even used non-geographical titles (*Burns' Country* and *Scott's Country*), seen by many of the diehards in Southampton as unforgivably mimsy. It was the appearance of the maps that changed the most, however. Gone was the drab, ration-book look of pre-war days, replaced by painted scenes from the areas covered within. Many were the work of Arthur Palmer, whose hallmark was melancholy, old-fashioned landscapes; a few, brighter and bolder, came from the paintbrush of J. C. T. Willis, later to rise through the ranks and become OS Director-General in the 1950s. The name that is most readily associated with between-the-wars OS cover artwork, however, is Ellis Martin. It is his maps that today's collectors get most exercised about, and for good reason.

It could be said that Ellis Martin single-handedly transformed the fortunes of the Ordnance Survey. After serving in the First World War, he joined the organisation in May 1919 as its first dedicated artist-designer, with a brief to beef up the look of the maps and their sales. He did both, quite spectacularly, producing gorgeous images of areas from the Cairngorms to Cornwall, the Thames through London, to the sharp peaks of Snowdonia. His covers for subject-specific maps, such as the 1927 total eclipse of the sun, aviation, population spread and ancient artefacts, were among his best; none better than a fastidiously detailed mosaic for a best-selling map of Roman Britain – a cover that was to be maintained in use until 1990, making it the last survivor of the 'golden age' of OS map design.

He is best remembered, however, for his designs that relaunched the most popular of the OS's general range of national maps, particularly the One Inch series. The years after the First World War saw a huge upsurge in day-trippers and tourists into the countryside, and Ellis Martin's maps perfectly encapsulated that enthusiasm. On the One Inch cover of 1919, we see a young man sat on a hillside, map outspread, overlooking a verdant valley. Leaning against a nearby bush is his trusty bicycle. Down below, framed by woods, a viaduct snakes across the scene and a small town hunkers down around its spired church (the illustration is an adaption of the view from Box Hill towards Dorking, but even when there wasn't a church spire in the scene, Martin was prone to adding one for effect). The young man, in his tweed cap, Norfolk jacket and plus fours, is the embodiment of the target audience: assured, casual (yet smart), independent and an indissoluble part of the scenery he surveys.

By the early 1930s, the hill-sitter was looking way too old-fashioned for the free-thinking, pipe-smoking chaps who were now the mainstay of the OS's public, so Martin redrew the exact same scene for the new age. Another young man, a hiker, replaced the Edwardian cyclist: his outspread map was bigger, but gone was the headgear and the scratchy outfit, to be replaced by a leisurely rake in rolled-up shirt sleeves and a tank top, casual trousers and a bulging knapsack on his manly back. Subtly, but with a typical eye for detail, Martin had even made the trees in the valley below grow a few feet in the intervening years, and had given the surrounding vegetation an extra bounce and lushness.

These covers followed the standard map-selling practice of picturing their target audience, much as the photographs on today's 1:25 000 Explorer maps tend to portray grinning punters cycling, sailing, kayaking or hiking. Another of Martin's 1930s covers for the One Inch series (mainly the Tourist and District maps) took this rule to its inevitable

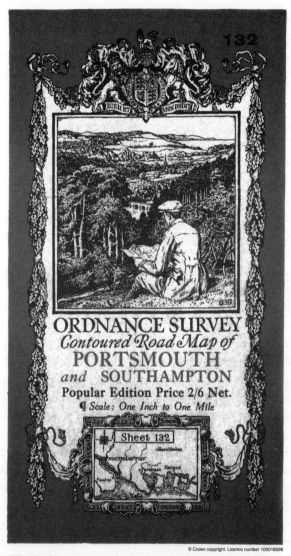

Ellis Martin's 1919 cover for the One Inch series; the tweedy cyclist was replaced by a knapsacked hiker for the 1933 update

conclusion, shoehorning every possible target map-buyer into the frame – as long as they were male, that is. The picture is dominated by a splendid young chap in the foreground, puffing away on his pipe as he leans languidly against a stone wall to consult his beloved Ordnance Survey. On the road ahead of him, a Morris car travels one way, a group of cyclists the other. In the distance, outside an inn at a country cross-roads, a touring bus sits waiting. This is the golden countryside, the map declares, and this is your passport to it, however you choose to arrive. Ironically, the 1930s was a tough time to be a hiker in rural Britain: massive areas of the finest countryside remained out of bounds; rights of way that had been used for hundreds, even thousands, of years were barred, for many landowners were loth to see the Great Unwashed from the cities stomping across their mountains and grouse moors. Violence erupted periodically, with many ramblers falling foul of over-zealous gamekeepers, most famously at the Mass Trespass on Kinder Scout in the Peak District, in April 1932. No hint of any of that kind of nastiness in Ellis Martin's dream-like portraits of a quintessential England.

Martin's images embody the romantic notion of the British countryside that held sway between the two world wars, the same one that had spawned iconic railway posters and the fantasy England at Bekonskot model village. Indeed, the wars sandwich his OS career with ruthless precision, for when the Second World War broke out, OS abolished his post and effectively sacked him. A third of the Southampton workforce was called up, and the Survey returned very readily to its roots as an outpost of the military, all thoughts of arcadian rambling banished. The Martin era was probably coming to an end in any case. His rather whimsical, rhapsodic designs may well have massively boosted sales to the public, but the maps themselves were riddled with minor errors, increasingly out of date and in need of a major overhaul. The triangulation system on which the national survey depended was, by now, almost a century and a half old; a new survey, using modern techniques, was demanded. In 1936, it began, the first concrete triangulation points appearing on the landscape. These were built as housing posts for the surveying equipment, ensuring absolute consistency and accuracy every time they were used, and hastening the creation of the National Grid.

❉

The building of the new trig points, around six and a half thousand of them, and the retriangulation of the entire country, was a mammoth undertaking. Because the pillars needed to be built on the highest points so as to be intervisible over long distances, the teams building them had to drag their heavy equipment, bags of chippings and concrete included, up mountains and hills, often in poor visibility and shocking weather. It took two weeks to construct one on top of Cadair Idris in mid-Wales, as the fog refused to shift so the surveyors could test the sight-lines. To make matters worse, there were no horses available locally to cart the equipment up and down the mountain, as it was August and the time for hay-making. In the end, the team managed to commandeer a nag from a coal merchant in Dolgellau (or Dolgelly, as they spelt it on the maps in those days). Similar problems presented themselves on Britain's highest mountain, the 4,408-foot Ben Nevis; building and testing that trig point necessitated a 22-day-long camp on the snowy summit. On Fair Isle, that speck of an island midway between Orkney and Shetland, one of the party had his shoulder dislocated by a vicious attack from an Arctic skua.

By the time World War Two had dragged to an end, Ordnance Survey was in a comparable state to Britain itself: knackered, battered and broke. Following the bombing of the Southampton HQ, staff were scattered around the country; it wasn't until 1969 that they were all finally reunited once more back in their home city. Ellis Martin's old office had been bombed off the map and, with it, his ideas on making the maps look aesthetically alluring. Instead, the wheel turned full circle: austerity Britain received austerity maps, with no hint of rural romanticism to clutter their functionality. And still the wheel turned: in the 1960s, graphic designers, rather than watercolour artists, began to play with the covers; in the 1970s, a new range of Tourist Maps was splashed with psychedelic scenes of the countryside as seen on an acid trip – see the (very) colour section; in the 1980s, the hitherto strictly utilitarian covers of the new Landranger series were plastered with pretty photos, now de rigueur for all OS products. And it worked. Just as Ordnance Survey started selling more maps when Ellis Martin's illustrations began to grace them in 1919, so did the sales of the Landranger series jump when the first photograph was used on its cover in 1984. Yet again, I find myself the exception to the rule. I was horrified by the new pictorial covers, and had a policy for a while of collecting only the pre-photographic examples, which effectively meant that I was deliberately going out of my way to buy only older, more out-of-date maps. Clever.

※

As ex-KLF Timelord Bill Drummond acknowledges in the opening quotation of this chapter, hours can be so easily, and pleasurably, lost in the idle perusal of Ordnance Survey maps. Look at them long enough, and you'll start to notice all kinds of tantalising details. Many of my happiest expeditions around Britain have been sparked off by something strange or unexpected on an OS map that has demanded closer inspection. On going to stay with relatives in West Yorkshire when I was about twelve, I badgered them into taking me on a trip down the M62, just because I'd noticed, on an upland section near the Lancashire border, the carriageways of the motorway splitting around a farm and was desperate to see it. Nowadays, Google 'Stott Hall Farm', or even just 'farm middle M62', and you'll be bombarded with maps and photos of the place, and even video interviews of the taciturn farmer who has to live there. When I first spotted it on the map, the only way to see it for real was to nag my Uncle Jim until he took me there.

There have been hundreds of odd little features to which the Ordnance Survey has opened my eyes, each one sending an initial jolt of electric curiosity through my veins and often inspiring a little adventure. Wonky hills, windmills, ancient barrows, tumuli and prehistoric cursus lines, remote railway stations, abandoned quarries, tunnels and even motorway spurs, odd-shaped settlements and coastal nodules, ravines, follies, good-looking woods, isolated churches or those that have long since lost their villages, stuff in 𝔊𝔬𝔱𝔥𝔦𝔠 𝔰𝔠𝔯𝔦𝔭𝔱, fords, Roman roads, well-placed country pubs, harbours, causeways and those mysterious blank spaces – reluctantly, and only recently, filled in since the advent of Google Earth and the like – that invariably indicated hush-hush military installations. I've pored over the map representations of Britain's most singular corners, such as the steadily vanishing Suffolk port of Dunwich, the Hanbury Crater in Staffordshire, which appeared in 1944 when an armaments store exploded in the biggest non-nuclear blast in history, the enforced emptiness of Salisbury Plain, or Inverie on the Knoydart peninsula, the only village on the British mainland inaccessible by road. I've even trekked many miles out of my way just to see what the Ordnance Survey had officially announced to be the most boring 1 x 1 km grid square of the entire 320,000 on the 1:50 000 Landranger series: SE 8322, just south of Ousefleet, between Goole and Hull. On the map, it contains absolutely nothing, save for a

Ordnance Survey's most featureless square kilometre in the land, at Ousefleet, near Goole

pylon line grazing one corner. In the flesh, it is one of those big-sky wildernesses that leave you feeling inches high, a land of ploughed black clods, mist and crows.

Fittingly, a recent map-inspired adventure came when I was in Hampshire, en route to visit the OS headquarters in Southampton. Over a cup of tea in my van, I was comparing my original early 1980s copy of Landranger number 185, *Winchester & Basingstoke*, with the modern version I'd just bought. Idly clocking the changes between them, something quite odd leapt off the paper. Inevitably, motorways provide some of the greatest differences between maps that span the last thirty years, and it was no different here. The M3 had blazed its trail across rural Hampshire and sliced around the eastern edge of Winchester. Looking at the new map, I could see the drastic cutting that had taken the new motorway through Twyford Down, a chalk and flint hill that sat by the side of the mysterious St Catherine's Hill, one of the city's most celebrated viewpoints. I remembered the brouhaha in the early 1990s about the project. It had been one of the most controversial of new roads, attracting eco-warriors, protest camps, stunts, marches, TV crews, security guards and police on mega-overtime, and acres of polarised newsprint. Yet, like the contemporaneous and equally fiercely resisted bypass around Newbury, thirty miles north up the A34, the Winchester M3 bypass had eventually been bulldozed through.

Only this was the second Winchester bypass, for the city had built one of Britain's very first, back in the 1930s, as can be seen on the 1959 OS One Inch, together with its contemporary Landranger equivalent, in the colour section. This dual carriageway, part of the A33, became one of the most notorious bottlenecks on the British road system. Worse, bends that were perfectly adequate for Austin Sevens couldn't cope with modern traffic speeds, and it was a regular site of fatal accidents. There it was on my 1980s map: a thick red road edging clumsily around the city's eastern margin. And there it wasn't on the new map. Not at all, not a trace, no sign that there ever had been a major dual carriageway there. I blinked. My eyes flitted from one map to the other. How could you lose a huge road like that and leave no trace, not a telltale cul-de-sac or a few odd sidings? Had the motorway been built over it, and somehow one or other of the maps had been plotted incorrectly? It's not unheard of for OS to locate things in slightly the wrong place: twenty years ago, a walker tried to sue them over a crevasse in the Scottish mountains that they had erroneously mapped nearly half a mile from its actual position. He'd fallen down it, where it wasn't supposed to be. A remote crack in the Grampians is one thing, however: to get the position so wrong of a major trunk road in southern England, less than ten miles from the Ordnance Survey HQ, seemed way too unlikely. For starters, the original bypass had run along the western side of St Catherine's Hill, the M3 on its eastern flank. They couldn't possibly have muddled them up. But I needed to go and see just what the explanation was.

I coursed down the M3 and was horrified by the sight of the huge wound in the chalk hill that speeds the motorway so heedlessly through on its course down to the coast. If there was a symbol of our willingness to trash the natural landscape just to shave a few minutes off our journey, this had to be it. During the 1990s, when I'd been attempting a side career in stand-up comedy, I'd done a few benefit gigs for anti-road protest groups. They were always fun: a couple of Levellers look-alike bands, some anguished bedsit warblers, a rainbow of hairstyles, clouds of dope smoke and the pub drunk dry of cider. The sight of the butchered hill had made me want to sign up to the cause once again. How could we be so gruesomely philistine?

Coming off the motorway, I parked up and set off to the place where, according to my 25-year-old map, the A33, one of Britain's first dual carriageways, ran. I began to doubt my map-reading abilities, as there was absolutely no sign of it to be found. Where it should have been, there were just grassy banks and trees, although many of them were saplings still in their plastic nursery jackets, so the first inklings that maybe, just maybe, the road had been grassed over and replanted bubbled up into my mind. I walked the swathe of greenery that, in places, definitely looked as if it was about the width of a large road. There were a few dog walkers and joggers around, and I stopped a couple to ask. Had these quiet water meadows, with swallows reeling on the thermals above us, been a main road until really quite recently? No one was quite sure, but some thought that yes, perhaps it had been. After about a mile, I came across a nature-trail map mounted on a board; this confirmed that, indeed, I was standing on 'the site of the former A33', a spot where I would have been mown down by speeding traffic just fifteen years earlier. It was quite eerie, and strangely exhilarating.

I began to climb St Catherine's Hill, keeping my ear open for the first growl of traffic from the motorway, but none came; had I not known it was there, I could have reached the top of the hill entirely ignorant of its existence. Even when I walked eastwards from the summit to seek out the grisly gash through its eastern flank, it proved to be amazingly well concealed and far quieter than I'd expected. My feelings flip-flopped, from the initial horror at driving through the hill on the M3 to unabashed admiration that such a phenomenal piece of engineering had solved a seemingly intractable problem, a problem for which maintaining the status quo was most definitely not an option. At the time that it was being considered and constructed, we'd heard so much about the downside of this vast project, the hatred and horror at the despoiling of the place. And yes, a truly civilised society would have tunnelled, not cut, the motorway through Twyford Down, but all the same, I don't recall ever hearing about the parallel work, to return old tarmac (which, I'd guess from its proximity, was far more of a disturbance to anyone on top of St Catherine's Hill) to a beautiful stretch of nature. Even for the locals I'd spoken to, it was already ancient, and largely forgotten, history. I guess I won't be asked to compère any road protest gigs these days.

Ordnance Survey's position at the heart of the British establishment does mean that we tend to hold its pronouncements as absolutely official, the very last word in any matter topographic. It is almost held to be entirely responsible for the size, shape and scope of the realm itself; that if something appears on an OS map, it is gospel truth. It hasn't always been that way, though. The longest-serving boss (1820–47) of the Ordnance Survey, Major-General Thomas Colby, made it his personal mission to clean up the maps' accuracy, heading off on hugely ambitious fact-finding tours – once walking 586 miles in twenty-two days – to see if the real landscape matched that depicted by the OS. All too often, it did not. Near King's Lynn, he noted that the map was 'done in a most slovenly manner; one wood was fully double its real size and more than twice its breadth out of its place. In short, there was too much sketching and that of very bad quality.'

Thanks to new technologies such as aerial photography (first introduced during the First World War), the massive retriangulation project that was finally finished in 1962 and, latterly, digital data recording, the accuracy of Ordnance Survey maps has improved immeasurably. Slip-ups still occur, however, mainly at the proofreading stage, most often seen in inaccurately spelled names and the use of wrong colours or symbols. Footpaths and rights of way are an occasionally thorny issue: the data is fed to the OS by local authorities, so that it's not uncommon to find a path marked that hasn't existed on the ground for decades. On the last series of the old One Inch maps, numerous footpaths were marked on Salisbury Plain that went right across army firing ranges; small wonder that every OS map carries the legend, in bold typeface: 'The representation on this map of any road, track or path is no evidence of the existence of a right of way.'

There's also the murky area of deliberate mistakes, or at least deliberate distortions, in OS maps, a subject it's nigh-on impossible to nail down. Map-makers through the centuries have purposely placed decoy or trap features in their maps to deter fraudulent copying. These can be a tiny made-up settlement, a non-existent slip road, an imaginary farm building or two, or – in the case of A–Z and other street maps – invented little cul-de-sacs placed in a suitably obscure position. Plagiarism has always been rife in map-making: even unintentional cock-ups have lived on for years thanks to their reproduction by rival cartographers lifting their information from others' originals. In John Speed's 1612 county atlas, he was unable to establish the name of the village of North Burcombe in Wiltshire, so wrote in the word 'Quære' (Query), to remind himself of the need to check it. This he forgot to do, and the fictional village of Query appeared on more than a dozen different maps of Wiltshire over the next 160 years, all of them claiming to be originals.

Ordnance Survey has to be ahead of the game in this area, for the jealous guarding of its copyright is its greatest single commercial asset; without it, the organisation would be bankrupt. A bright light was suddenly shone on this opaque area of OS cartography back in 2001, when the Automobile Association (AA) agreed to pay an out-of-court settlement of £20 million to the OS, in recognition of massive (the AA say 'inadvertent') plagiarism of OS maps over many years. More than 300 million individual copies of over 500 published maps and guides were found to be rip-offs of Ordnance Survey originals, ironically including the AA's plan of its own home town, Basingstoke.

Because the settlement took place only hours before the showdown was due to begin in the High Court, we were never treated to the prospect of Ordnance Survey having to detail exactly what it had spotted on the plagiarised maps to determine their origin. They've been no more forthcoming since. In something of a baptism of fire into her new job as OS Director-General, Vanessa Lawrence stated enigmatically at the time: 'There are design elements in the way we show things which are not obvious to either the user or the copier. When we see the two versions side by side, we can spot clues.' In other words, these are not deliberate mistakes that might impinge on the quality of the cartography, more little distortions, fingerprints or, as OS preferred to call them, 'a watermark'. Mentioned were tiny kinks in rivers, exaggerated curves in roads, fake outhouses on farms and misplaced apostrophes or slight spelling mistakes in names.

The £20 million settlement – which included past and future royalties – was the headline-grabber of its day, but both organisations have form in this area. Ordnance Survey has been hotly pursuing infringements of its data and surveying since the 1911 Copyright Act, and has a small team of copyright experts in HQ, whose job it is to spend their days scrutinising rival publications for telltale clues. In 1995, it won damages from two Norfolk publishers of tourist maps, Streetwise and Colour Maps International, but it was small beer compared with the AA case. The AA, meanwhile, had had to pay out an undisclosed sum to the Ordnance Survey of Northern Ireland just the year before the bigger British case, for exactly the same misdemeanour of lifting maps of the province's towns and passing them off as their own. 'Inadvertently', of course.

The AA case is something of a pointer to the Ordnance Survey's future, although with a huge and fundamental difference. With well over nine-tenths of the organisation's business now in the world of digital data, it is there that the battleground is now set. More than ever before, it *will* be a battleground, for proving intellectual or statistical copyright on electronic data is like nailing down blancmange. With the swiftly developing sophistication of Global Positioning Systems (GPS), and the plethora of free satellite imagery and mapping websites, it is going to be ever harder for OS to maintain its hold on the national topography. And that's before you even consider the political campaigns – most notably the *Guardian*'s 'Free Our Data' – to prise OS's gargantuan database from its paternalist clutches. Some data will be released in 2010, but it's unlikely to be enough to silence the campaigners who are seeking nothing less than Ordnance Survey's entire oeuvre out there in the public domain.

With so much of the OS's emphasis now placed in the digital realm, it's hard to see how its traditional paper map will survive. Already gone are the largest-scale maps, the hyper-detailed 1:2500 series, whose hard-copy publication finally ceased in the mid-1990s. Most startlingly, OS have been advertising to contract out their printing operation when they move to their new HQ on the outskirts of Southampton, projected to be sometime in the winter of 2010–11. It seems that, for the first time since their foundation over two hundred and twenty years ago, they will no longer have the capacity to print their own maps.

Ordnance Survey assures me that it is fully committed to continuing the sale of paper maps for its two most popular series, the 1:50 000 Landrangers and the 1:25 000 Explorers. No doubt that is its avowed intention, and as long as government agencies need printed maps for the likes of emergency planning, that should provide enough income to ensure the survival of even the lowliest sellers in the series. My more miserable hunch, however, is that, within my lifetime, the beautiful sight in a bookshop of complete rows of pink spines, covering land from the Shetlands to the Scillies, will become a thing of the past – though which will go first, the maps or the bookshops, is anyone's guess.

While OS itself vaults (mostly) smoothly into the digital age, the hunger for its paper maps will continue unabated among many of us who count ourselves as collectors. If I measure myself along the spectrum of obsession, I realise that I'm quite far down it, relatively speaking, for the only totality in map collecting that I've ever striven for has been to own, by fair means or foul, every 1:50 000 Landranger of England and Wales – a highly modest ambition of acquiring just 120 maps. I couldn't even raise my game and get obsessive about the Scottish sheets, and worse, I let quite a few of my older maps go, which marks me out immediately as a very amateur map addict. The serious ones would sooner sell their children.

The place to find the real hardcore among Ordnance Survey fans is the Charles Close Society (CCS), named after the inspirational OS Director-General who steered the organisation through the First World War and then successfully broadened it out into the civilian market.

The CCS is a wonder, its regular newsletters and publications proof indeed that there is no aspect of the Ordnance Survey or its maps too obscure to fascinate someone. I am, of course, a proud – if slightly awed – member, my fascination a low-wattage glimmer compared with the full-beam glare of some people, for whom obtaining every print-run of every edition of every map in every kind of cover is the only acceptable ambition.

You may scoff, but Ordnance Survey hobbyists are just the same as people who collect Bruce Springsteen records, Barbie dolls or the autographs of *Coronation Street* stars, namely somewhere on a scale calibrated from the enthusiastic to the autistic. The concept of the complete collection, including all the mis-cuts, misprints and outtakes, is the Holy Grail for extreme collectors, and the advent of the internet has made such exhaustive dedication that much easier. It's much easier to find your fellow Barbie/Bruce/autograph/map obsessives online, for they are almost guaranteed to be supremely computer-literate and conducting the majority of their human interaction that way in any case. However obscure the interest, there will be others who share it, and it'll only take a few minutes to find them. There will be a website or twenty, numerous blogs, Yahoo! groups and message boards, perhaps even occasional meetings out there in the real world. There is also the global marketplace element of the internet, which seems to mean that no one should ever throw anything away again, and that, however dull or tatty something is, the chances are someone somewhere will pay good money for it.

Such bespoke infatuation is all well and good, but it's not for me. I prefer to get my kicks – and my maps – in the dusty corners of second-hand bookshops, the thrill of a sudden chance discovery in a battered cardboard box far outweighing the clinical efficiency of the click of a computer mouse. In my day, all that were fields.

The town of Baarle, splintered between Belgium and the Netherlands

4. BORDERLINE OBSESSION

> I have always loved the moments of travel when, brought to a
> halt by a striped barrier, approached by unfamiliar uniforms,
> you feel yourself on the brink of somewhere unknown and
> possibly perilous.
>
> ~ Jan Morris, *Trieste and the Meaning of Nowhere*

Where there's a map, there's a border. Often, it's the boundaries – political, topographical, cultural, linguistic, historical – that are a map's
raison d'être: a show of muscle, a graphic illustration of change or simply
a bold, bright statement of territorial integrity. And how they fascinate
us: a map addict adores his borders, knows them intimately, and craves
to visit them and the places that straddle these hallucinogenic divides.

Borders may begin as lines on the map, but all too soon they
deepen into cultural and even physical reality, to the extent that they
can sometimes be seen from space. Look on any website showing
satellite imagery of the globe, and you can often see how a border on
the map can be clearly delineated in the landscape, as neighbouring
countries prioritise different uses for the land and alternative agricultural practices. The starkest example is between the American states
of Montana and North Dakota on the one side, and the Canadian state
of Saskatchewan on the other (see colour insert), but, merely from the
aerial evidence, you could also plot the international borders between
Russia and Finland, around the Russian exclave of Kaliningrad, and
between Namibia and Angola. You can pretty much trace the entire
outline of Kuwait without any labels needed.

Britain is a land that takes its borders very seriously indeed: its constituent countries, their counties, regions, districts, ridings, hundreds, palatines, commotes, wapentakes, liberties, rapes, cities, towns, boroughs, constituencies, wards, dioceses, deaneries, archdeaconries, parishes, even postcode districts – all can inspire fierce loyalty and raise passions among map aficionados. And although there's nothing particular to see, save for the occasional signpost or flag, perhaps a subtle change in tarmac, we love also to visit these borders, to see and feel them, jump across them and back again, to linger on the edge of two, or more, places at the very same time. It appeals to two contradictory sides of our character in the very same moment: the urge for order and neatness, together with our need, occasionally, to hang in limbo.

Of course, the Americans do it bigger and better: they've managed to create an entire national park and a major tourist attraction, pulling in half a million visitors every year, out of nothing more than a remote spot in the desert, which just happens to be where the states of Utah, Arizona, Colorado and New Mexico all meet at right angles. Four Corners, as it's known, has a car park the size of Wiltshire, an interpretive centre, restaurants and gift shops galore, as well as an almost permanent queue of people waiting to climb the monument where the exact borders meet and photograph their loved ones straddling the four states. The most popular pose is like something out of the game of Twister, each foot and hand in a different state and a daffy grin to prove it. It's easy to scoff, but I know full well that if I'd been growing up within two days' travel of the place, I'd have made my dad's life hell until he finally took me there.

It's the odd and anomalous boundaries that we love the most, and there's a steady stream of us touring them for no other reason than that they exist on our well-thumbed maps. Take Europe's wonkiest border, which can be found in one of its straightest corners, the wealthy farming flatlands straddling Belgium and the Netherlands. This was a place that I was bursting to see ever since becoming aware of its existence. The small town of Baarle bestrides both countries, despite being five kilometres on the Dutch side of the border. Within and around the town, there are twenty-one separate exclaves of Belgium, which, in turn, contain nine further enclaves of Holland: the smallest of these thirty angular parcels of land being half a field, not quite two-thirds of an acre. It's a situation that's been nearly a thousand years in the making, from a succession of medieval and modern treaties, agree-ments, land-swaps, sales and stand-offs between the Lords of Breda and the Dukes of Brabant. Just walking through Baarle's neat streets means that you will cross and re-cross the border numerous times, and the authorities have kindly assisted the visitor by marking these frontiers in the pavements with lines of + + + + + markings, painted either side with B or NL accordingly (there's going to be some almighty tarmac inconvenience when Belgium finally disintegrates).

Baarle's mad borders are its single biggest asset: without them, the place would be a slumbering country town unnoticed by practically anyone. As it is, it's a regular photo opportunity for Dutch and Belgian royalty or politicians to announce mutual accords in the town (the Enclave Room, through which the border runs, in Den Engel Hotel is the usual backdrop). Tourists flock to Baarle, to emulate the same pose as their masters with a foot either side of the divide. The + + + + + fron-tier symbol, scored in so many pavements, repeats itself ad nauseam on posters, shop signs, logos, town literature and almost all of the postcards available. Baarle is a border-collector's wet dream.

Officially, it's not one town, but two: Baarle-Hertog (Belgium) and Baarle-Nassau (the Netherlands), and there's double everything. Two town halls, two burgomasters, two fire departments, two national phone companies with boxes side by side, two websites for anything (.be and .nl), two languages (Flemish and Dutch), two police chiefs both sat in the same building with their respective flags at the front of their desks. Houses identify which side of the line they're on by their number plaques – rectangular red, white and blue for Dutch, oval black, gold and red for Belgium – although some houses have their front door in one country, their back door in the other. Some houses have in the past even moved their front doors to change nationality and take advantage of better fiscal arrangements on the other side. Even graves in the cemetery are marked with little metal flags to identify which side of the line the deceased hailed from.

In some other parts of Europe, a situation like this could be horribly explosive, but in this plump, placid arable landscape, it's all accepted with a shrug, a wry smile and a weather eye on the tourist coaches packing the town's car park. Not that the divide is merely academic: the 'problem' of Baarle has occupied huge amounts of governmental concern over the centuries; spats and smuggling were commonplace, while the impasse in divvying up some of the local agricultural land has resulted in some wonderfully uncultivated, and ecologically rich, terrain in an area otherwise sprayed and cropped to within an inch of its existence. These days, the effect is most commonly seen in retailing, for Baarle's shops seem to have settled firmly into their appropriate national sectors. In the Belgian parts of the town centre, it's all chocolate emporia, chip shops and tobacconists urging Dutch strollers to stock up on cheaper Belgian fags. Just up the street in the Netherlands, it's mainly banks, home-interiors shops doing dull things in pine and – proof indeed that you're in Holland – a sex shop (which, like most Dutch shops, looks as if it's run by the council), its earnest window display of lubricants and mannequins in nasty nighties enough to bore anyone off sex for life.

For the map addict and border-spotter, Baarle's pièce de résistance is the interactive 3D maquette, or model, of the town centre, housed in an octagonal glass house just inside a Belgian enclave. There the town lies in perfect miniature until you press a button and the two countries separate horizontally, the Belgian bits rising up an inch or two over their Dutch neighbours. Or so I thought at first, before realising that Belgium stayed still, while the Dutch parts sank, which, considering

Holland's eternal battle with nature, seemed hellish tactless. A hint perhaps that, behind the postcards and we're-all-Europeans-now camaraderie, there was some deadly serious national one-upmanship going on in sleepy Baarle.

If you took a straw poll of the tourists ambling contentedly around Baarle, you'd likely find that a fair number of them had gone out of their way to visit some of the other weird borders snaking around our continent. The chances are, every one of these tourists has been a map aficionado from a very early age, for that is where this strange interest is incubated. It starts with noticing the little nodules of enclaves, exclaves and tiny countries or counties in the family atlas. It progresses through hunting out larger-scale maps to get a closer look and digging out weighty reference volumes in the local library to find out a little more about them. Before long, you're harassing your poor parents to take you to see these far-flung places: anything from a lengthy diversion on some Sunday outing in order to take a look at Flintshire (Detached), to trying to persuade them that the family holiday this year really should be in northern Italy, because then you can bag San Marino (and, at quite a push, perhaps the Vatican City and/or Monaco).

That's really all it's about: bagging them. Just as climbers in the Highlands brag about bagging their Munros, we map addicts collect countries, counties, enclaves and exclaves, storing them up in our heads with guarded jealousy. We will – and do – go hundreds of miles out of our way to add a Luxembourg or a Liechtenstein to the list. We might only be there for a matter of hours, but that's not important. We've been, it's been seen, it's ticked off. All too often, though, these are not places to linger. After all, somewhere whose principal attraction is its odd borders is unlikely to provide much else in the way of entertainment, once you've sent a few postcards ('Look where we are!') and admired the profusion of brass plaques for dodgy banks making the most of the local feudalism and tax-free status. More often than not, tiny countries are a crushing disappointment. I remember cajoling a companion on my first InterRail holiday, at the age of twenty, into a lengthy detour to visit Andorra. As well as its obvious appeal as one of the continent's micro-states, I was hopeful that it might prove to be something of a European Tibet, a mountain kingdom far from the pressures of our grubby lives, a repository of the highest spiritual and cultural order. We sat on a bus that zigzagged its way at the speed of a glacier up into the Pyrenees, only to find that the country was a hideous duty-free shopping mall, five thousand feet up, swarming with crazed people ramming their car boots full of cameras, fur coats and bottles of Pernod. All there was to do was get pissed on cheap cocktails and feel faintly conned and very sick on the bus back down the hairpin bends.

Collecting mini-countries is how a border-spotter's dependency begins, but you're soon on to the hard stuff with me and all the others in Baarle: the enclaves, exclaves and other freakish anomalies of the European map. The internet has taken the sport to unheard-of levels: virtually everyone sweating their way up the 5,368-foot peak of Sorgschrofen Mountain in the Alps is only doing it so they can photograph themselves at the rock on the summit that marks the point where the borders of Germany and Austria cross each other, creating the exclave around the village of Jungholz. These days, they then post their photos straight on the web. There are whole websites dedicated to pictures of smiling young men – who you know probably still live at home with their mums – grinning at different signposts marking these cartographic exceptions to the rule.

Such hangovers from medieval treaties and inbred parochialism are much more than mere diversionary footnotes to geography, however, and not all are as cheerily twee or geared towards tourism, gambling or shopping as Baarle, Jungholz, the Spanish exclave of Llivia in France, and German Büsingen or Campione d'Italia in Switzerland. Enclaves and exclaves have played, and continue to play, a hugely disproportionate role in world affairs, often proving to be either the impossible-to-shift grit of some ancient dispute or the spark that ignites a new one. Some of the most famous – Danzig, Kaliningrad, Berlin, Dubrovnik, the Gaza Strip, Nagorno-Karabakh, Chechnya, Ossetia, Gibraltar, Ceuta and Mililla – are bywords for stand-offs, wars and misery stretching back centuries. You'd think that progress and globalisation were quietly ironing out these aberrations on the map, but quite the opposite is true. Many more new enclaves and exclaves were created in the late twentieth century than were disposed of: the break-ups of the Soviet Union and Yugoslavia alone unmasked twenty brand new ones in Europe and western Asia, some desperately fractious.

Some have been ironed out, yet their ghosts refuse to budge. There is no modern border quite as infamous as the Berlin Wall, despite dividing the city between the Soviet and western sectors for only forty years, the physical wall a mere twenty-eight. Its destruction in November 1989 was the single most graphic and joyous proof that this divided city, its divided country and its divided continent, could finally be reunited. Only tiny stretches of the Wall remain today, yet its influence plods doggedly on. No Berlin street map is complete without a line marked 'Course of Wall' running across it. Maps, aerial photos, postcards and posters showing the Wall in aggressive situ outsell all others; lumps of masonry of dubious provenance are still the most popular city souvenirs of the city; the few remaining kilometres of graffitied concrete are photographed thousands of times daily; museums about the Wall and the city's brief divide draw in coachloads. Districts that were once in the eastern sector still underperform against those in the west, and everyone still uses the division to state where they live, work and play, or where they are going. As the vicious reality of partition recedes further into history, its iconic status only grows. We are absolutely fascinated by it, and becoming ever more so.

The first time I went to Berlin, I was obsessed with scouring the city for the scars of the Wall, and on finding them, feeling some kind of strange rush before hurtling off to look for the next. Back home, I

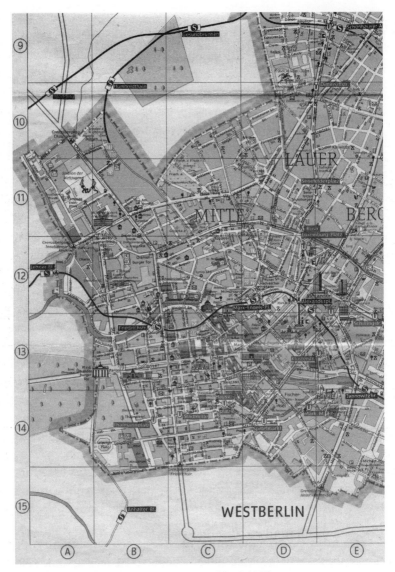

An East German map of Berlin from the days of the Cold War

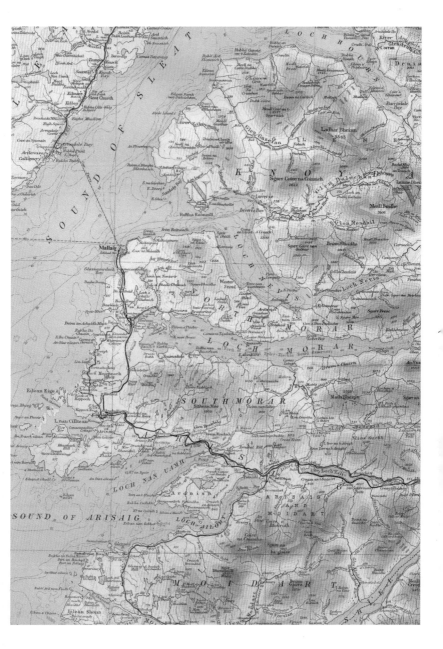

Bartholomew maps got better and better the higher (and deeper) they went: those of their native Scotland were exquisite (see page 20).

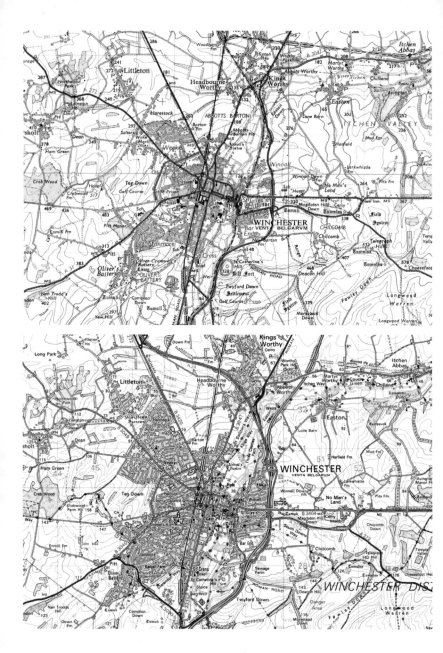

The vanishing trunk road (see page 122): the A33 on the outskirts of Winchester, 1959 (above) and 2005 (below).

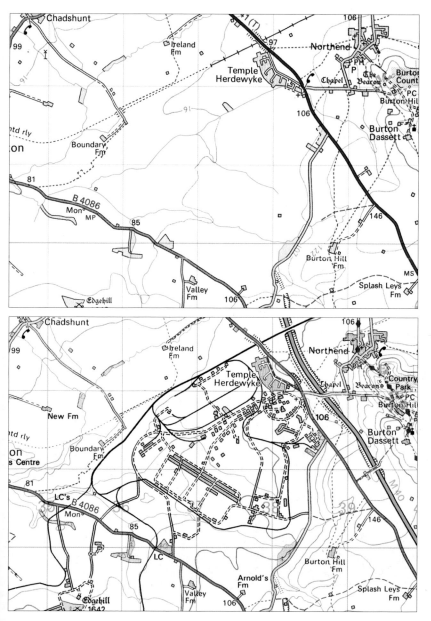

Now you see it, then you didn't – the Kineton armaments depot in Warwickshire (see page 168), on the OS Landranger map no. 151 of 1979 (above) and 2008 (below).

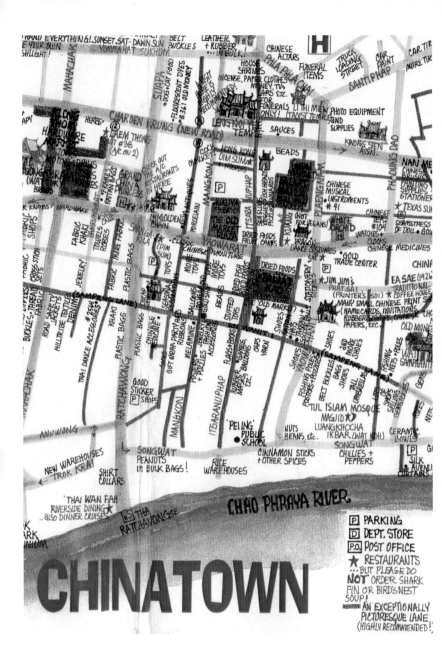

Organised chaos: Nancy Chandler's map of Bangkok (see page 267).

ORDNANCE SURVEY
"ONE-INCH" MAP OF
THE CHILTERNS

Price Three Shillings Net
Published by the Ordnance Survey Office,
SOUTHAMPTON

Women only rarely appeared on Ellis Martin's covers for the Ordnance Survey (see page 261).

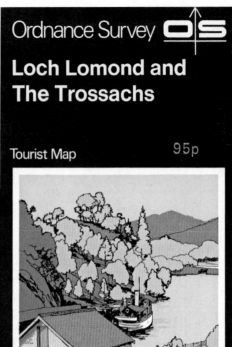

Ordnance Survey **OS**

Loch Lomond and The Trossachs

Tourist Map   95p

The area covered by the map is indicated on the back cover

Ordnance Survey

Lake District

Showing part of National Park Boundary

Tourist Map

The area covered by the map is indicated on the back cover

OS covers get groovy ... the countryside as seen on a 1970s acid trip (see page 120).

A line on the map, here the USA–Canada border near Scobey, can soon become a very definite line on the ground (see page 131).

The ruler-straight Central Line (red) and its beguiling 'Escalator Link' at Bank, before both were destroyed by the arrival of the Docklands Light Railway (see page 25).

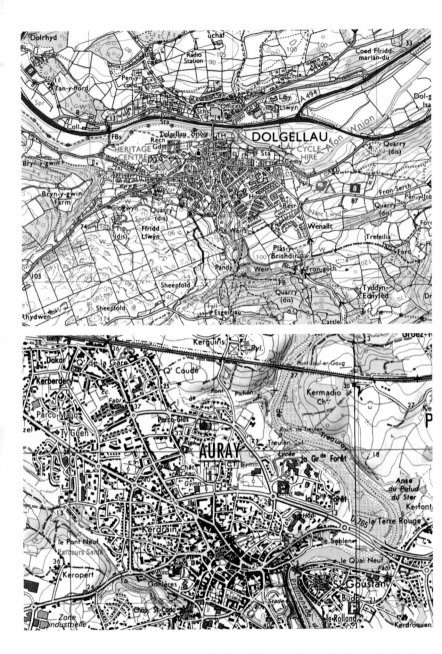

Ordnance Survey (above) versus L'Institut Géographique National (below): for once, the Brits win hands down (see page 46).

lost days gazing at maps, photos and YouTube videos of the city, before, during and after its divide. Best was the progression of historic tube maps, showing the system growing, splitting, contracting, reuniting and finally growing again, plus the shaky home movies of the *Geisterbahnhöfe* (ghost stations), the U-Bahn and S-Bahn stops in the eastern sector that lay on lines connecting different parts of the western zone. These used to be sealed, while armed Ossi (Eastern) guards loitered on dimly lit platforms to make sure that no one got on or off as the train ambled through. Some stations straddled the border, so that platforms and exits had to be divided or sealed accordingly. In a few places, there were parallel railway lines belonging to the two different halves, necessitating huge fences between them, lest anyone tried leaping from a train or peering too hard at their unknown neighbours.

Because these *Geisterbahnhöfe* were sealed so suddenly in 1961, they were perfect time capsules when they came to be reopened in 1989 and beyond. The tourist industry and the nostalgia freaks are gnashing their teeth that at least one wasn't preserved that way: although signage in Hitler's 1930s Gothic typescript has survived in many of them, the main motivation in 1989 was to erase the city's hideous division, not to slap on a heritage order and glorify it. The same happened at the legendary Checkpoint Charlie, which was swiftly demolished on the Wall's demise. A naff replica has now been rebuilt for the tourists to pose at. Our fascination with this short-lived border is not going to go away, and it is not going to help Berliners overcome what they call their *Mauer im Kopf*, the 'wall in the head', for that is as defined and almost insurmountable as the physical original.

— ·— ·— ·—

Everyone's mental landscape consists of *Mauern im Kopf*: those decreed from on high and woven into our personal history, as well as those drawn on no map at all, a place or a moment where we leave the familiar or comfortable and enter the unknown. Our towns, villages, fields and cities are full of such invisible borders – places we just don't go, that are on the other side. My partner grew up precisely three and half miles, as the crow flies, from where we now live. Until, at the age of twenty-nine, he started seeing me, he'd never once been to this village. It lies across the other side of a divide that's drawn on no map, but is as real yet invisible to the casual eye as a country-house ha-ha. In Wales, such divisions are manifold: the concept of one's *milltir sgwar* – square mile – is deeply ingrained in the culture, so that attitudes, physical appearances, even specific words in the Welsh language change from village to village, valley to valley.

It's far from just a Welsh thing, however. At the age of six, living on a modern housing estate in suburban England, my mental map of it was crystal clear. One street in particular was a no-go area; I felt supremely daring even taking my bicycle up it, and would execute a swift U-turn out at the first sign of a twitching curtain or returning car, my heart pounding. There was no specific threat or bad memory connected to it; it just didn't feel like territory I could be familiar with. As my bike shed its stabilisers and began to take me further into the town and the surrounding countryside, there were numerous places that were crossed off my mental map as being out of bounds: streets, roads, lanes, closes and even leafy avenues where I'd never go. My dad once bought me a street map of our home town, and I remember staring at the parts that frightened me or left me cold, learning the names of the 'enemy', prepared only to get to know them vicariously from the map. Sometimes this was because of singular dangers: a grumpy old man who'd once shouted at or tried to grope me, a family that scared me, a building that spooked me (there were plenty of those), the home of someone that terrified me at school (ditto). Often, they were for no good reason at all, just a vague sense of unease which I couldn't understand and didn't want to go any deeper into. Frequently, these no man's lands necessitated considerable detours, but I was always happier to do that than face these often invisible demons gurning out of the map at me. To some extent, I still feel that today: there are roads I dread having to take, so soaked do they seem in some unspecific melancholy or foreboding.

Borders of the mind, unmapped and mostly unseen, are the ones that most affect our lives on a day-to-day basis. The shops we go to, the streets we walk down, the parks and towns and stations and riverbanks we use, all dictated by a sense of there being a line over which we do not like to cross. Gang warfare has always depended on such identification with place: the divide between where you can and cannot go is sometimes literally a matter of life and death. Such brutality is not only confined to obvious culprits such as drug-dealers or racketeers: six people died in Glasgow in 1984 because of a turf war between ice-cream vans.

— · — · — · —

If you hail from this corner of the world, it would seem that there's barely room for many imaginary boundaries, for the swiftest of glances at the globe will show that no continent does actual borders quite like the Europeans. Many national or sub-national boundaries in the Americas, Africa and Australasia follow natural features and, where they're a bit thin on the ground, it was out with the ruler and a steady line along some parallel or other, often for hundreds, even thousands of miles – the cause of many a subsequent problem, it must be said. In Europe, millennia of scrapping over every last inch of turf has produced borders that wriggle and squirm across the map like a nest of vipers. For those of us in Britain, where the principal borders – between England, Wales and Scotland – have remained substantially the same for well over a thousand years, what is most amazing about those on the European mainland is how fluid they seem. Compare maps of 1750, 1850, 1950 and today, and very little seems to have stayed the same. Some change on a bewilderingly regular basis; if someone born in 1870 had lived into their late seventies in the same Strasbourg house, they would have changed nationality five times, being bounced like a ball between France and Germany.

To sample the borders of Europe, I recently went InterRailing again, this time with my partner and thankful indeed to have already ticked Andorra off my list. The trip took us from Paris to Corfu. Direct, it's just a shade over a thousand miles, although our journey more or less doubled that, crossing fifteen international borders in the process. These were marked with varying degrees of boot-stomping and pass-port-stamping. Some – France into Belgium, into Holland, into Germany; the Czech Republic into Slovakia – passed by unnoticed, the change in country marked by little more than a change in signage on the station platform. Some involved long waits at dusty frontier halts, a couple of platforms and a customs shack in the middle of a field. Claques of uniformed officials banged up and down the train, shouting 'Pass!' at anything that moved. Finally, the train would shudder its way out of the station, before creaking to a halt twenty minutes later at the frontier station on the other side of the border, where we'd go through the whole process again.

By far the most intimidating crossings were of borders that weren't even there two decades ago, namely between the member states of the former Yugoslavia; each involved unyielding stares, lengthy scrutiny, a few staccato questions, lots of muttering between armed officials, and finally a large stamp being flourished to ink the pages of Her Britannic Majesty's passport. As each new state has peeled off the rump of the old country, it seems that their greatest growth industry has been in scores of uniformed officials to police their shiny new borders. As ever, the people attracted to such a career (job description: glaring, mumbling, making people feel very uncomfortable, possessing the ability to wear big boots and silly hats with no shame or sense of irony whatsoever) are the kind that you know had sand, soil and shit kicked in their faces throughout their childhood, but who have been getting their revenge in regulation nylon slacks ever since. Crossing twice into

Serbia was especially cheerless, for, although border guards anywhere look like serial killers in the making, the chances are that here they actually were hurling their neighbours into shallow graves just a few short years ago, and would relish the chance to redeploy such skills on smart-arse Western tourists, especially those scribbling it all down in a notebook.

Using the ex-Yugoslav railway network was a ghostly experience, for it reeked of the painful recent past. Stations that, not so long ago, were bustling with activity to destinations far and exotic, have been reduced to spectral affairs, one or two trains a day going any distance at clod-hopping speed (the tracks are in a terrible state of repair), plus the odd local rumble through the suburbs. The station at Skopje, Macedonia's magnificently mountain-ringed capital, was the most sombre. A huge earthquake in 1963 levelled the city and a new elevated central station was built as part of Tito's plan to create a socialist architectural Utopia on the plain of the Vardar River. The ten-track station under a giant tubular roof once hummed with the chatter of those whisking away to Athens, Salonica, Pristina, Belgrade, Sofia, Istanbul, Zagreb, Ljubljana, Vienna and all points between. Now, everything stood semi-derelict and forlorn, the destination-indicator board had flicked its last long ago, the cafés and waiting rooms stayed locked, the platforms deserted. The only flurry of life came when the occasional train dragged slowly in: briefly the station flickered and crackled, before collapsing back into torpor.

Ironically, the happiest border crossing of all was the one that we'd been most nervous of and was logistically the most difficult to organise, namely crossing from Montenegro into Albania. Montenegro's dusty capital, Podgorica (né Titograd), is only fifteen miles from the border. There's a railway line to Shkodër, northern Albania's biggest town, but no trains currently use it. There are no buses, either, so the only way to do it was to find a taxi that would take us to the frontier, walk through it and hope that there would be someone on the other side to take us further. We asked at our Podgorica hotel about finding a taxi. The young girl on reception, who had been a great laugh and a rich mine of information up to this point, stared incredulously. 'Why you want to go to Albania?' she barked. 'You are drug smugglers, yes? Spies? Trafficking of people?' 'Er, no,' we protested weakly. 'Just we're so near, and it would be a shame not to see the place.' This didn't wash at all. 'I hate Albanians with all of my heart,' she spat. We'd heard much the same from almost everyone we'd met in Macedonia and Serbia too.

Consequently, it was with some apprehension that we lugged our rucksacks to the border post, having been dropped there by a Montenegrin taxi driver who couldn't wait to get away. Sat in his little booth on the Albanian side was what looked like a regulation border guard, not much more than five feet tall and with a fussy little moustache. I groaned at the sight. He eyed us warily, before taking our passports from us and studying them very carefully. On reading the words UNITED KINGDOM OF GREAT BRITAIN AND NORTHERN IRELAND on the cover, he broke into a huge grin. 'Ah, Anglia!' he chuckled. He stood up. 'Anglia! Meester Bean, Norman Wisdom, Tony Blair!' Fancy coming from a country known only for three gurning clowns. I did a weak Norman Wisdom impression, which had him in fits of laughter and calling over his colleague to meet us. As we stumbled our first few steps into what used to be called 'Europe's last Stalinist state' (and where, by a miracle of raw capitalism, a taxi instantly appeared to hurry us on our way), the wheezing giggles of the two loveliest border guards in existence echoed behind us. It was a very accurate omen. There were many more laughs to be had in Albania than in painfully self-conscious little Montenegro, uptight Serbia or anywhere else we'd found in the Balkans.

Because of the suited-and-booted brigade at every border in Eastern Europe, it was impossible not to be minutely aware of the divides between countries, as they stood on the map of 2008. Only twenty years ago, the picture would have been very different, and it could well be again twenty years hence. For the map of Europe with which I was travelling told only a fraction of the story. There were a whole host of ghost nations and their borders stalking us as well. In the current configuration, we went through Belgium, the Netherlands, Germany, the Czech Republic, Slovakia, Hungary, Romania, Bulgaria, Serbia, Macedonia, Bosnia-Herzegovina, Montenegro and Albania. We also travelled, in a parallel age – it may be past or future; perhaps both – through Wallonia, Flanders, Brabant, Westphalia, Saxony, Prussia, Bohemia, Moravia, Ruthenia, Transylvania, Wallachia, Rumelia, Dacia, Thracia, Dalmatia and Illyria. It sounded more like a wander through the *Notting Hill Book of Baby Names*.

— · — · — · —

If the borders of the countries of mainland Europe are in a state of almost perpetual flux, so it seems are some rather nearer to home, those of the British counties. For the most part, these have changed little for seven or eight centuries, until the end of the Second World War, that is. Since then, however, it's been an almost constant round of reviews, commissions, recommendations, enquiries, submissions, task forces, changes, counter-changes and a bewildering quantity of Acts of Parliament. And we're still not happy with the result. Far from it; there's almost no subject guaranteed to light up the letters pages of local newspapers and online forums quite as spectacularly as the question of county boundaries and county loyalties.

Just like the greater map of Europe, the old county map of Britain contained a stack of anomalies and historical quirks. It had its Luxembourgs in the shape of Clackmannanshire, Rutland, Radnorshire, Kinross-shire and the Soke of Peterborough; its Danzigs and Dubrovniks in the clutter of enclaves and exclaves that had built up over centuries. The last of these to go, in 1974, was the detached part of Flintshire, otherwise known as the English Maelor, a tiny and oddly shaped nodule on the map that worried me enormously as a youngster, so abandoned and alone did it seem in the pages of the family atlas. It fascinates me still: I made one of my Welsh television programmes about the Maelor, despite the fact that no one there could watch it, for the little exclave pokes out into England, TV signal and all, and is connected to the rest of Wales by only the most slender of necks. As a local historian there told me in the programme, 'When, in the 1990s, the boundaries were being redrawn yet again, the only option not presented to the people of the Maelor was the one that they probably wanted the most – namely, to be transferred over the border and into Shropshire or Cheshire. Very few people here feel any real affinity with Wales.' As it was, the poor sods ended up as part of the new unitary authority of Wrexham County Borough, a fate you wouldn't really wish on your own worst enemy.

The Maelor has been an exclave of Flintshire ever since it was given by the county's progenitor, Edward I, as a gift to his beloved wife, Eleanor of Aquitaine (and as a nod back to the area's previous incarnation as a widow's dowry under the native Welsh ruler, Gruffudd Maelor). This act of gentlemanly generosity over seven hundred years ago has entirely coloured the culture and the flavour of the place, even today, for there is a neither-here-nor-there quality to the Maelor, an island remoteness that belies its firmly inland location. No one has captured this quality better than the late Lorna Sage, whose sublime memoir, *Bad Blood*, recalls growing up in the Maelor village of Hanmer, 'a time warp, an enclave of the nineteenth century', where 'most engagements were really contracted between legacies and land, abutting acres, second cousins twice removed, or at least a tied cottage and a tea service'.

It was tidying up the many little islands of one county lost in another that first interested the government in fiddling with county borders; the Counties (Detached Parts) Acts of 1839 and 1844 rid us of scores of these outliers, although dozens still lingered, being abolished piecemeal throughout the next century or so. There were some strange bedfellows that surely needed sorting out: the villages of Icomb, Worcestershire, and Great Barrington, Berkshire, sat just five miles apart, both distant outposts of their respective counties deep within

Gloucestershire. Even after the clean-up, Worcestershire still had eight lumps – four in Gloucestershire, two in Warwickshire, one in Stafford-shire and one in Herefordshire – remaining outside the main county border. The most celebrated of these was the county's 'second town', Dudley, which wasn't transferred out of Worcestershire until 1966. Bizarrely, from 1889 to 1929, the parish of Dudley Castle was an exclave of Staffordshire, surrounded by an exclave of Worcestershire, itself surrounded entirely by Staffordshire.

This was nothing compared with the situation in Scotland, however. Until the Local Government (Scotland) Act of 1889 tidied it up, the county map reflected its origins in the battles and bargainings of the clans and lairds, with numerous exclaves, some quite signifi-cant, on the map. Most remarkable was the county of Cromartyshire, which had grown out of the lands owned by the Earls of Cromarty, and was nothing but twenty-two completely separate parcels of land strewn across the entire width of Scotland, as if the whole county had been dropped and smashed by a fleeing giant. Only one nugget, around Ullapool on the west coast, was anything like a decent size at 183 square miles, slightly larger than Rutland, albeit in one of the least populated parts of Britain. The other twenty-one exclaves varied in size from twenty-eight square miles down to a tiny fifty-one acres at the tip of the uninhabited Gruinard Island, later infamous as the place where anthrax was tested on sheep in the Second World War.

The perpetual tinkering around with counties reached something of a peak in 1974, a landmark year for the map addict: two general elec-tions (those constituency maps won't just colour themselves, you know), the launch of the Ordnance Survey's new 1:50 000 series in its startling pinky-purple jacket, as well as implementation of the most radical change yet in British counties. Cleveland, Merseyside, West Midlands, Avon, Strathclyde, the Central and Borders regions, Mid, South and West Glamorgan, Greater Manchester, Humberside, Tyne and Wear, and Hereford and Worcester were all created in a governmental bloodrush of

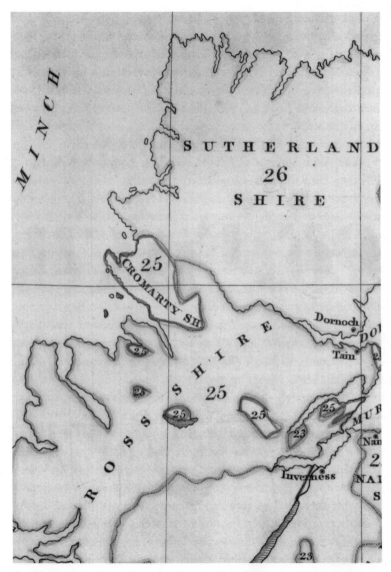

'As if the county had been dropped and smashed by a fleeing giant': Cromarty-shire

clean lines, smooth edges and practical good sense. Sounding as though they'd been conceived and developed deep within the brutalist womb of a 1960s civic gulag, their birth wiped out at a stroke boundaries and loyalties that had worked quite adequately for centuries. Needless to say, the kind of people who get terribly exercised about such matters detested the new counties from the word go and lobbied tirelessly for their removal.

I was seven years old at the time and deliriously excited by the fact that, without moving so much as an inch, I had ceased to be a child of industrial north Worcestershire, but was now a proud resident of Hereford 'n' Worcester, the Sonny and Cher of English counties. I knew all the stats: how my county's highest point, for instance, had rocketed from a fair-but-middling 1,395 feet (the Worcestershire Beacon of the Malvern Hills) to a super, soar-away 2,307 feet (a ridge, slap on the Welsh border, in the Black Mountains) just by the stroke of a pen. Never mind the fact that, by any definition, Kidderminster was a whole world away from the dark peaks of the Borders. It counted, it was official, and I hugged it close to my chest. I recall proudly announcing this revelation to my dad and step-mum, who just gawped in slack-mouthed incredulity at the weird shit that was tumbling from their little boy's lips.

Even without the Ribena goggles of my childish enthusiasm, I still feel that the 1974 reorganisation has been rather unfairly done over. Faced with the dog's dinner of administrative borders that John Major and the Boundary Commission have bequeathed us now, those reviled, abandoned 'new' counties are starting to take on a glorious sheen of logic and clear thinking. Unlike our present system, the 1974 counties, and Scottish regions, were supremely easy to remember and to understand, with everywhere being served for one set of needs – mainly education, social services, transport – by its county council, the rest by its more local district council. And while some of them were undoubtedly a streamlining step too far, there was unshakeable sense in many, particularly in metropolitan areas. After all, London – a metropolis that had once been carved up between Surrey, Kent, Essex, Middlesex and the City – had been redrafted as a single unit (the London County Council) as far back as 1889, and then expanded into Greater London, taking in more of each county and a slice of Hertfordshire for good measure, in 1965. What works for the capital was sorely needed in our other great conurbations. Until 1974, the urban West Midlands was cloven between three counties: Warwickshire, Worcestershire and Staffordshire (and, historically, the towns of Halesowen and Oldbury were in an exclave of Shropshire). Bristol was sliced in two between Gloucestershire and Somerset, the Newcastle/Gateshead sprawl between Durham and Northumberland. There was obvious room for improvement.

While the 1970s names and boundaries smelled of corduroy jackets on polytechnic lecturers, their 1990s replacements stank of the fudge and the focus group: truly the millennial way. On every decision, all it took was a few well-organised, very vocal protestors to whip up enough letters of support and the Boundary Commissioners collapsed in a funk. The result is there for all to see: I doubt if even the most avid, aspergic map addict could rattle off a complete list of current administrative British counties and county boroughs, a moniker that includes such mighty shires as Wokingham, Neath-Port Talbot, Renfrewshire *and* East Renfrewshire, Stockton-on-Tees, Halton, Thurrock, Rhondda Cynon Taff, the infamous Bath and North-East Somerset (aka BANES, with woeful accuracy), Lincolnshire, North Lincolnshire and North-East Lincolnshire, but no other separate Lincolnshire from any non-northern point of the compass. Barely anyone knows where they all are, fewer still care. The administrative county map of Britain now looks as if it's been left scrunched up under the stairs and nibbled by mice.

— · — · — · —

Nowhere is the post-war saga of county boundaries as defined or passionate as it is in Rutland, that Lilliputian East Midlands county

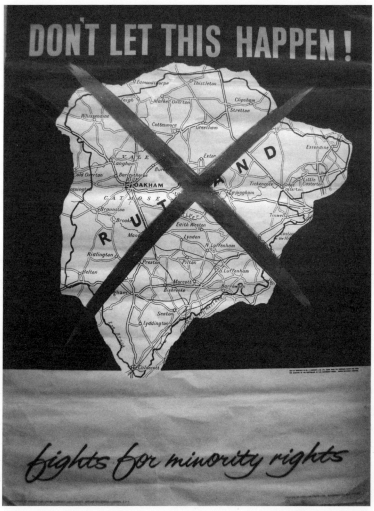

A poster from the Save Rutland campaign, as it swings into action in the early 1960s

that many people would probably struggle to place accurately on the map. 'Have we been there?' would be the brow-furrowed question, possibly followed up with: 'I think we passed through it on our way to Norfolk once. Or was that Retford?'

Rutland may be tiny – in England's smallest shire, you're never more than seven miles from the border – but this is its greatest asset as much as its most obvious potential weakness. Everywhere you turn, it's Rutland this and Rutland that: like small men and yappy toy dogs, it makes an awful lot of noise for its diminutive size. Local people think of themselves as Rutlanders or Ruddlemen first, English second. Being British tiptoes in behind, being European comes precisely nowhere.

Nothing ever unites a cause so magnificently as a threat to its very existence, and so it has been with Rutland. Since the Second World War, every one of the many government reports has recommended its abolition and incorporation into one of the neighbouring counties of Leicestershire, Northamptonshire or Lincolnshire. A county of just 36,000 inhabitants, they boom, is unviable and unsustainable. To offer the full range of goods and services demanded of a modern local authority is too prohibitively pricy and complicated for somewhere with such limited resources of manpower and revenue. The threat was seriously floated in 1962, when a government investigation recommended the abolition of a number of smaller counties. Rutlanders swung into action with a boisterous campaign to save their shire: a mock-up of naval warship HMS *Rutland* was placed in the middle of the county town, Oakham, bunting and a big banner declaring that 'Rutland Expects' flapping above it in the breeze. Various enthusiastic campaigners, often in military uniform, would megaphone passing shoppers from the pretend poop deck with the importance of saving their county status. One charming photo in the Rutland County Museum shows the ship in situ, with a comely maiden from the local girls' grammar school in front, coyly holding up a placard that told the world that 'Rutland Fights for Minority Rights'. When the campaign achieved its objective, and Rutland was (temporarily) spared the chop, the mock warship was quietly mothballed, but those who stashed it away knew all too well that it would probably be needed once again in the near future. And so it proved.

Rutland's fighting spirit – and its plywood warship – was called on as never before as the swinging 1960s shuddered to a halt. First, there was the dastardly plan to create Europe's largest manmade reservoir in England's smallest county. 'Don't Flood Rutland' and, rather more obliquely, 'Don't Reduce Rutland to a Tow-Path', were the rallying cries for the campaign against a 3,100 acre artificial lake, almost the size of Windermere, at the tiny county's heart. Newspaper headlines panicked about everything from parking problems to an influx of water-borne midges and flies. But voices in favour of the new reservoir – and the projected boom in tourism and property prices for houses with an unexpected waterfront view – began to sound, and in 1970 Royal Assent was given to the plan. By mid-1977, Rutland Water was open for business and the hamlets of Nether and Middle Hambleton had vanished beneath it. The larger settlement of Upper Hambleton remains to this day, isolated on a thin, ghostly finger of land poking out into the reservoir. The Water's most famous spectral landmark, the lonesome Georgian church of Normanton, sticking out from the southern shore, looks as if it should tell the sad tale of a village recently lost beneath the waves, but the rest of Normanton was already long gone: the entire village had been demolished in 1764 under the orders of Sir Gilbert Heathcote of Normanton Hall, so as to improve the view from his splendid portico. Now *that's* Rutland.

Ironically, by the time the local great and good had gathered to toast the opening of Rutland Water, the county from which it took its name had finally seen the waters close over its head. Rutland had managed to survive the tentative county cull of 1965 that had seen off the Soke of Peterborough, the Isle of Ely and Middlesex, but they were no match for Ted Heath and his determination to streamline the county map of Britain. In 1974, Rutland was annexed by neighbouring Leicestershire, being reduced to the status of a mere district council. Grinding salt into the wounds, Leicestershire County Council jobsworths even went round ripping out the Rutland signs and dumping them all. One by one, they were reclaimed and reappeared on the roads, where they still sit quietly today.

This being Rutland, however, the fight was only just beginning. The county never felt at home in Leicestershire: its modest population accounting for just 5.5 per cent of the new merged entity, its bucolic issues ignored by the pressing needs of a largely urban authority, whose principal city is due any day now to become the first in Britain with a majority brown and black population. It's a long, long way from the quiet, honeyed – and overwhelmingly white – conservatism of Edith Weston and Tixover.

Over the next two decades the groundswell of dissatisfaction with Leicestershire rule grew thunderous. Combining the increasing thirst for nostalgia, the growing scepticism towards politicians at all levels and the gulf in understanding between the rural population and its urban, multicultural counterpart, the campaign almost ran itself. Every grumble and grievance was easily exploitable with the answer of: 'It would all be all right if only Rutland regained its independence.'

The i-word is a real facet of Rutland's identity: independence. They talk about it a lot, and chuck it around like verbal confetti. To a Ruddleman, it's a word to stiffen the sinews, and it's very telling. Here in Wales, politicians – even those from Plaid Cymru, for whom independence is their raison d'être – tiptoe around the word as if it might blow up in their faces, which indeed it might. No such reticence in Rutland. In the 1960s, they'd called out and marched to 'Fight for Minority Rights'. In the late 1980s and early '90s, such a slogan sounded either too monochrome or – heaven help us – as if they were proposing an enclave for Muslims or gays, so it was clear, simple and blunt: 'Independence for Rutland' went the cry. You get the feeling that if total secession from the UK was on offer, Rutlanders would grab it with both ruddy hands and the county would become a British Liechtenstein or Andorra, making its way in the world by selling postage stamps and duty-free, together with a little light tax evasion. At one point during the 'independence' campaign, they even issued Rutland passports as a PR offensive: the Republic of Rutland certainly has a bit of a ring to it. Its first piece of legislation would be to revoke the ban on hunting, its second the one on smoking.

In the end, the only independence on offer was that of a separate county council, which is hardly the stuff to get the pulse racing. It was enough, however, to take the county on its latest journey, as the Boundary Commission announced yet another comprehensive review of local government in the early 1990s. From the outset, Rutland was vocal in its demand for reinstatement on the county map, but the Commissioners showed no inclination to acquiesce. In 1995, there came a surprising volte-face when, out of nowhere, Environment Secretary John Gummer announced that he would allow the county's reinstatement as a unitary authority. The burger-forcer had become the burghers' hero, although rumours persisted that the nod had come from a higher authority, namely Prime Minister John Major. His constituency of Huntingdonshire had, until 1974, been a separate county (albeit with Peterborough tacked on the top for its last nine years), before being swallowed wholesale by Cambridgeshire. There was a half-hearted campaign running to reinstate Huntingdonshire, and Major thought it would be expedient politically if he backed it. To do so, he had to acknowledge the far greater strength of feeling in nearby Rutland, so he backed both horses. His own fell at the first fence, but the Rutland Pony powered on to the finishing line. On the strangely apposite date of 1 April 1997, Rutland was reborn. It's a date still celebrated in the county as – you guessed it – Independence Day.

Except, it isn't quite that simple. Rutland exists as a local authority, though not as a county in the eyes of the Post Office or in any of those choose-your-county boxes that you have to tick if buying something on the internet. The official name of the local authority is the gloriously tautological Rutland County Council District Council. To preserve its nominal independence, Ruddlemen have to pay one of the highest council taxes anywhere in Britain, with fairly patchy services in return. Furthermore, and with a grim sense of inevitability about it, those shrieking the loudest for 'independence' swiftly consolidated their own positions on the fledgling County Council District Council, and almost as swiftly descended into a mire of corruption and nepotism.

In Rutland, as in every place where localism is most politically charged, much of the campaign's impetus came from incomers. While it's an expedient pose for some, it is surely meant sincerely by many who, having come from elsewhere, truly value the distinctiveness of their chosen habitat and are desperate to see that not lost. This is certainly the case – and with good cause – in Rutland. Like the kernel of a nut or the bud of a new leaf, the 150 square miles of Rutland hold the essential imprint of England, or at least one particular version of England, the kind that likes its beef to be dripping with blood and its Saturday afternoons doing something with horses – either riding them, chasing small creatures with them or slapping money on them. Rutland is at the heart of English hunting country, it is modestly famous for its illustrious public schools, and, save for a few limestone quarries, industry's grubby mitts have barely touched it. Since universal suffrage, and even during the Labour Party's high-water marks of 1945 and 1997, Rutland has never elected anything other than a Conservative MP.

I knew that I had to take a trip to Rutland the day a mate told me that it was the wife-swapping capital of England; the Land of Rut indeed. My friend lives about fifteen miles away over the Leicestershire border, and told me of Rutland residents in her social circle who regularly find themselves at parties where a fumble in the hot tub is just for starters. These Rutlanders are commendably lacking in coyness, as you'd expect from people who spend large parts of their lives hanging around in the company of tons of quivering horse flesh and randy dogs. Lack of prudery, and a honest get-on-with-it lustiness, are undeniably central facets of the true rural existence – not the *Move to the Country* version, with its Chelsea tractors and stripped pine, but the real, horny-handed version, more Massey Fergusons and stripped housewives. Rutland, true to its agricultural heritage, just likes to get 'em off and get on with it.

It was a bank-holiday weekend when I rolled into England's mini-shire, and it was hard work finding somewhere to camp. By a stroke of luck that seemed to indicate that it was all meant to be, the only place available at the last minute turned out to be in the very village that I'd been reliably informed was the erotic epicentre of this libidinous little county. I pitched camp and wandered down into the village, through a typical bank-holiday torrential downpour. By the time I arrived at the pub, I was soaked. Thankfully, I was wearing a cap, so at least my head was relatively dry.

'Bollocks! He's already got a hat on,' hollered a bloke at the bar as I entered the pub. 'Well, sorry, mate, you're going to have to get yourself another one.' Only then did I notice that everyone was wearing a strange, and usually ill-fitting, piece of headgear. Three or four red-faced fellas sat at the bar beneath vast panamas. A lady in a trilby was swaying cheerfully by the dartboard. And my inquisitor peered out from under the rim of a white fedora. 'Er, what's it for?' I ventured. 'Oh, it's a charity thing,' he replied. 'Distressed greyhounds or some-thing. Go in that room' – he gestured towards the back bar – 'and pick yourself a hat for the night. Put 50p in the bucket.' I meekly did as I was told, and came back in sporting a floppy summer hat, something I'd been meaning to buy anyway since getting painfully sunburned on my thinning scalp the previous week on a Norfolk beach. Bargain.

The hats definitely helped break the ice. According to my source, many of Rutland's wildest parties originate in fancy dress: it's not hard to see where a gathering is going when there's someone in a PVC basque being led around the room on a dog chain; you're not expecting Twiglets and a tombola after that. Although a pub full of people in daft hats isn't quite so obviously designed to crank up the libido, there was something pleasantly anonymous about everyone being semi-obscured by their hat, making conversation and shameless flirting a whole heap easier. I told one woman that I liked the top she was wearing. 'Yeah,' she drawled, thrusting her chest out. 'I 'ave got great tits, 'aven't I?' She had, and was using them to devastating effect, particularly on the farm lad that I was hopelessly trying to chat up.

Like all good parties, time melted away into an impressionistic sweep of colour and raucous laughter. An Elvis impersonator serenaded us: as he was being paid, and as he had evidently put a lot of work and time into his stiff quiff, he was the only person in the pub allowed to get away with not wearing a hat. He was good, and just got better and better as the evening, and more especially the beer, wore on. Folk were amazingly friendly, and quite happy to chew the fat with a total stranger in a floppy hat. At one point, I was dancing like a loon to the ersatz Elvis, and noticing lots of hands covertly stroking lots of thighs – but, sadly, not mine – all over the pub. I'd make a useless undercover reporter, though, because with alarming speed at some-time after midnight, the world suddenly started to spin and I had to get out into the fresh air – the perils of being a crap drinker. As I whirled, green-faced, from the pub, the bird with the self-declared great tits grabbed my arm: 'You going? Well, if you wake up in a few hours' time, come back. We'll still be going here.' Rutland, oh Land of Rutting, you get my full respect for partying beyond the call of duty.

Of Rutland's future, one thing is sure: it will retain its 'independence', even if it's largely cosmetic. No fool politician is going to open up the can of worms marked 'abolition' in the foreseeable future. Such things matter in fretful old England these days: hanging on to the trappings of self-determination and localism, the baubles and the beads, the flags and the signposts, while trying to ignore the growing feeling that it's only a matter of time before a barcode is tattooed on your fore-head and your entire day could be reconstructed from CCTV footage.

The harsh realities of modern life, though, come knocking here as much as anywhere else, and all too literally. The weekend I was there, the *Rutland Mercury*'s front-page splash was about the very village I was camping in. An extended family of Romany gypsies was hoping to set up permanent base there on a small parcel of land that they owned: two rival petitions – one hotly against them, one supporting their cause – were doing the rounds in the village. The 'anti' petition had chalked up over 400 signatures, the 'pro' one a rather less impressive 96. Now, the police were wading in and asking everyone to desist. Not desist collecting signatures per se, but desist from knocking on doors to collect them. 'We are encouraging people ... across the Rutland area not to open the door to strangers,' the local inspector was quoted as saying. That's going to do wonders for community relations; keep everyone bolted indoors, muttering conspiratorially to themselves.

This tiny storm-in-a-teacup hints at the darkest cloud looming over England's dwarf fiefdom. Rat-race refugees – or rather, race refugees – are eyeing up Rutland's rustic exterior and deciding that it has the edge over the various local sprawls – Leicester, Peterborough, Corby, Northampton – from which they hope to escape. Even with the slump, the local housing market remains feverish. With two-bedroom ex-council houses going for two hundred grand, few local youngsters have a snowball in hell's chance of making it on to the first rung of the prop-erty ladder. While these pressures can be found all over the country, Rutland's strident declaration of its independence and shrink-wrapped status can only exacerbate the problem: the more it makes of its unique-ness, its separateness, its crystallised Englishness, its 98.1 per cent whiteness, its dyed-in-the-wool Old Toryism and its diminutive size, the more eagerly it will be lusted after by that rootless band of malcon-tents who twitch uncontrollably at the sight of anything multicultural and who are permanently searching for a bubble where it's still 1959.

Rutland's is an extraordinary story. The county's civic motto of *Multum in Parvo* (Much in Little) is flaunted at every turn, and it underpins the identity of the place with unerring accuracy. To people in neighbouring, 'normal' counties, Rutlanders have the reputation as being rather above themselves and a mite snooty, as befits anyone who is part of a small clique, and in English terms, to be from Rutland is a clique that's only marginally larger than being a paid-up member of the royal family. Size, it's said, isn't everything, but it sure is in Rutland. This monumentally proud, strange and utterly fascinating little county is like no other, and it's all down to its pint-sized dimensions. In other words, the very uniqueness of the place, its every idiosyncrasy, comes from nothing more than a few random lines swirled on the map over a thousand years ago.

— · — · — · —

It seems that our attitude to our county borders has gone much the same way as our attitude to architecture, where each generation trashes the work of the one immediately prior to it. If that's the case, we can look forward to endless rounds of boundary reviews, a situation designed to please only indolent politicians and their pet tub-thumpers in the regional media. Plus antiquarian map dealers: old county maps have become the mainstay of much of the trade, adorning a steadily increasing number of downstairs toilets and hallways, office foyers and CEO suites, particularly in companies doing their utmost to turn our urban environment into America Lite.

By far the most popular sets among the many old county maps on offer are John Speed's Tudor series and Thomas Moule's early Victorian extravaganzas. Stunningly attractive syntheses of art and cartography, they are for sure, but they also have their own misty-eyed hunger for the past, so that it is *our* nostalgia for *their* nostalgia that drives the booming sales. Both Speed (1542–1629) and Moule (1784–1851) give us portraits of Britain at different high-water marks in our history, carefully editing out any details that left people unsure or apprehensive about the present or the future. Speed's 1612 county atlas, the *Theatrum Imperii Magnæ Britanniæ* ('Theatre of the Empire of Great Britain'), is a fine example of cartographic triumphalism. At that moment in history, the 'Empire of Great Britain' had spread no further than these islands; indeed, when he started working on the maps, Scotland wasn't even part of this self-declared empire, and when it became so at the union of the two Crowns in 1601, Speed had hastily to amend his plans by introducing one map of the newly formed Great Britain, together with just one map of Scotland as a whole. This compared very poorly with the county-by-county maps of England and Wales, and poorly even by comparison with the four maps of the different Irish provinces.

Speed's plans dwell fulsomely on all aspects of empire, both ancient and contemporary. His county plans bristle with civic pride and are dotted with depictions of royal residences, battles historical and legendary, aristocratic heraldry, Roman coinage and seas crammed with full-sailed battleships securing British coasts. Each county map comes with lavish notes, where truth is not always allowed to get in the way of his exuberant imperialism. On his Sussex map, he states as fact that 67,974 men were killed at the Battle of Hastings in 1066, despite our certain knowledge that it was conducted with considerably fewer than 10,000 soldiers on either side. Much of the mythology, enduring appeal and over-popularity of Stonehenge can be laid at the feet of John Speed, for he used it as the prime symbol of an ancient British empire, illustrating his map of Wiltshire with a massive drawing of it and wildly attributing it to the same kind of national heroism that his whole atlas was attempting to evoke. According to Speed, Stonehenge was 'erected by Aurelius Ambrosius, King of the Britaines, about ye yere of Christ 475 AD' as a memorial to his troops killed there by the 'treachery of ye Saxons'. Other monumental stoneworks, such as nearby Avebury, don't even merit inclusion on the map.

Even more telling are the English county maps of Thomas Moule, published as a complete collection for the first time in 1836. Like Speed's atlas of two centuries earlier, Moule revels in proud patriotism and historical embellishment for each county. Embellishing most of the maps are chivalrous knights, high Gothic columns, pilasters and alcoves, stately homes and medieval cathedrals, bucolic scenes of cheery peasants at the water's edge or herding stout cattle. Yet when the maps were published, the country was industrialising and urbanising at breakneck speed, with a concomitant revolution culturally and socially. The 1832 Reform Act, massively extending the franchise, had been bludgeoned through Parliament in response to considerable agitation; by the end of the decade, the Chartist movement was demonstrating fervently in favour of universal suffrage. Demonstrations, riots and fatal over-reactions by the authorities had placed the matter of workers' rights centre stage. Canals had connected all corners of the country and created the first industrial conurbations, and now railways were accelerating that process in unimaginable ways. In the decade up to 1831, the populations of both Manchester and Liverpool had risen by nearly 50 per cent. When the London–Birmingham railway opened in 1838, some five million people used it in its first year. Everything was changing, but you'd never have known it from looking at Moule's maps. They were a Picturesque flourish of lost lands and ways of life; in their day, they were already soaked in a wistful nostalgia. Now they seem doubly so.

— — — — —

Russell Grant, the diminutive astrologer, has become an unlikely champion for the old British counties. The interest started when he was a youngster, seeing his home patch of Middlesex so summarily disposed of in the mid-1960s. Twenty years ago, the publishers of his best-selling horoscope books told him that they would, as a reward for his prodigious and profitable output, publish any book of his choosing, fully expecting some vanity job. Instead, he produced a tome called *The Real Counties of Britain*, which sold oodles and has been updated and reprinted numerous times since. I interviewed him about the subject in Dolgellau, the solid old county town of Meirionnydd (Merioneth) for 438 years, until it was subsumed by Gwynedd in 1974. We did the interview sat on a bench by the River Wnion, Russell's stumpy legs quite unable to reach the ground, which looked unintentionally hilarious when it appeared on screen. He was eloquent and passionate for his cause. 'When I produced the book,' he told me, 'it really touched that part of the British psyche that needed to belong, that had allowed us to belong to a distinct area, and that had been the way for centuries, before the government began to muck them around. Those changes basically took away people's sense of belonging; they often bore no resemblance to the familiar patches. Everything had to be bigger, which is not necessarily better at all, and they're still tinkering with them now.' He got quite agitated about the Ordnance Survey and how it is instructed by its government paymasters only to show the borders of local authority areas rather than traditional counties, but his greatest ire was saved for those individuals who include Torfaen, Medway, Thurrock or Inverclyde in their addresses: 'As if the people who empty your dustbins warrant that kind of respect!' he spat, his little legs swinging furiously.

Russell Grant is a leading light in the Association of British Counties (ABC), the rather more respectable campaign championing this persistent issue. Its more shadowy, renegade counterpart is the direct-action group CountyWatch. Although it's gone a little quiet in the last couple of years, CountyWatch hit many a headline in the mid-2000s by storming around the country and ripping up any county signs that were marking the borders of modern administrative areas instead of the traditional boundaries of the old counties. It was an inspired idea, gaining acres of publicity, annoying the hell out of local council jobsworths and absolutely delighting the sort of people who write at least one letter a week to their local paper.

Despite my fascination – and sentimental enthusiasm – for the old borders, I won't be slipping on a balaclava and joining CountyWatch on a nocturnal patrol around the Yorkshire Ridings just yet. It's a very fine line between getting rightly exercised about such matters and a whole hornet's nest of petty obsession and some pretty dodgy politics. No surprise that many of the CountyWatchers are also active in hysterical (and often fabricated) campaigns about saving the pound (both kinds), the ounce, the yard, the mile, the pint, the sausage, the pork pie, real ale, Kendal mint cake, the countryside, Union Jacks on car number plates, hunting, shooting, fishing, Orange parades, school uniforms, parish councils, 'God Save the Queen' and the fancy dress of the Westminster Parliament.

Such obsessive upholders of tradition are themselves an age-old tradition, something probably worth preserving but not getting too excited about, like morris dancing or a half-arsed chorus of 'Auld Lang Syne' to see in the New Year. Absolutely every age has spawned its naysayers and nostalgists, folk who can only see the past in soft focus and the present through narrowed, bloodshot eyes – it's a debilitating ailment that many a map enthusiast has succumbed to; as we saw, Alfred Wainwright suffered an acute case. Today's bunch are the people who thought that BAN BLAIR was a cogent campaigning slogan and sprayed it over bridges, walls and roads like lusty tom cats. They see a sinister European plot behind everything and go right off the deep end about political correctness *gone mad!*, the BBC, multiculturalism, the 'gay mafia', the 'Jewish mafia', the 'Scottish mafia', global warming, secularism, Guardianistas, the 'Islamification' of Britain, New Labour, Cameron's Conservatives and the LibDems. Which, you might think, leaves them electorally disenfranchised, but you'd be very wrong. These hecklers of modernity are just as good at inventing new political parties, and appointing themselves as leaders, as they are at creating vociferous new pressure groups. The angry nationalist right seems to schism on an almost weekly basis, so that nearly all of these dreary dissidents have passed through at least a couple of tiny political parties in much the same way that London drinking water is said to pass through numerous kidneys on its way to your glass. There's always a gaggle of them standing in any high-profile by-election, blinking tetchily out from behind their bottle-bottom spectacles and homemade rosettes as the returning officer announces their 37 votes. Policies range from a mild harrumphing about modern life being simply beastly, to outright Holocaust denial and support for eugenic solutions. It's a long way from worrying where Berkshire ends and Oxfordshire begins. Or is it?

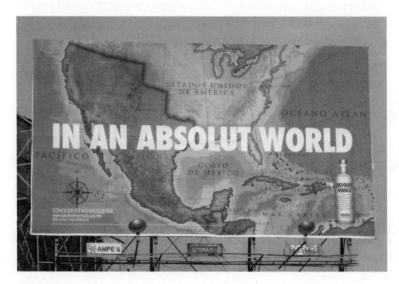

The controversial Absolut vodka ad, showing Mexico in its pre-1848 borders

5. THE POWER MAP

So Geographers, in Afric-maps,
With savage-pictures fill their gaps;
And o'er unhabitable downs
Place elephants for want of towns.

~ Jonathan Swift, *A Rhapsody*

If history is written by the winners, then it's they that get to draw the maps too, often in the immediate aftermath of victory. Maps have been used for political and propaganda purposes since they were first drawn in the sand with a stick, and have facilitated every war in history. Great leaps forward in cartography have almost always had a military catalyst, not least in our own Ordnance Survey, whose name is a blast from the fledgling days of the Empire, when the Board of Ordnance surveyed and mapped the south-eastern coasts of Britain in case of an invasion by Napoleon.

We like to think that maps are factual and somehow true, that they have little or no agenda, but that can never be the case. Their representation of reality can only ever be selective and subjective. Every cartographer has to decide what to include on their map and, perhaps more importantly, what to exclude. Emphasis of one feature over another requires choice and thus bias, and absolutely no map is too trivial or inconsequential not to upset or offend somebody. When, in 2005, the BBC changed its weather map, a very British storm-in-a-teacup ensued. Gone was the two-dimensional flat elevation of the

British Isles, to be replaced by a tilted view taken from somewhere above France. The effect was to emphasise the southern and eastern parts of the country, with a much-reduced Scotland receding into the distance. Within days, the BBC had received over four thousand complaints and questions were being tabled in both the Edinburgh and Westminster parliaments. Faced with such pressure, the Corporation could do little but back down gracelessly, reduce the angle of the tilt and restore some measure of Caledonian cartographic pride. Not that it did anything for the weather up there.

Different emphasis – on roads, say, over railways, or south-east England over Scotland – could be described as a cartographic economy with the truth. But maps also tell barefaced lies. Near where I grew up was a government rocket-research establishment, spread over hundreds of acres behind massive fences patrolled by shadowy guards. On the Ordnance Survey, none of this was shown: just empty fields and the odd wandering contour. That was it. A few miles from where my grandparents lived in Leamington Spa was another huge military base, the Kineton armaments depot, three or four times the size of the rocket establishment. Occasionally we'd go for a walk on nearby Edge Hill, from where you'd have the most fabulous panoramic view over the base, its watchtowers, hangars, roads, railways and clusters of sinister buildings. As can be seen from the example in the colour insert, the gap on the map was even more marked there: so huge was the site that the void in the middle of pastoral Warwickshire looked, if anything, even more suspicious on the OS than any accurate rendition of the base would have. Most ridiculous of all, when we went on holiday to Scarborough, a favourite trip was over the moors to see the vast golf balls of the Fylingdales early-warning radar station. Again, the map showed nothing. I began to comb my growing OS collection for other obvious empty spaces, and discovered that there were dozens. They were all secret sites of one sort or another. In a country the size of Britain, who did they think they were kidding?

This was at the height of the Cold War, however, and propaganda was everywhere. I remember the relish with which my school geography teacher, a luminary of the local SDP and fresh back from a holiday in West Berlin, brandished an East German map of the city in our startled faces. On it, the western sector was blank, almost devoid of any feature at all. 'How stupid must the communists be,' he boomed, 'to deny the existence of a city that everyone can see for themselves, just by looking across the river?' Fair point, but we weren't averse to doing exactly the same thing on our own maps. And were it not for the satellite imagery of Google Earth and the like, the British government would still be demanding that our maps maintain their secretive black holes. It was only in 2006 – some seventeen years after all Berliners were finally able to see every street of their city represented on the map – that the policy was quietly dropped, as the Cabinet Office spokesman put it, 'because of the availability of this information from open sources'.

The policy of blanking out military establishments from the map had lasted almost eighty years. In 1927, Prime Minister Stanley Baldwin ordered that 'no work of defence shall appear upon any map on sale to the general public'. In a largely vain attempt to conceal the policy, he further decreed that 'no blank space shall appear, but the natural physical features of the country shall continue to appear'. Sometimes, that worked, but for the larger sites this often looked ridiculous and, even to the amateur eye, highly suspicious. Paranoia reached new heights during the Cold War: almost five thousand specific 'key points' (as defined by MI5) were wiped from the map during the 1950s and '60s, lasting, in most cases, well into the 1990s. The ambiguous – and ubiquitous – OS label 'Works' also stems from this time, as it was decided not to specify the business of any factory, lest such information prove useful to the all-seeing enemy. It was a bit late for that. The Russian maps of Britain from this era, based wholly on the OS and with other information provided by aerial photography and local spies, managed to specify the activity of thousands of mines, quarries, mills and factories, as well as fill in the blanks of the military sites.

Since the end of the Cold War, but more especially since the advent of the internet, this highly secretive door to the innermost workings of the state has been flung open quite spectacularly. Some former top-secret sites are now busy tourist attractions, many others the target of 'urban cavers' and intrigued locals. It is a huge area of study: there is so much that the government kept from our eyes and our maps, often for reasons far short of defence of the realm. Learning about such places will have you looking at both maps and the landscape in a wholly new way. The net, of course, is the medium for this, as the kind of men who love maps, secrets and conspiracies are also, handily, very good at building websites: the collection of the irrepressible Alan Turnbull, accessed from www.secret-bases.co.uk, is a jaw-dropping place to start. Be prepared to lose a whole day, though.

The early 1980s was not a great time to be a nervous, impressionable teenager. With Reagan's buffoonish finger on the button, the concept of Mutually Assured Destruction being wafted around and government leaflets dropping on the doormat telling us that we should stockpile some tomato soup and paracetamol in case the bomb was dropped, every day brought something new to feel terrified of. In the middle of all this, our local paper ran an April Fool's joke that the toilets being built in the new shopping centre were actually a nuclear bunker for the great and the good of the area. Little did any of us know that the real thing was only just up the road, the secret Regional Government Headquarters built in the Drakelow sandstone tunnels just north of Kidderminster. This was one of the second range of emergency centres, under the main command of the vast complex beneath Corsham in Wiltshire. At one stage in the 1960s, military top brass advised the government that, due to worries about Corsham's ability to withstand an H-bomb attack, it should be quietly leaked that Drakelow was the principal site for the main government headquarters, so that they'd come and blast us instead. Much as I would have felt very proud of the idea of Kidderminster as the de facto – if brief, and probably final – capital of Britain, if I'd known that at the time, I wouldn't have slept a wink between the ages of about eleven and fourteen.

⚔

If most cartographic falsehoods stem from emphasis and exclusion of often quite tiny details, then distortions of the truth can be found on the largest possible scale. The problem of perspective – basically, how to represent our spherical planet in two flat dimensions – has for centuries riven minds and caused controversy, none more divisive than the thorny question of how to represent the entire globe itself. Any attempt to portray the world in this way necessitates a compromise between accurately showing the shape of continents and accurately showing their size; one or the other has to give. Precisely where to strike that compromise has been the central question for centuries, although it's only in the past forty years that the debate has become heavily politicised and surprisingly bitter.

The Flemish cartographer Gerardus Mercator produced the most famous world projection in 1569, a literal transposition of the globe in cylindrical form, and then rolled out as a flat sheet. Its main purpose was as a nautical aid, as the lines of navigation remain true. For centuries, this remained the gold standard of world maps, even though it hugely boosts the apparent size of landmasses towards the northern and southern latitudes at the expense of those nearer the Equator. To compound its sins, as Antarctica is usually shorn off, the northern hemisphere commonly accounts for about two-thirds of the map, massively exaggerating the size of Europe, Russia and North America. On the Mercator Projection, Alaska (0.66 million square miles) and Brazil (3.28 million square miles) appear to be much the same size, but things get even more distorted the nearer you get to the poles: Greenland (0.8 million square miles) and Africa (11.6 million square miles) also appear to be pretty equal in area.

In 1973, Arno Peters, radical German writer and film-maker, with a dissertation in propaganda techniques, startled the hitherto sleepy world of cartography by publishing what he claimed was a brand new way of looking at our globe. Launching the modestly named Peters Projection in a blaze of publicity, he rounded on what he called the imperialist and even racist overtones of the Mercator map, claiming that his new piece of work, which puts a much elongated Africa centre stage, was an important building block in overcoming such entrenched attitudes. Developing-world charities and damp liberals everywhere loved it, and the Peters map became an essential feature on the wall of every scruffy pressure-group office and lefty student bedsit in the West. It was an instant icon, the Doc Marten of maps.

In Britain, the radical *New Internationalist* magazine has been banging the drum for the Peters Projection for decades, inveigling new subscribers for nearly thirty years now with the offer of a free Peters world plan if they sign up. It was enough to hook me in as a student and the map took pride of place on my wall, between the Coal Not Dole placard and some knick-knack from the Nicaragua Solidarity Campaign. Since the early 1980s, the *NI*'s subscription offer has flagged up the Peters map freebie by rubbishing the Mercator Projection as 'a colonialist, Eurocentric view of the world'. When the magazine first published the map in 1983, it ran a regular column that invited its readers to snitch on any Mercator Projections that had been spotted in public places, as if poor, long-dead Gerardus was something dodgy hanging around a school playground. In America, the Peters map made little headway beyond the offices of the hardcore, until it featured in a 2001 episode of hit drama *The West Wing*, in which an earnest representative of the fictional Organisation of Cartographers for Social Equality appeared, demanding that the President champion the cause of the Peters Projection map to help the USA atone for its imperial misadventures. Sales of the map in the States rocketed in the aftermath of the show's airing.

Many organisations and individuals have clung to the Peters map like a set of right-on rosary beads, refusing to countenance that there is anything wrong with it, and even denouncing those who question its provenance, accuracy or aesthetic as being bullies and racists. But it isn't quite that simple. For starters, in the razzmatazz with which he first presented the map to the world back in the 1970s, Arno Peters rather forgot to mention that his projection was a near-identical copy of one produced over a century earlier by Scottish clergyman James Gall – indeed, most cartographers now refer to the image as the Gall–Peters Projection. Neither did he mention that, for all his bluster about righting the wrongs of the cartographically oppressed, the only latitude on the map that is an accurate representation of size and scale is not around the poorer countries of the Equator, but near the 45° line, which, in the southern hemisphere, passes almost entirely through the sea (save for briefly grazing Chile, Argentina, New Zealand and the Crozet Islands, uninhabited except for a French research station and about five million penguins). In the northern hemisphere, by contrast, the 45° line passes through such downtrodden corners as the USA, Canada (even forming their mutual border for 150 miles south of Montreal), France, Italy, Croatia, Russia, China and Japan.

Then there is the not unfamiliar irony of someone from the West making quite a name for themselves (and, in Peters' case, a fair bit of money) out of lambasting others to take the problems of the developing world seriously. Once the guilt-tripping marketing machine had been cranked into action, the 'Peters Equal Area World Map' (as

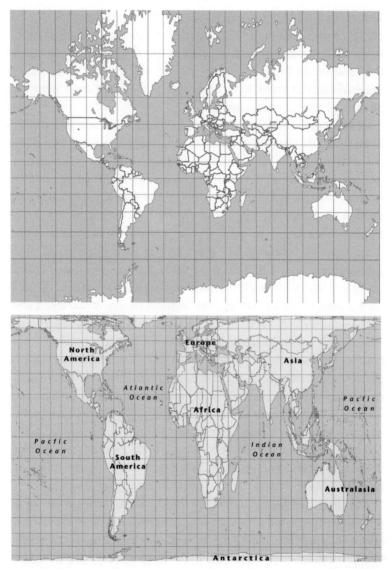

Mercator versus Peters: the fight for the soul of world mapping

it is now promoted) was flying off the press to decorate schoolrooms, offices, international agencies and ideologically sound bedrooms the world over: to date, nearly 100 million have been sold. Perhaps the most strident criticism, however, has to be an aesthetic one: there's something uncommonly ugly about the Peters map, with its stretched centre and squashed extremities. As rival cartographer Arthur Robinson so pithily put it, the Peters map is 'somewhat reminiscent of wet, ragged long winter underwear hung out to dry on the Arctic Circle'.

Like many coming from an immovably ideological position to prove a point, Arno Peters deliberately picked a fight that wasn't really there. Usage of the Mercator Projection was already dying out when he seized on it and denounced it so shrilly, in order to flag up the difference of his own map. Thirty-five years on, the debate is still often presented as Mercator versus Peters, the great cartographic slugfest between the Eurocentric imperialists in the one corner, and the progressive internationalists in the other. In creating and sustaining this illusion of a fight for the soul of world mapping, Peters has been enormously successful. Not to be churlish, he has succeeded too in asking important questions about the way we perceive the world thanks to its mapping, and what implications that has for global geopolitics. Geography professor Thomas Saarinen collected more than 3,800 sketch maps of the world by children from forty-nine countries for a *National Geographic*-sponsored research project in 1999; most, even from kids in developing countries, hugely over-inflated the size of Europe and placed it far more centrally than is truly the case.

✕

The Mercator versus Peters argument has split and electrified the world of cartography for decades. It's astonishing to see just how vehement the debate has become, and what mud has been flung from both sides in its course. Imagine, then, just how many feathers can be spat when the entire world is turned upside down, with south at the top and north at the bottom. In *The West Wing* episode mentioned earlier, this is the pièce de résistance of the representatives of the Organisation of Cartographers for Social Equality in their presentation to the President's press secretary, the elegant Claudia ('C. J.') Cregg. 'But you can't do that!' she squeals as the topsy-turvy map loads on to the screen. 'Why not?' asks one of the evangelising cartographers. ''Cause it's freakin' me out!' Cregg shoots back.

She's got a point. Your first view of the world 'upside down' is startling; dizzying and disorienting in fairly equal doses, laced with a hint of the unspecifically offensive. Remember how, as a child, you'd hang upside down or do a handstand and the most familiar faces looming up at you would appear as freakish as if they'd just landed from Planet Zog? How odd do the eyes look below the nose and mouth? Is that a smile or a frown? Try the same effect looking at the whole world. The cosy and familiar has been upended and turned into something entirely alien: a made-up landscape worthy of Tolkien or the Reverend Awdry. It's not just that Australia is at the top, Europe and North America at the bottom, it's that the shapes look so suddenly strange and fantastical. The archipelago of Indonesia leaps into pole position, Africa, India and South America all taper upwards like giant fir trees, the Iberian peninsula thrusts out from Europe like an angry skinhead, Madrid is above London, which is in turn above Edinburgh. Most disconcerting of all, the whole world seems to be resting its substantial weight on just two countries, Canada and Russia.

Move the focus closer to home, and the effect is just as startling. The island of Britain viewed upside down challenges almost every assumption we hold about our own geography. Politics too: a map like this takes us right out of the equation, for the focus is no longer on the parts of the island that are manmade and man-dominated. Just as globally, it's the thinly populated lands of northern Canada and Russia that suddenly hold our attention, at home it's Scotland that demands respect and closer scrutiny. Although England is clearly still the larger constituent country of Britain, it looks a far closer-run thing upside down, for Scotland's bony bulges appear far more prominent. It's amazing that they've not yet begun marketing such a map as a souvenir north of the border.

The frontispiece of Robert Macfarlane's masterful *The Wild Places* consists of a map that is almost the exact antithesis of the BBC's weather map. It has the British Isles upside down and viewed from somewhere over Rockall, far to the north-west of Ireland. This has the effect of grandiosely emphasising what passes for wilderness in our temperate little lands, places that Macfarlane tells us will only be found 'far north or far west; for to my mind, this was where wildness survived, if it survived anywhere at all'. Macfarlane's map brings the ragged coasts of western Scotland and western Ireland to the fore and the archipelago of Hebrides, Inner and Outer, basks most becomingly in its unaccustomed limelight. Conversely, the commuter lands and manicured countryside of the south and east disappear into a vague distance. Without even turning a page, it is unambiguously clear what and where has captured Macfarlane, and from what angle he will be taking it.

Although a number of medieval charts and maps had south at the top, in modern times the 'upside-down' map of the world first gained prominence in – of course – Australia. It was created by Stuart McArthur of Melbourne, who drew his first south-up map in 1970 for a primary school geography assignment. His teacher told him to redraw it the 'right' way up, if he wished to pass the module. At fifteen, he went on a school-exchange programme to Japan, where he encountered American students who taunted him for coming from 'the bottom of the world'. These slights to his country's place on the globe spurred him on to produce and market the first modern south-up map, the *McArthur's Universal Corrective Map of the World*, launched on

Australia Day in 1979, when he was nineteen. It's sold over 350,000 copies. Stuart's text on the original map is written in pure teenage, testosterone-lashed Ocker:

At last, the first move has been made – the first step in the long overdue crusade to elevate our glorious but neglected nation from the gloomy depths of anonymity in the world power struggle to its rightful position – towering over its Northern neighbours, reigning splendidly at the helm of the universe.

Never again to suffer the the perpetual onslaught of 'down under' jokes – implications from Northern nations that the height of a country's prestige is determined by its equivalent spatial location on a conventional map of the world.

This map, a subtle but definite first step, corrects the situation. No longer will the South wallow in a pit of insignificance, carrying the North on its shoulders for little or no recognition of her efforts. Finally South emerges on top.

So spread the word. Spread the map!

South is superior. South dominates!

*Long live **AUSTRALIA – RULER OF THE UNIVERSE!***

Stuart McArthur not only turned the globe upside down, he moved the traditional east–west axis so as to place Oz centre stage. It's a commanding image, especially for a European, who suddenly finds himself resident of a tiny knot of seemingly irrelevant little countries in the distant bottom-right corner. Shifting the left and right axes is a very common way for different cultures to represent the world with themselves as near to the centre as possible: it's general practice on world maps in the old USSR, Japan, China and around the Pacific Rim. It's often the norm too in the USA, despite the fact that, in order to place themselves in the middle, it necessitates a particularly savage split of the landmass of Asia, with territory up to India and the west of China and Russia on the right-hand side of the map, while Japan, South-east Asia and the east of China and Russia come in from the left. Some territories – usually around Bhutan and Bangladesh – virtually disappear into the margin. To reproduce a globe on a flat page, there obviously needs to be a vertical division somewhere, and if the main reason for the map is to show the landmasses of the world and their relative positions, the only elegant way to do that is by drawing the line down the Pacific or Atlantic oceans. But that, of course, wouldn't have the Americans in the middle; lying between these two great oceans, they are condemned to living on the far left or far right of most world maps, so they have to butcher other continents to ensure that the spotlight remains on them.

⚔

It *is* all politics: you can see why Arno Peters got his sackcloth *unter-hosen* in such a twist. In that regard, the received wisdom of the north-up, Europe-centred plan (on the Mercator Projection) can be seen to be very heavily loaded indeed. After all, there is no scientific or inherently topographical reason for north being at the top of any map. Until the Middle Ages, east – the direction of the rising sun and the presumed location of Paradise – was generally placed at a map's upper edge: it's from this that the term *orientation* arises, i.e. to place yourself in relation to the orient, the east. North overtook east as the upper direction of choice from the adoption by mariners of the North Star as their principal point of navigation. Look at the Earth from space, and there is no natural up or down – indeed, the famous photo of the planet, known as the 'Blue Marble', from the 1972 Apollo 17 space mission, was inverted to fit the traditional view. The original had the South Pole at the top, but that was deemed by NASA to be too controversial for public consumption.

With the benefit of modern political hindsight, we can look at almost any early map and see just how stacked it is, even if we cannot always be sure why. The *c.*1400–1420 Evesham map of the world, for example (with east and Jerusalem at the top), bolsters every facet of early English nationalism under Henry IV: newly seized Calais is shown as far bigger and more important than Rome or Paris, while the island of England stretches along the entire western coast of Europe from Scandinavia to the Mediterranean. And it is England alone that is shown, as a discrete – albeit fairly shapeless – island, dotted with important-looking settlements, particularly around the wool-wealthy Abbey of Evesham, for whom the map was commissioned (and mysteriously including the minuscule Devon hamlet of Taddiport; it's assumed that this is where the map-maker hailed from). Wales and Scotland are shown as separate offshore islands, almost entirely featureless and wholly removed from bustling, powerful England.

Quite why the Evesham map-maker went to such lengths to separate the three British countries is a mystery, although it undoubtedly reflected – and fuelled – the febrile constitutional atmosphere of the day. In 1406, King James I of Scotland was captured en route to safety in France and kept hostage by the English Crown for eighteen years. At the same time, Owain Glyndŵr was mounting his rebellion in Wales which, at its height, saw almost all of the country under his command. The Evesham Map was clearly more of a political poster than an accurate topographic representation, for common knowledge of the real size and shape of Britain was firmly in the public domain by the time it was drawn, as can be seen from the most celebrated and accurate early medieval plan of Britain, the Gough Map, published some forty years earlier in about 1360. It is full of telling detail, showing over six hundred settlements, two hundred rivers and a road network of some three thousand miles, including distances between the major towns. It provided the basis for all British maps for the next two hundred and fifty years, until the Tudor golden age of cartography.

Like the much-harrumphed-over BBC weather map of six and a half centuries later, the Gough Map is massively skewed towards southern and eastern England: the shape of the coast of Lincolnshire, East Anglia, Kent, Sussex and Hampshire is astonishingly accurate and beautifully delineated. The West Country, Wales, north-west England and Scotland do not fare so well. Wales looks like a cancerous lump on the western edge of the plan (at the bottom), with a tiny fraction of the detail shown elsewhere. Around London and Oxford, numerous roads are carefully pinpointed. In Wales, only one is shown, and that is a route that hugs the coast and connects the recently built 'iron ring' of Edward I's castles, from Flint to Rhuddlan, Conwy, Caernarfon, Cricieth, Harlech and Aberystwyth, thence into the less troubled lands in the south. The inference is clear: inland Wales is not safe for travellers, who are best advised to scurry from one English plantation town to the next. Scotland fares even worse: as well as bearing the immortal legend 'Here Dwell Wolves' in the Highlands, it is as shapeless as an old sock and, apparently, has no roads at all. (Incidentally, there is *no* surviving map that contains that legendary motto 'Here Be Dragons', although there are plenty of historic maps illustrated with dragons and all manner of other beasties. The only example that has ever been found is on an early sixteenth-century globe, which states *hic sunt dracones* near the east coast of Asia. This is often optimistically translated as 'here are dragons', but it is far more likely to be a reference to the Dagroian tribe of Sumatra. Sorry.)

Map-making played a pivotal role in the growing British Empire; at its late Victorian peak, it was the map of the world, with huge swathes coloured imperial pinky-red, that was the chief icon of Great Britishness – on the Mercator Projection, naturally, as it made Canada look enormous. All empires have used the same techniques, as two sites in Italy demonstrate: the *Galleria delle Carte* (Gallery of Maps) in the

Vatican and the *Sala delle Mappe* (Map Room) in the Doge's Palace, Venice. The Vatican gallery is a long corridor decorated with forty-four monumental sixteenth-century maps of Italian regions and cities, together with other Church holdings. Its intent is clear: a bold, brilliant use of space and decor to induce a feeling in the viewer of overwhelming intimidation by the sheer power of the papacy. The Venetian map room has an even more explicitly political edge. Its eighteenth-century maps, copies of ones lost earlier in a fire, are sumptuous in their execution, detailing all the known lands of the world, with particular emphasis on Venetian domains and those visited by Venetian explorers, most notably Marco Polo. Visiting dignitaries to the secretive headquarters of the all-powerful, paranoid Venetian republic would have passed through the *Sala delle Mappe* on their way to see the Doge, having already been dazzled and humbled in equal measure by the *Scala d'Oro* (Golden Staircase) and numerous other rooms and corridors of unprecedented ostentation. As political strategy, it was meticulously calculated and stunningly effective.

Such cartographic empire-building often depends on gross exaggeration, which can afford great opportunity for satire – witness the distorted map of the 'World According to George W. Bush' that did the email rounds a couple of years ago, or the Ronald Reagan version of two decades earlier, which became a best-selling poster across the world. On this, the UK (and Ireland) were marked as Thatcherland ('a subsidiary of Disneyland'), a reduced, grey Canada became Acidrainia ('a wholly owned US subsidiary'), 'Our China' (i.e. Taiwan) was much the same size as 'Their China', the 'Japan Corporation' was in the shape of a car, while Israel was massive and dominated the Middle East. Such cartoon frivolity has an absolute basis in historic cartography.

That joke maps can so swiftly make their point in such a clear, graphic way is testament to the visual immediacy of a map, and the information that it contains. Inevitably, such swift potency can cause equally speedy controversy. In early 2008, Absolut Vodka used a map of pre-1848 North America, when Mexican territory extended far north and east into what is now the USA, as an advertisement in *Quién*, a Mexican celebrity gossip magazine, and on a few street billboards. Over the map, where Mexico and the Estados Unido de América (USA) are of pretty much equal size, the legend simply states 'In An Absolut World'. This was swiftly picked up in the States, and thanks to wall-to-wall news TV stations, radio ranters and internet forum boards, the story went ballistic. The *Los Angeles Times* ran a poll on people's attitudes to the advert: nearly two-thirds of the 70,000 respondents voted for the option 'The ad is an affront to Americans. I'm going to be boycotting the product.' Thousands made their fury known on the paper's website, as well as in just about every other internet forum going, expletive-filled home movies on YouTube included. Reading them is a salutary reminder of just how explosively potent one map can be. It's also very funny. Comments such as 'I'll be pouring my Absolut down the drain today – what a bunch of morons' came thick and fast, with the emphasis firmly on the thick. Mind you, that contribution is a masterstroke of literacy and wisdom, compared with many, such as this extract from an email sent to Absolut HQ that the sender proudly shared on the message boards:

> *I JUST TOOK MY HALF FULL BOTTLE OF ABSOLUT VODKA AND POURED IT IN MY TOILET!! AND THEN I TOOK A SHIT ON IT!!! I SHIT ON YOU AND YOUR DISGUSTING COMPANY WITH NO BRAINS. I WILL INFORM EVERY (REAL) AMERICAN CITIZEN AT EVERY OPPORTUNITY ABOUT THIS INJUSTICE. YOU JUST ALIENATED MILLIONS OF POTENTIAL CUSTOMERS OF WHICH A MAJORITY WILL NEVER RETURN TO PURCHASING YOUR PRODUCTS. FUCK YOU!*

And that was far from the worst. Many conservative American commentators quickly adopted their own version of the map, showing a vast razor-wire fence along the entire modern USA–Mexico border, under the same strapline as the original.

A cynic might think that Absolut achieved everything and more they could have wanted from their map advert: huge publicity for the brand and thousands of hours of excitable airtime around the world, all for a modest initial outlay in one Mexican magazine and a few roadside hoardings. It was the stark clarity and utter unambiguity of the image that lit the controversy: a map can do this more quickly than almost anything. Maps that show some change to the status quo seem to tap into something very deep, particularly for conservative-minded individuals: fear of change, of shifting borders, of losing land and identity. The virulently anti-EU stories that fill the pages of the *Sun*, *Daily Express* and *Daily Mail* often use very simple maps to demonstrate how they claim the EU intends to carve up or destroy the UK. They have all recycled parodies of the old *Dad's Army* title sequence, which showed swastika-headed arrows sweeping across a map of Europe to the northern coast of France, where they were repelled by a plucky Union Jack arrow taunting them from the coast of impregnable Albion. This image has been used time and again by right-wing papers, the Nazi arrows being replaced variously by French, German, Russian, East European or EU flags, the € symbol, pictures of gypsies, Trabant cars and even strange foreign food. A picture, in this case a map, really is worth at least a thousand words.

In some ways, the Absolut advert harks back to the eighteenth- and nineteenth-century heyday of the caricature map, the staple of parodists, from those who hawked their pamphlets in the city streets of Georgian England to the earliest satirical magazines, most notably *Punch*, established on the cusp of the Victorian age in 1841. James Gillray (1757–1815) was the greatest exponent of the first wave, and it is no coincidence that his two most celebrated images both employ maps.

Both deal with the aftermath of the French Revolution. The first, from 1793, flicks a bullish two-fingers at the French: a map of England, personified into the figure of King George III, forcibly expelling a great fart of brown 'bum boats' over to the coast of France. The source of the mass elimination is halfway down the south coast, most probably Portsmouth, the chief naval base. George III's rounded backside is represented by Sussex on the map, his rubicund face replaces the county of Durham, Northumberland is his nightcap, Kent and Cornwall his feet. By contrast, the French coast is depicted as a mean, cadaverous face in profile, with the eye at the Seine estuary, the Normandy peninsula as the nose and Brittany as the chin. England is shown crapping straight into France's mouth (see the beginning of Chapter 2 for the actual map).

Even more famous is a later Gillray cartoon from 1805, entitled 'The Plumb-Pudding in Danger'. The pudding in question is the globe, which British prime minister William Pitt the Younger and French emperor Napoleon Bonaparte are excitedly carving up between them. This image has been much used as a graphic illustration of the iniquities of imperialism, for, at first glance, Gillray seems to be damning his own country as much as the French. Closer inspection reveals that the wild-eyed Napoleon is busily helping himself to the countries of Europe, while the daffy-looking Pitt is being left to slice off only the seas.

Many maps have used the same technique as Gillray, in his 'bum boats' satire, to anthropomorphise countries and territories, and usually for explicitly political ends. These can be both damning and alarmist, such as in Fred W. Rose's famous 1877 'Serio-Comic War Map', showing Russia as a vast octopus whose tentacles are spreading in all directions and throttling, or threatening to throttle, a top-hatted Persia, a furious Turkey, a comatose Poland and a simple-looking Finland. Hungary is raring to have a pop at the Russian octopus, but is being held back by his elegant sister, Austria. Although the main point is clearly made, Rose could not resist a few other cartographic digs: Sicily consists only of wine barrels, Spain is fast asleep, Greece is a crab nipping at the Turkish Empire from below, Belgium the figure of King Leopold II counting his money, and Ireland a monk with 'Home Rule' on the brain – quite literally, for the words are written on his hood. Rose's map was hugely successful, and he returned to the same theme to update it at other points in his career.

Although these maps personifying nations were usually employed in a negative manner (many British ones showed a corpulent, drunk Prussia and a huge, savage Russia), they could also be given a positive, uplifting spin. Ireland, for example, often portrayed in British anthropomorphic maps as a thug or thicko, could be transformed into the shape of the beautiful Erin, her calm gaze rallying those who fought for her cause. Such an image became especially popular with Irish expatriates in America, as well as those fighting for the cause at home, who revered not just Erin, but other sentimental personifications of Ireland as a woman or mother, including Queen Maeve and Cathleen ní Houlihan.

In the popular British children's atlas *Geographical Fun: Being Humourous* [sic] *Outlines of Various Countries* (1869), Ireland has reverted to its less uplifting cliché, portrayed here as a stout peasant woman carrying an uncommonly ugly, ape-like, red-haired baby on her back. She is, the accompanying verse assures us, '... happy in her baby's smile/No fortune her's – though rich in nature's grace/Herrings, potatoes and a joyous face'. *Geographical Fun* was a huge seller, found in the nurseries of most late Victorian children, who lapped up its blunt stereotypes about everyone who had not had the good grace to be born English. For that was to be truly blessed, as the map-portrait of England, a classical figure of Britannia, and its accompanying verse ('Beautiful England – on her Island throne/Grandly she rules – with half the world her own') makes ringingly clear. By contrast, Scotland is shown as a cadaverous bagpiper struggling into a fierce wind and Wales as Owain Glyndŵr wittering on about 'King Arthur's long, long pedigree/And cheese and leeks, and Knights of high degree'. France is a hook-nosed old crone admiring herself in the mirror, Spain a dusky señorita making indecent eyes at a Portuguese bear, Germany a studious young woman who can't stop herself dancing frivolously, Italy a sinister revolutionary and Prussia a gun-toting buffoon looking the wrong way.

Over the centuries, Europe has accounted for the vast majority of the world's controversial cartography. It's only two decades since the European map that many of us had grown up with was shattered into fragments as the countries of Eastern Europe broke out from behind the Iron Curtain; it was seeing the first maps from which Czechoslovakia, East Germany and Yugoslavia had vanished that brought home the enormity of what had just happened. And as for the USSR, it was quite unimaginable that the great monolithic block of colour at the continent's right edge had suddenly fractured into so many oddly shaped, and even more oddly named, little shards. For any map aficionado, the maps and atlases from their childhood have a certain permanence, as if they have been hewn from ancient stone. I'm sure my great-grandfather would have felt the same about the disappearance of the Austro-Hungarian Empire and Prussia, the radical revision of the shapes of Romania, Greece, even Denmark and France. The map of the New Europe still looks odd to me now.

Eastern Europe is a fascinating place for a map addict, not just to chart the changes in national borders before and since Communism, but to see the physical alteration, born of sweeping social engineering, within a country. We think that the map of Britain, or of any of our great cities, is almost unrecognisable from sixty years ago, but in truth our essentially conservative approach to planning and development has kept the shapes remarkably consistent, even if most towns and cities have bloated massively, especially those fed by the arteries of motorway. The maps have changed far more dramatically in Eastern Europe. Millions of people have been shunted around into instant new towns, old ones razed to the ground and whole zones cleared for industrial or military use.

Nowhere is this more palpably displayed than in Romania's National Museum of Old Maps, a collection donated to the nation by former prime minister Adrian Nastase. Among the dozens of luscious manuscripts from all over the world, the most sobering is a municipal map of Bucharest itself from less than fifty years ago. There, on the south side of the city centre is the capital's grand arsenal, sat on top of a small hill. Around it runs a warren of medieval streets and cuts, dotted with churches; an area not dissimilar to the famous, and fascinating, Lipscani district just across the Dâmbovita river. All gone now, all traces removed, swept away by the megalomania of Nicolae Ceausescu. In 1971, the President visited North Korea and was stunned by the gargantuan scale of civic planning in the capital, Pyongyang. He returned to Romania, determined to do the same in Bucharest, and set about sweeping aside an entire quarter of the city in order to build a new municipal district of wide boulevards, government buildings and housing for the Party faithful. The centrepiece, on the old arsenal hill, was to be his great legacy, a parliamentary palace of unprecedented size and ostentation, a building that's claimed to be second in size only to the Pentagon. When the Ceausescus were overthrown and summarily executed on Christmas Day 1989, the cost of the building had almost crippled the country, but it was still far from finished. Questions were posed as to whether this obscene monument to the former president's self-aggrandisement should even stay up; there were compelling arguments, both political and financial, to bulldoze it into history. Fortunately for Ceausescu's palace, the mob that took over the country on his execution were the same old Stalinists at heart, and loved the palace with as much passion as their erstwhile guru. So on went the work, and on it goes even now; the building is still only 90 per cent complete.

✄

The Eurovision Song Contest, that orgy of spangles and bad hair, is as good a place as any to see the ancient fault lines across our continent flicker annually into life. A map was published in the *Independent* shortly after the 2007 contest, won, on its first attempt as a solo nation, by Serbia. Originally produced by an English father for his daughter's school project, the map was a neat graphic illustration of where the winning country had garnered its 268 votes from. On an outline plan of European nations, each country that had given Serbia a maximum tally of *douze points* was shaded in black, each that had given it ten a dark grey, eight points a lighter grey, and so on through the monochromatic spectrum to virginal white, for any country that had awarded Serbia the celebrated *nul points*. There was a big, black blot, like an angry ink stain, over the Adriatic and leeching into central and Eastern Europe. The further you got from it, the paler the shades became until it faded out altogether at the fringes of our fractious continent.

The map became something of a symbolic cause célèbre to para-noid Western European Eurovision fans. Visual proof, they crowed, of the conspiracy that has hijacked the contest since those from the other side of the Iron Curtain had been allowed to play. They'd crashed the party, behaved with the most appalling rudeness to the generous hosts and then run off with the silverware. Never able to resist the rumble of a passing bandwagon, Liberal Democrat MP Richard Younger-Ross tabled a motion in Parliament 'that this House believes that voting in the Eurovision Song Contest has become a joke as countries vote largely on narrow nationalistic grounds or for neighbour countries rather than the quality of the song, and that such narrow voting is harmful to the relationship between the peoples of Europe; and calls for the BBC to insist on changes to the voting system or to withdraw from the contest'.

Where politicians were duty-bound to moderate their language slightly, no such restriction in cyberspace. Eurovision websites, debate forums and social networking sites were aflame with indignation and hatred. Calls for two separate Eurovisions – one for the West, like the good old days, and one for the East – were made by numerous screaming queens, often punctuating their hysteria with observations about how the 'dirty gypos', 'illiterate spud-pickers' and so on had stolen their baby. If it wasn't quite a call to resurrect the Iron Curtain, it was a fervent desire to see a ruched velvet one parting the two sides of the continent once more.

But Eurovision has only ever been about politics. In its fifty years of broadcasting tone-deaf kitsch to the world, the stitch-up votes and mutual point-swapping have been as precisely political as any international summit communiqué. Eurovision is the continent's way of slapping a country on the back, only marginally assisted by the quality of the song proffered. Thus it was that Israel (that well-known European nation) triumphed twice in succession in the late 1970s, as the Begin–Sadat Peace Accord was chewed over on nightly news bulletins. One of Yugoslavia's final acts as a nation was to win the 1989 contest, just before the growing cracks split asunder and the region descended into butchery. Ireland's spectacular run in the early 1990s, winning four contests between 1992 and 1996, was two-pronged: a thumbs-up for the first paramilitary ceasefires of the Peace Process and a more general acceptance that, for those few short years, the country really was the coolest place in Europe, before the *ker-ching!* of dollars drowned out the music. Even Britain has reaped handsome rewards from political voting: was it really any coincidence that our last win, on 3 May 1997, came just thirty-six hours after the country had so joyously ejected the Conservative government from office after eighteen long years? Eurovision was the rest of the continent cracking open the champagne with us.

The East European surge in recent years is inevitable, given that they are so excited to be there and throw their all at the competition, their top talent included. In contrast, over the last decade, we've sent a motley pack of session singers, chisel-jawed fag hags and *Pop Idol* rejects to fly the flag on our behalf. There's a gap as big as the North Sea between the British paranoia about Eurovision (that the Commies have hijacked it) and the reality (Serbia would have won in 2007 anyway, if only the votes from Western European countries had counted, and – for crying out loud – since when was Serbia, the tinder-box of the Balkans, a natural depository for anyone's sentimental affection or political boosterism?). Like the breathless certainty that England is almost guaranteed to triumph in every football tournament, we believe that winning is our rightful position, even if every shred of evidence points the other way.

⚔

So to our nearest neighbour, the most successful Eurovision nation of all, Ireland. In a study of the politics of mapping, nothing has been so delicate in recent times as the way in which partition and the civil war in the north of the island have impacted on the way it is mapped. Take this encounter, from 1987:

> *[The British soldier] showed me his map, making sure that none of his comrades could see what he was doing. The map was incredibly detailed, every house, every field, every road carefully denoted and described. It would be impossible to go wrong with such a map. Different colours made everything clear. He laughed when I explained my plight with maps. I showed him my Michelin and my Ordnance Survey, and he shook his head in wonder at how out-of-date they were. His was the map I should have, he said.*

This comes from *Bad Blood: A Walk Along the Irish Border*, by the Dublin-based novelist Colm Tóibín; his tale of walking the divide between the Republic and Northern Ireland at a time when bombs and beatings were the stuff of daily life. In the book, Tóibín moans regularly about the inadequacies of his Michelin map, eventually swapping it for an Ordnance Survey, which he found 'even more useless'. By contrast, the British Army, tooled up and patrolling the fields and farms of the borderlands, were equipped with pinpoint accurate maps, ones that were entirely unavailable to mere mortals.

More than anywhere else in these islands, Ireland demonstrates the often thorny politics and unequal power of mapping. Until very recently, the standard of maps available to the public, on both sides of the border, was lamentable: hardly surprising, when they were based on antique surveying carried out by officers of the British Ordnance Survey in the early years of the nineteenth century. The 1801 Act of Union had ramped up British expansionism in Ireland; map-makers, if not quite the vanguard of the colonialists, came hotfoot behind. Brian Friel's masterful play *Translations*, premiered in 1980, caught this epoch beautifully: the starkest of culture clashes between the English military cartographers and the rural Irish population. The greatest flashpoint was language: the indigenous population, educated in the hedge schools in Irish, Greek and Latin, saw the place names so integral to their lives ridden roughshod over as the surveyors clumsily rendered them into English, a language few locally had any knowledge of.

I spent a deliriously happy few months bussing, hitching, walking and cycling around Ireland in the late summer of 1991, four years after Colm Tóibin's disoriented ramble along the border. If the basic principle of a map is to prevent you getting lost, the Irish Ordnance Survey wasn't much help. The Half Inch (to the mile) series was the best you could get back then, and while OS maps on my side of the Irish Sea were slickly modern and metric, their Irish brethren looked as if nothing had been added or changed since the days of horse-drawn carts. The tang of antiquity was not just stylistic. A note at their bottom said it all: 'Altitudes are given in feet and are referred to Ordnance Survey Datum of 1837 which is a Low Water of Spring Tides observed in Dublin Bay on the 8th April 1837.' In other words, the topographical data was collected two months before an eighteen-year-old Princess Victoria stumbled nervously on to the throne, at the beginning of her 64-year reign.

The maps were rubbish, but that only served to highlight the happy difference between here and there. I revelled in their primitiveness, even when lanes that definitely existed on paper were either nowhere to be found or faded out into impenetrable clouds of nettles and horse-flies. One blazing day, I set off by bike from a hostel in west Cork to explore the coves and lanes around Clonakilty, hitting the town itself for a bite of dinner before the last, easyish seven-mile trundle in the fading light back to the hostel. The map showed me a perfect route as I bumped along lanes and through hills flooded by a rich, red sunset. Deep in the nape of the green slopes, a plume of pink-grey smoke was twirling heavenwards from the chimney of an impossibly cute cottage. My soul sang as I climbed briefly off my bike to lean on the fence and take in the scene. The fence was heavily electrified. A surge of current flung me on to the tarmac, grazing my knee, sending my heart racing, my temples throbbing, my guts to liquid and my legs to jelly.

Wobbling off on the bike, my leg bleeding and heart still threatening to snap, I shortly came to a crossroads that wasn't on the map. With precious little daylight left, and no bike lights, I struck out in the direction that seemed most sensible, and became increasingly lost. A good hour after leaving Clonakilty, I hit a mystery junction where a sign told me that the town was still only three kilometres away; there were more than five miles to go, and I finally limped up the hill to the hostel in coal-black darkness and a panicky sweat. Needing human reassurance, tea and sympathy, I floundered into the hostel kitchen, where a group of travelling girls were having a lovely, cosy time together. They turned to me and smiled. 'I just got so lost on my bike,' I whimpered at them. 'I've been all over the place trying to find my way back. The map's wrong. And I got an electric shock.' My voice trailed away to a barely audible stutter: 'And I'm really, really knackered.' Instead of jumping to put the kettle on and toast me a comforting crumpet, my fellow hostellers stared at me with rictus smiles. 'Excuse me,' one of them ventured in a thick German accent, 'no English.' They turned back to their games and laughter, warmth and comradeship.

Irish mapping has come a long way since even 1991. The old Half Inch maps that steered me blindly around the country were being gradually replaced by a 1:50 000 series, modelled fairly extensively on the British Ordnance Survey's system introduced in the 1970s. Based fairly extensively, but, this being Ireland, not overly much. Since my first visit to the Republic in 1976, it's been a source of fascination to see how, little by little, the Irish have distanced themselves from the Brits in the wallpaper and furniture of their national identity. When it comes to designing things like maps or new stamps, coins, banknotes, phone and post boxes, road signs, road markings, car tax discs or number plates, 'not looking like a British one' seems, altogether understandably, to have become bullet-point number one on the design remit. So determined were the Irish to leapfrog the Brits and become New Model Europeans instead, they even took the decision to replace the mileage distance on road signs with kilometres. Only, this was done at a very Irish pace, so that, even today, you will come across multiple fingerposts at junctions with a glorious jumble of signs in different colours and typefaces, and even different systems of measurement on the same post.

The remnants of Ireland's troubled history can still be seen on its maps, none more so than those that cover the 224-mile border between 'the north' and 'the south'. Let's get those terms, anathema to the ears of any map addict, out of the way from the start. The island of Ireland's most northerly point is Malin Head, in County Donegal, in the Republic. Nothing in 'the north' comes anywhere near as far up the map. Neither should the province attached to the UK be known as Ulster, for that is the name of one of the island's four provinces, and includes three counties (Donegal, Monaghan and Cavan) in the Republic as well as the six in Northern Ireland. Whichever way you talk about this border, it is a tale of confusion, obfuscation and downright sadness, from this foggy nomenclature to the spiky matter of its carto-graphic representation.

Maps from the 1960s through to the turn of the new century paint a stark picture of communities divorced from their roots and hinter-land, innumerable ancient roads and lanes 'spiked', cratered or block-aded off the map. Colm Tóibín describes one such former crossing in *Bad Blood*:

> *I had no trouble spotting the border, which someone had gone to a lot of bother to make impassable. The track was blocked with rusted barbed wire and huge blocks of concrete with rusted iron fenders sticking up from the concrete at all sorts of angles, like a building after a bomb. A few yards away there was a second block of concrete and more iron fenders, and then the bridge over the stream which was also blocked. The bodies of a few abandoned cars lay among all this debris. Even on foot it took a bit of an effort to climb over. A motorbike would have considerable difficulty; for a car it would be impossible. The border was blocked.*

Many remain closed to this day.

The awful, chilling watchtowers that suddenly reared up out of the gentle greenery may have gone, but the scars remain on the map as much as the land. On a 1:250 000 tourist map from 1990 of the north of Ireland, there are regular gaps of twenty and thirty miles between approved crossings, slicing natural communities apart with all of the brutal efficiency of the Berlin Wall. The road-numbering system in the two countries is also different – British A roads become Irish N (national) roads and Bs become Rs (regional), though occasionally a British A is deemed to be no better than an Irish R, or vice versa. One seven-mile stretch of the main road from Clones, County Monaghan, to Cavan Town crosses the border four times, meaning that the road starts as the N54, becomes the A3 for a couple of miles, briefly returns to its N54 status, then quickly becomes the A3 again before finally going back to the name by which it started. Not that many people were travelling it in the 1970s, '80s or '90s – none of the border crossings was approved and the road had been rendered impassable by the British army, meaning that the journey from one Republic of Ireland town to another necessitated a hefty detour down back roads.

Since the mid-1990s, the jagged breaks in the maps of the Irish borderland have been gradually healed, although not all of the most minor routes have been reinstated – or, indeed, are ever likely to be. Not that that, of course, is sufficient in itself to heal the wounds that years of forcible, armed partition have wreaked; the 'borders of the mind' – far more insidious than anything on the map – will be in place for generations yet. Clones, County Monaghan, is a good example: once a thriving market town and important railway junction, the trains were all withdrawn overnight in 1959 (when the only cross-border service left was that between Dublin and Belfast), a presage for the even greater disruption caused from the 1960s onwards by the steady, forcible closure of most roads that straddled both sides. The town was divided from its natural County Fermanagh hinterland, its economy collapsed and its once vibrant music scene evaporated. Its residents became used to being stopped and searched (on both sides of the border), and, in an area very equally spread between the two countries and the two religious communities, 'The Troubles' became a no-go public topic, fuelling all manner of corrosive private paranoia and suspicion, leaving the area as somewhere regularly identified as one of the most insular in Ireland.

In these post-settlement days, the better quality of mapping, once available only to the military, has finally been made accessible to all. There are still political fault lines running through the system, however, ones that have been solved in uniquely Irish ways. The new 1:50 000 series of the Ordnance Survey of Ireland (OSI) and its Northern Ireland counterpart, the OSNI, uses a united numbering system for the maps, going west–east, north–south, from number 1, in the north-western corner of Donegal, through 15 for Belfast and 50 for Dublin, to number 89, at County Cork's southern tip. Those that cover an area solely under the jurisdiction of the Republic are published by the OSI, and are called the Discovery series. Those wholly in the northern province – called the Discoverer series; see, *we're different* – are produced by the OSNI (in rather better covers, it should be said). The OSI maps show their grid covering the entire island, with no visible border; for the OSNI, only the grid of maps covering Northern Ireland (and neighbouring County Donegal) are shown: as in so many areas of Norn Iron life, there's scant acknowledgement of any land mass to the south or west of its border.

The problem, as ever, comes along these border areas. Say you're off to visit Belturbet, County Cavan, for its glittering annual Lady of the Erne beauty pageant (first prize an 'all expenses paid' week in, er, Belturbet). Although there's almost certainly no reason to leave the town, in the unlikely event that you fancied a little spin into the countryside, you'd go and pick up the local OS. That would be the number 27 map, *Upper Lough Erne*, covering a roughly 50:50 split of the two sovereign states, but published by the OSNI. Should buying such a product be a peace process too far for you, help is at hand, for the OSI have an almost identical map – number 27A, *Cavan, Fermanagh,*

Leitrim, Monaghan – available too. The split between the OSI and OSNI along the Donegal border seems to have been achieved quite happily, but it all goes to pieces further east, with a stack of huge overlaps and outright repetition. The politics of mapping this hateful divide go a lot further than whether to label it Derry or Londonderry (or, as many agencies have done, reach the ultimate in unsatisfactory compromises by labelling the city Londonderry, but the county Derry; never the other way around).

For all the back-slapping and eye-popping scenes of Ian Paisley and Martin McGuinness doing their Chuckle Brothers routine, there is one part of Ireland where the map still lies through its teeth. Buy any street atlas of Belfast, or print off a city map from the internet, and it will show you the confident, cosmopolitan city of the marketing men, all shiny new shops and buffed heritage. This, we're told, is the peace dividend writ large. On none of the official maps is the heavy cost of that shown, in the shape of the city's thirteen miles of walls, fences and impenetrable barricades known, with Orwellian Newspeak, as the Peace Line. Erected as a temporary measure to keep the two communities apart in the early 1970s, it has instead been repeatedly beefed up and extended, even through the years of ceasefire and subsequent peace when all of the other border barriers were being steadily dismantled. Now the Line, or rather Lines, for there are bits strewn throughout Belfast, are towering in their scale, great forty-foot-high blockades scything through gardens and across streets, dwarfing the houses below them. Some remain the original vast panels of grey steel and razor wire, and have been prettified with murals and even ironic trompe l'œils of painted streets receding into the distance, like the backdrop to an old movie. Others have been thoroughly institution-alised as fence-topped red-brick walls, planted with tumbling shrubs to soften the blow. And none appear on the map, despite the fact that their presence forces any pedestrian, cyclist or driver to make a massive detour.

In parts of west Belfast, where the oldest Peace Lines appear, you can just about plot part of their course on the map from the pattern of truncated streets and disconnected neighbourhoods. In most areas, the streets are still shown as whole and continuous, even if they are entirely impassable. For the most part, you're best off checking the internet, using a satellite-image map where you can bounce between the maps and the aerial photos. They tell very different stories: the photo an absolute statement of fact and the map not even so much as a half-truth.

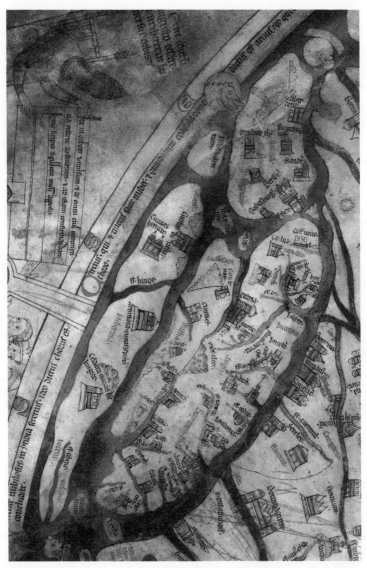

Britain and Ireland on the Hereford Mappa Mundi

6. GOD IS IN THE DETAIL

It is not down in any map; true places never are.
~ Herman Melville, *Moby Dick*

Man's eternal need to define God has meant that the Almighty has had almost as big an influence on the history of mapping as that other great human impetus, war. The two are, of course, indissolubly linked.

Maps are used to demonstrate God, in an attempt to quantify and codify the divine, but they can also encourage us to stray into the territory of acting like tin gods ourselves. There is something superhuman in the unfurling of a map, a feeling that you are, in some small way, lord and master of all you survey. It's not just the wartime generals gathered round enormous charts, using canes to push model tanks and men hither and thither with deistic determination; perhaps the same surge of power comes for managing directors of contract-cleaning businesses, gleefully tapping the British map on the wall of their Portakabin HQ as they demonstrate to Gerald from Admin and Tracy from Accounts the next advance into new postcode districts.

This latter image has sprung to my mind a lot lately, with regard to the omniscient god of today, Tesco. At the moment, I'm happy to live in the least Tescoed part of Britain south of the Scottish Highlands. It doesn't impact on my life in the slightest, as the nearest store is a full hour's drive away, which always gives me a smug little frisson when I overhear the anguished debate in middle-class circles about its sweeping predominance. The county of Powys, occupying a quarter of Wales, contains not one branch of Britain's biggest supermarket: it was repeatedly mentioned as a contributory factor in some recent lifestyle survey in which our county was declared to be the happiest place to live in Britain. Not for long, though. In one fell swoop, Tesco has announced new stores for Llandrindod Wells, Welshpool, Newtown and Machynlleth, a four-pronged offensive that I feel coldly certain all began at a map. Somewhere deep in its headquarters, there's surely a huge wall-mounted plan of Britain, about fifty feet high and flagged with every branch of Tesco, Tesco Metro, Tesco Express, Tesco Ultra, Tesco Plus, Tesco Gold or Tesco Whatever. Every time executives passed it, they glowered at the great void in the middle of Wales, and swore to fill it with their flags. The deities of the cult of BOGOF have pronounced, and we will tremble before them.

The god-like feelings somehow seem more acute the greater the scale of the map being scrutinised. There is something almost voyeuristic about the Ordnance Survey's largest-scale maps, those at a whopping 1:500, just over ten feet to the mile. Here, you can poke your nose into every outhouse, manhole cover, lamp-post, public toilet, shop, pub and railway station platform. The original series even showed ground-floor room divisions within any public building. In these days of hovering over satellite imagery of our neighbours' back yards, searching for swimming pools to crash or pondering the suburban ubiquity of those circular trampolines, such close-range cartography might seem quaintly archaic, but its stark clarity and detailed annotation still have the power to shock. How far do you go? Lewis Carroll, in his phantasmagorical last novel, *Sylvie and Bruno* (published in two volumes in 1889 and 1893), floated numerous bizarre ideas and inventions, many of them satires of the obsessions of the late Victorian age. One such obsession was maps: their prosaic ubiquity was something that the theosophically minded Carroll evidently rather disapproved of and, in this novel, took to its warped conclusion in the form of a map with 'the scale of one mile to the mile'. This leads to the abandonment of maps altogether, as it is noted that 'we now use the country itself as its own map, and I assure you it does nearly as well'. The conceit was reprised by Jorge Luis Borges in his one-paragraph story 'On Exactitude in Science' (1946, but purporting to be from a piece entitled *Travels of Praiseworthy Men*, from 1658, by the fictional J. A. Suarez Miranda):

> *In that Empire, the craft of Cartography attained such Perfection that the Map of a Single province covered the space of an entire City, and the Map of the Empire itself an entire Province. In the course of Time, these Extensive maps were found somehow wanting, and so the College of Cartographers evolved a Map of the Empire that was of the same Scale as the Empire and that coincided with it point for point. Less attentive to the Study of Cartography, succeeding Generations came to judge a map of such Magnitude cumbersome, and, not without Irreverence, they abandoned it to the Rigours of sun and Rain. In the western Deserts, tattered Fragments of the Map are still to be found, Sheltering an occasional Beast or beggar; in the whole Nation, no other relic is left of the Discipline of Geography.*

Carroll and Borges lightly satirise the map-maker's obsession with topographical exactitude; imagine what they would have made of subsequent developments in cartography, let alone the revolution of GPS and satellite technology (though Lewis Carroll would perhaps have loved the chance to zoom into close-ups of schoolyards from the comfort of his armchair). Maps encouraging *us* to feel like gods of all we survey are a comparatively recent phenomenon, for, although the pursuit of topographical 'truth' has always been a major impetus in the creation of maps, many other strands – cultural, artistic, political, geodetic, religious – have fed their development too.

✝

The godlike 1:1 map is the extreme end of cartographic obsession, and is as far as can possibly be imagined from the earliest Western maps. In these, topographic understanding was entirely subsidiary to our place before God Himself: the map, like every other art form, was considered, first and foremost, to be an allegorical representation of the divine. In the Christian tradition, they were little more than crude – if very beautiful – propaganda, for the rough shapes of Europe, Asia and Africa were well known by the early medieval period, but such knowledge was largely ignored when it came to drawing the maps. Indeed, demonstrating too great a passion for scientific understanding, such as of the actual shape and dispersion of the continents, was harshly persecuted as pagan and heretical; as Lloyd A. Brown puts it in *The Story of Maps*: 'The lamp of scientific knowledge, a tremulous flame at best, was obscured for a time by the blinding light of religious ecstasy.' 'For a time' is putting it mildly; the suppression of scientific understanding by ultra-zealous Christianity began in about the fourth century AD, and it is something we are still struggling with seventeen centuries later.

The first Christian map of the world dates from the middle of the sixth century, part of the *Topographia Christiana* ('Christian Topography') of Cosmas Indicopleustes of Alexandria. Cosmas converted to Christianity after a long career as an itinerant merchant; he had sailed many of the world's seas and visited numerous countries in Africa and Asia (his second name means 'sailed to India'). Unfortunately, the 'blinding light of religious ecstasy' rather eclipsed his extensive first-hand knowledge, and the eleven-book *Topographia*, although it contains much useful geographical information, is an extended religious tract that twists every piece of evidence into fitting his newly acquired dogma. Cosmas's map shows the Earth as a flat, rectangular shape – precisely that of a tabernacle, in fact, the house of worship described to Moses by God during the Jewish Exodus from Egypt. This notion was nothing more than an extremely literal interpretation of the words of St Paul (Hebrews 9: 1–2: 'Then verily the first covenant had also ordinances of divine service, and *a worldly sanctuary*. For there was a tabernacle made; the first, wherein was the candlestick, and the table, and the shewbread; which is called the sanctuary'). The ocean forms a border, in the middle of which is the rectangular landmass, with a few seas, most convincingly the Mediterranean, nibbled out of it. Paradise is to the east, beyond the ocean.

Cosmas explains further in the accompanying text. The world, he states, is flat, shaped and laid out exactly like the tabernacle described in St Paul's Letter to the Hebrews, with the heavens forming the shape of a curved lid above. He is especially vitriolic towards those who believe that the planet is spherical:

> *Here then the Pagans are at war with divine Scripture; but, not content with this, they are at war also with common sense itself and the very laws of nature, declaring, as they do, that the earth is a central sphere, and that there are Antipodes, who must be standing head-downward and on whom the rain must fall up.*

He is even more vicious in his denunciation of the idea that the Earth and the heavens rotate. The sun, he explains, vanishes every night because it disappears behind a vast conical mountain in the extreme north, while the revolution of the stars at night is simply a waggish illusion laid on by angels hanging around in the firmament as they wait for the Resurrection. Despite the belief of the 'pagans' that the sun is many, many times the size of the Earth, Cosmas confidently declares that to be rubbish; it is, he declaims, only around six hundred miles wide.

Cosmas's tabernacle-shaped Earth resurfaced in other maps over the ensuing centuries, although many cartographers, using different biblical references, chose to draw it in other ways. The idea of a square or rectangular Earth, though not necessarily in the shape of a vast tabernacle, was said to be decreed by Isaiah 11: 12 ('And he shall set up an ensign for the nations, and shall assemble the outcasts of Israel, and gather together the dispersed of Judah from the *four corners of the earth*'), while those who preferred the idea of the Earth as a vast, flat disc could call on Isaiah 40: 22 ('It is he that sitteth upon *the circle of the earth*, and the inhabitants thereof are as grasshoppers; that stretcheth out the heavens as a curtain, and spreadeth them out as a tent to dwell in').

In the Western Christian tradition, there was little progress in cartographic detail from the sixth century until the turn of the fourteenth: nearly all of the six hundred or so surviving maps from this period plough the same well-worn furrows. At least the circular maps hint at the reality of the Earth's shape, and they are often spectacularly elaborate and beautiful to look at. Most of these are in the form of what became known as T-O maps, from the tradition of dividing the three known continents in a T-shape, contained within a larger O. Occupying the half of the map above the top of the T is Asia, the bottom-left quadrant Europe and the bottom-right Africa, although there are also symbolic meanings in the T as a crucifix and the three continents mirroring the Holy Trinity. Some scholars of the time claimed the existence of a fourth continent, in the Antipodes, but they were fiercely denounced as heretics. The maps are full of divine codes and symbols, landscapes of life and death as much as physical geography. Jerusalem is always placed at their centre.

✝

The more lavish of these early medieval world views are known as *mappae mundi*. The term *mappa mundi* is not, as is commonly assumed, 'a map of the world', but 'a cloth of the world': a subtle, but important, distinction. The finest of all *mappae mundi* can be found in Hereford Cathedral, an example that can be dated fairly precisely to the tail end of the thirteenth century, as both of the brand new castles at Conwy and Caernarfon are shown. The Hereford map, a substantial 54 x 64 inches, was inscribed on a single piece of vellum, one of the reasons

A basic T-O map

that it has survived so well. The map became the centrepiece of one of the greatest ecclesiastical controversies in recent times: its near sale, by Sotheby's at public auction, in 1988. This was the desperate act of the Dean and Chapter of Hereford Cathedral, who, at the time, were faced with spiralling debts. In order to secure the future of the cathedral's other great early medieval relic, its enormous chained library, they decided to sell the map.

Uproar ensued – Sir Roy Strong called it 'one of the most terrible and vulgar ideas I have ever come across' (a line you suspect he might use most days about something or other). Petitions were raised, debates raged in Parliament. Like many other people, the furore made me go to Hereford to see this great medieval monster for the first time, which, considering the fact that the city was only a short, direct train ride away from where I grew up, was perhaps some kind of proof that it just wasn't taken seriously enough, even by local map addicts. The threat of its imminent loss certainly changed that: I was one of tens of thousands of extra visitors pouring into the cathedral to view the Mappa Mundi. At the eleventh hour, a huge anonymous donation arrived in Hereford (it transpired to be from J. Paul Getty Junior), the map was withdrawn from auction and plans were mooted for a new, purpose-built centre to display and explain both the Mappa Mundi and the chained library. This opened in 1996, and it's a splendid exhibition, offering much better presentation and interpretation of both treasures than they ever had before in their dark, dusty corners of the cathedral.

While not doubting that the Dean and Chapter were in a horrible position back in 1988, their reasoning for singling out the medieval map for disposal was deeply spurious. This boiled down to their theory that the Mappa Mundi had no intrinsic link to Hereford, a wild reinterpretation of the facts as far as they can be ascertained. Unusually for a medieval map, we can be confident of the identity of its creator, for his name is written clearly in a corner: Richard of Haldingham and Lafford, now better known as Holdingham and Sleaford in Lincolnshire. Church records show that there was one Richard de Bello working as a clergyman at Lincoln Cathedral between 1278 and 1283, and that, two decades later, there was a Canon Richard de Bello at Hereford Cathedral. It is more than likely that they were one and the same, or at least closely related, explaining the map's early arrival at Hereford, and rather blowing apart the Dean and Chapter's assertion. Was seven hundred years in the same place not a strong enough case to make for its retention there?

As the top of the map represents the east, where we can see both a figure of Christ and the location of Paradise, the shapeless lump representing the island of Britain can be found in the north-western corner, in the bottom left of the vellum. Tucked away on the River 'Wie', Hereford is printed on the map, although many theories believe it to have been a subsequent addition once it arrived in the city, for the annotation of the name is quite poor and ragged compared with that of nearby Gloucester and Worcester. Also pointing to later supplementation, the only mountains shown in Britain are the Grampians of Scotland, Snowdon in Wales and the Clee Hills in Shropshire (a modest 1,772 feet), a most unlikely triumvirate. This is thought to be another local reference, although the Clees were home to strategically important lead mines, which may have boosted their candidature for inclusion on its own. Each city name is accompanied by a pictogram of a cathedral, tower or castle; if its size and scale gives some indication of the importance of the settlement, then London is by far the most significant place, followed by Lincoln (this was drawn by a local lad, after all) and, surprisingly, Berwick-upon-Tweed and Chester. Their apparent stature is more symbolic than literal: with trouble rife in both Scotland and Wales, these border towns were given some cartographic steroids in order to be seen flexing their muscles at the troublesome neighbours.

Even were they not wedged down in a corner, Britain and Ireland would be but incidental players on the Mappa Mundi. London, for all its swagger, pales into insignificance next to Europe's two greatest cities of the time, Paris and Rome, basking nearer the glow of the all-important *Mare Medi Terranea* ('Sea at the centre of the Earth', or Mediterranean). Someone didn't take too kindly to this, however, for France bears the marks of repeated scratching and scribbling: an overly patriotic verger during one dull Evensong in the Hundred Years' War, perhaps. Inevitably, the major city of all is Jerusalem, depicted as a huge battlemented circle, full of turrets and doors, at the apex of the three continents and the entire map.

On a document as richly detailed, elaborate and antique as the Mappa Mundi, you would expect to find the odd tiny mistake: a mislabelled town in an obscure part of the world, a river connecting the wrong settlements, an illustrated beastie placed on the wrong continent. To find, when there are only three known continents, that two of them have been named incorrectly, is a surprise. The labels for Europe and Africa, clearly scribed in gold, are the wrong way round. Was Richard the map-maker suggesting Africa-Europe as one giant land-mass to counterbalance the mighty Asia? Was he, like the creators of intricate Persian carpets, incorporating a deliberate mistake to show his own fallibility in the face of God's perfection? Or did that part of the labelling get done on a particularly weary Monday morning?

Far more eye-catching than any of the places marked on the map, even the Holy City, are the vast range of monsters and beasts that freckle the margins and some of the land ranges. As well as the biblical images of the jaws of Hell, Adam and Eve, Noah and company in their Ark on Mount Ararat, the stable at Bethlehem and the Red Sea parting to allow the Israelites through, there are a stack of weird, and sometimes grue-some, depictions. In Asia, we see a sciapod, a human figure with a giant nine-toed foot that he is using as a parasol. Nearby are a manticora, with the body of a lion, face of a man and tail of a scorpion, a Minotaur, dragons, giants and pygmies. Over the Baltics and Russia are a selection of cannibalistic horrors, including men with dogs' heads and two semi-human figures feasting on the flesh of their parents. The weirdest of all are reserved for Africa: human-like creatures with no heads, but eyes and mouths in their chests, or their arms sticking out of their heads, or with four eyes, or no ears and horribly deformed feet, or with sealed-up mouths or shown feeding their young to the serpents. The continent is also home to troglodytes, hermaphrodites and the deathly basilisk.

This menagerie of horrors was more than folksy superstition or innocent embellishment. It was directly inspired, as were similar adornments to Christian world maps over most of the previous millen-nium, by the third-century fantasist Gaius Julius Solinus, mockingly known as 'Pliny's Ape' for his slavish, if selective, use of Pliny's ency-clopaedic *Naturalis Historia* (*c.*AD 77); 'he lifted only the nonsense' (Lloyd A. Brown, *The Story of Maps*). Nonsense it may have been, ridicu-lous hearsay and fabrication designed only to titillate and terrify, but that suited the early Church perfectly, and the ferocious beasts of Solinus could be found on maps right up until the fourteenth century. Just as pedagogic Christian mapping had quashed earlier geographic under-standing of the actual shapes and layout of the world, so it did much the same for any conception of what might be found in nature. The fact that the most horrific creatures were almost always depicted in the 'uncivilised' parts of the world (Africa, Asia and the far north) incul-cated a fear and prejudice which took very deep root.

†

It's not as if this thousand-plus-year hiatus of ignorance was an inevitability, or the best that could be made of the limited knowledge and resources available at the time. Far from it. Many cartographic truths had been established in the Graeco-Roman era, most notably by Claudius Ptolemy of Alexandria (c.AD 85–165), eminent mathe-matician, geographer and astronomer. The first of his works was the *Almagest*, a thirteen-book exposition of the mathematical theory behind the motions of the sun, moon and planets, whose findings were not superseded until the seventeenth century. In about AD 140, he produced the eight-book *Geographia*, which took the same mathemat-ical approach in detailing the coordinates of around eight thousand places across the known world in what we would now call a system of latitude and longitude. He used his data to produce twenty-seven maps in the *Geographia*; none of the originals have survived, but countless cartographers have plotted them according to his exacting instructions. He knew the Earth to be spherical, worked out the problems of differ-ent projections, used meridians, parallels and grids and introduced perspective, or the idea of different scales for different maps, depend-ing on whether these were plotting small regions congested with names and settlements or wider, less populated tracts of land. He was vehemently dismissive of the notion that the lands were entirely encir-cled by a mythical, heavenly ocean, calling it 'a fallacious description, and an unfinished and foolish picture'.

If the Christian lands of Europe preferred to spend the next millennium or so in a fog of pious ignorance, the pursuit of knowledge about the shape and structure of the world, and how this could be conveyed in maps, was enthusiastically pursued elsewhere. Third-century Chinese mathematician Liu Hui developed sophisticated surveying techniques that enabled height, depth and comparative perspective to be measured and plotted. In the Islamic world, Ptolemy's *Geographia* was translated into Arabic in the ninth century, and formed the basis of many new studies and maps. These were often far more accurate and detailed than Ptolemy's raw data, for they took his theory and added their practice as explorers, missionaries and tradesmen, as well as developing contemporary skills in surveying and triangulation. It was also in the Muslim parts of the world that Ptolemy's data was sketchiest, so they were easily able to improve on that. European cartography right up until the eighteenth century depends far more on Islamic groundwork and theory than anything produced by its own people. The size of the Earth, for example, was pretty accurately established by tenth-century Persian scholar Abū Rayhān al-Bīrūnī six hundred years before Europeans managed to come up with the same figure.

Maps helped to define and sustain the fundaments of biblical creationism; they also played their part in finally challenging them. The literal interpretation of Creation reached its inevitable conclusion in 1650, when the Primate of All Ireland, Archbishop James Ussher, published a work stating that God had created the world on Monday 23 October 4004 BC, and, as detailed in the book of Genesis, finished it by Saturday night. Soon, this bold assertion was included in all reprints of the King James Bible and thundered from the pulpits and in schoolrooms. Into such a world came William Smith, whose lifelong obsession was to map Britain from below. Despite terrible hardships, this he finally achieved, producing the world's most advanced geological map of the whole of England and Wales, and part of Scotland, in 1815. Proving the antiquity of the rock strata on which we live was a major leap forward into accepting and understanding the concept of evolution, over forty years before Charles Darwin published *On the Origin of Species*.

✝

The Renaissance had dragged Europeans up to speed in cartography as in all other branches of the arts and sciences, although it had taken a fair while for the influence to seep across the English Channel from the revolutionary continent. In British map-making, the Tudor age of the sixteenth century was particularly productive, honed from a curious mixture of greater intellectual freedom and the ruthless power struggles of Henry VIII. His break with the papacy in Rome, in order to establish the Church of England and grant himself a divorce, necessitated a far more bullish defence strategy, which he swiftly realised demanded better maps: the coasts, in particular, were surveyed and mapped with an attention to detail not seen again until the turn of the nineteenth century. Following Henry's death in 1547, Crown and country descended into a bloody battle for political and religious supremacy, which reached an uneasy truce of sorts, eleven years and three monarchs later, on the accession of Elizabeth I.

Although Elizabeth re-established the new Protestantism as the religion of state, she strove hard to distance herself from the opposing fundamentalisms of her predecessor siblings, Edward VI and 'Bloody' Mary I. Despite Pope Pius V's excommunication of Elizabeth in 1570, Catholics and their worship were tolerated; furthermore, the arts and sciences blossomed, the first stirrings of imperial adventure united the nation, and a new generation of maps, spearheaded by Christopher Saxton's luxuriant county series of the 1570s, came to symbolise the confident, increasingly literate new England. In 1588, this was rocked by the thwarted invasion of the Spanish Armada and its attempt to force Catholicism back into the country. The inevitable reaction was a further uprising of anti-Catholic sentiment, both officially and among the population at large. Some fine Tudor maps display this with unblinking honesty, most notably those collected, drawn and annotated by William Cecil, Lord Burghley (1520–98), the lynchpin of Elizabeth's court for all but the last few years of her long reign.

Burghley was a first-rate example of an Elizabethan map addict. From an early age, he collected plans and maps, both professionally and for pleasure. His official residence at Theobalds, near Cheshunt, was lavishly decorated with maps, charts and cosmographies, including a map of the heavens that occupied the entire ceiling of the Great Hall and incorporated an animatronic sun. He was a passionate exponent of the idea that maps could demonstrate military, economic or political landscapes more effectively, and more swiftly, than any other tool of communication. As Elizabeth's chief courtier, he made it his job to map the location of the gentry, squires and officials of England and Wales, right down to the lowest level of authority, the Justices of the Peace, either by annotating the plans produced by Saxton or drawing his own. This intelligence-gathering occupation, described as 'a geographical index to the government's friends and enemies', came into even sharper focus after the skirmish with the Armada, when Burghley painstakingly marked with a cross every Catholic and Catholic-leaning family, to be carefully watched and monitored. This was the first example of the minute mapping of religious difference for political motives, a dismal, if inevitable, trend that has survived and thrived to this day, from Belfast to Bosnia to Basra.

☿

The turbulent swings between Protestantism and Catholicism dominated the next century of English life, and provided a covert impetus for one of our most celebrated national maps, John Ogilby's *Britannia* (1675), often described as 'the world's first road atlas'. It is a stunningly beautiful work: a mile-by-mile strip map of the country's seventy-three major roads, 7,500 miles of them in all. The detail was unprecedented, with villages, towns, hills, woods, commons, fords, bridges, churches, large houses and inns carefully plotted at one inch to the mile. Today, they are among the most highly valued of all collectable British maps, celebrated for their aesthetic charm and detailed portrait of every route and rut of the landscape.

It seems that there was a great deal more to them than their aestheticism and pragmatism. Recently, I took part in a BBC Wales television series, *Terry Jones' Great Map Mystery*, which traced four of Ogilby's routes across Wales. The former Python has made some terrific TV histories with author and director Alan Ereira, often unearthing new evidence that sheds light on old times, and this was no exception. Why, they pondered, was the very first map in *Britannia* the route between London and Aberystwyth, of all places? It's a small enough place today, but in the seventeenth century it was a tiny, remote fishing hamlet. Close reading of the accompanying text, and examination of the details on the maps, led them to the startling conclusion that *Britannia* was a cartographic blueprint for a French invasion of England and Wales.

Ogilby started the volume shortly after King Charles II had signed the secret Treaty of Dover (1670) with Louis XIV of France, knowledge of which didn't come into the public domain until 1830. Charles had grown up in France, and much admired – and desired – the absolute monarchy, rooted in Catholicism, enjoyed by the Sun King, Louis; such authority was in stark contrast with his piecemeal Restoration powers in England. The Dover treaty laid plans for Charles to declare publicly his Catholicism and for French troops to help back this with a swift invasion. *Britannia* supplied all the options for this invasion, indicating, for instance, that a 'back door' attack through Wales would be far more likely of success via Aberystwyth than the more obvious ports of Holyhead or Fishguard. Interspersed with the best potential routes for marching armies were those connecting pilgrimage shrines, another nod to the Catholic undertones of the atlas, and the location of metal mines for armaments. In the course of the series, Terry Jones interviewed

Professor Ronald Hutton, eminent historian of this era, who agreed that this interpretation was significant and highly plausible.

Back in the previous century, at the same time that Lord Burghley was producing his Here Be Papists maps for the Elizabethan court, a wealthy Midlands family were doing much the same, albeit for precisely opposite reasons and in the rather more glamorous medium of heavy woollen cloth. The result was the staggeringly lovely Sheldon Tapestry Maps, still largely extant today. Ralph Sheldon and his family were devout Catholics; their two houses, at Beoley in Worcestershire and Weston Hall in Warwickshire, would have been squarely marked with a cross on Burghley's maps, for they were well known and wealthy too. Ostensibly, the four tapestries, each about 20 x 16 feet, were woven in the late 1580s to decorate his newly built pile at Weston. Sumptuously colourful and packed with detail of the Midland counties of Worcestershire, Warwickshire, Gloucestershire and Oxfordshire, they purport to be nothing more than a joyful celebration of both the locality and the new excitement around cartography, for much of the information (including a few mistakes) came directly from Christopher Saxton's recently published county maps.

Loyalty to the Crown and to England is ostentatiously displayed throughout the tapestries, in copious royal crests, woven verses, decorative border flourishes and even a reproduction of the title page from a Protestant reformers' tract. It seems, perhaps, that they were trying just a little too hard to throw cynics off the scent, for some people have declared the tapestries to be the cartographic equivalent of the priest's hidey-holes that could be found in many local houses, most famously Harvington Hall. Large houses belonging to families of fellow Catholics feature prominently, and with some exaggeration, on the maps. Furthermore, some (most recently Robert Macfarlane in *The Wild Places*) have claimed that the large Catholic houses, and some smaller but easily identifiable residences, are augmented on the tapestries with a thin red thread. With the sometimes violent religious upheaval going on around them, the maps could have possibly represented potential escape routes (they are some of the first English maps to show roads) and safe houses. 'The Armada had been only a few years earlier,' states Richard Ovenden, keeper of special collections at Oxford's Bodleian Library, where most of the remaining tapestries can be seen. 'Perhaps the Sheldons were hedging their bets.'

It's a great story, although, according to Sheldon tapestry expert Dr Hilary L. Turner, it is just a story. She told me, 'I have never quite understood the statement that the tapestry maps had a practical use in "mapping safe houses". Practical - how? Each tapestry measured approximately sixteen feet high and twenty foot across - scarcely pocket size and a little difficult to unroll while escaping in the saddle, surely?' She quickly demolishes the rest of the theory: 'The link between the houses shown on the tapestries is that most of them belonged to the Catholic Sheldon family or to their friends and relatives - not that all of them were practising Catholics. Many major residences owned by other Catholic families weren't shown at all. Robert Macfarlane's information is also incorrect. Most buildings, whatever their function or size, were outlined by a single black thread. Red roofs, yes; the two Sheldon houses - Beoley (on the Warwickshire tapestry) and Weston (on Warwickshire and Worcestershire), together with Milcote (Warwickshire) - have short red lines dividing floor levels. Occasionally there is a red-outlined window - but on no clear sectarian division. Sorry - but the Catholic connection is not one which should be stressed.'

The bigotry that was mapped for so long as a central tenet of Christianity did all it could to put me off the Church, although I did dive headlong into a brief phase of happy-clappiness at the age of sixteen (beer, blow and blokes soon cured me). This momentary lapse does suggest at least a penchant for the spiritual search, and, yet again, maps came to my rescue in the shape of a growing interest in paganism.

Thankfully, this didn't really kick in until my thirties, so I'd outgrown the crushed-velvet-and-pewter-jewellery school of witchcraft before it even began. My best mate couldn't really understand it, until one day suddenly exclaiming, 'Oh, I *see*! Paganism's really mappie, isn't it?'

It is. Go to any pagan event or gathering, and there will be a stash of well-worn Ordnance Surveys to be seen in every battered Volvo estate and camper van in the car park. I was thrilled to find that my anorak obsession was now bathed in the uplifting glow of spirituality, for this wasn't just idle perusal of maps and even idler ambling around the country following those maps, it was a Journey with the Ancestors to ancient Places of Power. One time, the annual weekend moot of the Society of Ley Hunters took place in a nearby village, and that was a twenty-course map banquet. Having listened to the speakers and talked with many of the participants, I galloped home to sit cross-legged on the floor with a ley guide, a pile of OS maps, a pencil and a ruler. Before my eyes, networks of lines materialised, running through tumps and forts, churches and standing stones, wells and crosses, especially in the parts of the country that I'd always been most drawn to, way before I knew my Imbolc from my elbow. I took to walking some of the ancient hollow ways and tracks, such as the Wessex Ridgeway and the Golden Road in the Preseli Mountains of Pembrokeshire. They had a definite quality that set them apart from your workaday rights of way, something more settled, solid and beyond. On the Ridgeway, I felt the feet and hooves of thousands of years by my side, heard the Babel of languages and sighs of the eternal winds. Having thought that I'd exhausted most of the possibilities of a map, it came alive in an entirely new way.

Tracing sacred landscapes, alignments and their many features has underpinned years of both my work and my leisure time. Living in the mountainous part of Wales has helped, for the landscape is so much less trashed than it is in most parts of England, despite the best efforts of the Forestry Commission. Many of the lines and tracks that Alfred Watkins identified in his seminal 1925 book about leys, *The Old*

Straight Track, have already been lost to the plough and the bulldozer, though plenty survive. And Watkins was no tie-dyed loon, I was relieved to see. Amateur beekeeper, landscape photographer, pillar of the community, Herefordshire dry through and through, his voice barks at you off the page: 'You must use Government Ordnance maps. One mile to the inch is the working scale. Other maps of two or four miles to the inch are quite useless, save for checking long leys.' Amen.

Of course, paganism, in its infinite varieties, attracts the same demagogues, nutters, fundamentalists and desperadoes as any other faith system, and it's always they that get the attention and the bad press. As a way, however, of regaining some spiritual dimension in our relationship with the land, our lore, our past and our future, it is essential, and no surprise that it's regularly cited as the country's 'fastest-growing religion'. We have lost far too much of the idea of sacred landscapes, of landscape at all, of journeying and pilgrimage, of the cycle of the year, of darkness and death in everything as well as light and life, and our societal plight only confirms it. Besides, Ireland, Scotland, England and Wales are such fine countries in which to practise a little light paganism, for there is so much to discover, in the heart of London as much as in the wilds of Connemara. Even the most unlikely places can throw up some thrilling Earth Mysteries. Even somewhere as unlikely as Milton Keynes.

☿

Like the proverbial prophet unrecognised in its own land, Milton Keynes likes to believe that it is loved globally, but scorned – or at the very least, severely patronised – locally. There is some truth in the suspicion. Town planners and students of social architecture from Japan, China, Germany, the USA and Scandinavia, in particular, seem to adore the place and flock there regularly to admire its rectilinear precision. Some love it so much that they set up their businesses and livelihoods there. Domestically, however, Milton Keynes is invariably just a weak punchline, usually accompanied by mentions of round-abouts and concrete cows.

Britain's New Towns are our ultimate map-born conurbations. Older settlements that had grown up along rutted routes, or where roads crossed each other, at fording or bridging points of rivers, on estuaries, nestled into strategic defence points and so on, had all evolved without any help or hindrance from cartographers: most were mapped substantially for the first time only when the Enclosure Acts came into force during the eighteenth century and every last inch of land was recorded and divvied up on huge charts between the landowners. The New Towns were conceived, incubated, born and brought up with maps as their constant nursemaids: if ancient, organic settlements were evolution and practice way before theory, the New Towns were theory only, on a vast scale, hypothesis made massive over whole swathes of post-war austerity countryside.

The main grid pattern of Milton Keynes was agreed at the tail end of the 1960s, and then it was just a matter, quite literally, of filling in the squares. MK's grid is not as stiff as you'd often find in, say, an American city: it wavers and fluctuates across the Buckinghamshire country-side as if the whole pattern were a flag rippling gently in an English breeze. Furthermore, the alignment is wonked from a straight north-south pattern, going more south-west to north-east: so the H roads are not quite horizontal, nor V roads absolutely vertical. This slight kooki-ness has also led to one of MK's strangest celebrated facts, that the whole city is aligned, like an ancient stone circle or burial chamber, to the sunrise of the summer solstice. I'd heard it said so often, but never by anyone who'd actually seen it. I had to have a look for myself.

Well, the first thing to report is that it works. Kind of. The line angled to the north-east, the location of the solstice sunrise on 21 June, runs right through the city centre. From its westernmost point bang in the middle of Milton Keynes railway station, the line heads along the two-mile Midsummer Boulevard, the High Street of MK, becoming a ruler-

'Very not Stonehenge': Milton Keynes just after sunrise on the Summer Solstice

straight path that crests up to a viewpoint over Campbell Park. Rather impressively, the line then continues invisibly, right up the nave of a glorious cathedral of trees, across a roundabout (inevitably), through the Millennium stone circle and its outlying heel stone before spluttering its last on an island in the middle of the artificial Willen Lake. It's the Asda own-brand version of the Grand Axis through Paris.

You have to hand it to them for trying. To underline the point, Midsummer Boulevard's parallel neighbours are called Silbury and Avebury boulevards, and there's an open-air square in the middle of the vast shopping centre that has bollards marking the position of the cardinal points of the compass and the sunsets and sunrises at midsummer and midwinter, together with a complicated sundial and accompanying explanation panels. I was trying to photograph these features when I was snapped out of my mood of all-time-is-now reverie by the arrival of a security guard. 'What are you photographing?' she fired at me. 'Well, this square,' I stuttered. 'Why are you photograph-ing it?' she barked back. Something inside me died. 'Why are you asking me?' I whimpered. 'Control spotted you on the CCTV and told me to come and check you out,' she told me with that blank hostility that comes with a monogrammed polyester cap. As answers go, ones like that make me feel like vomiting, but instead I could only tell her that I was a visitor in her city, and was doing what visitors often do, namely photographing the sights on offer, even if they were as apparently few and far between as in Milton Keynes. 'What's there to photograph here, though?' she rattled. 'Well, all the stuff about the solstice alignment,' I explained, expecting an 'oh right' in cheerful recognition. 'What do you mean?' she shot back. 'What solstice thing?' My answer seemed only to have made matters worse: she was now glaring at me as if I was perhaps a reconnaissance scout for the Wiccan equivalent of al-Qaeda. I explained the stuff around the square, and even took her round to show her a bit of it. Not once in the time that she'd been a security guard in that centre had she ever thought to wonder what those bollards, plaques and sundial were all about, but Control would doubtless have given her one hell of a bollocking if she'd wasted valuable teenager-taunting time getting to know her surroundings.

Milton Keynes has built these fabulously Old Religion touches into the New City, but no one knows about them, not even the locals. The day prior to the solstice, I'd tried to find the city's tree cathedral – the exact same size, shape and layout as Norwich Cathedral: in other words, not something you can lose behind a litter bin. I knew I was in vaguely the right area, but could find no one to ask as I hovered by the side of a busy H or V road. On the other side was some nauseous confection of turrets and towers, a kiddies' theme park that went by the name of Gulliver's Kingdom. The car park was packed. I darted across the main road, hiked through the cars and approached the baseball-capped girl in the ticket office. She smiled mechanically. 'I'm just trying to find the tree cathedral,' I explained. 'It's near here, I think – do you know where it is?' She didn't, but fair play, she took me inside to ask all her colleagues. There was much head-scratching and puffing of cheeks, but no one had the faintest idea where it was. Only one of them had even heard of it.

I walked back out, through hordes of disgruntled parents being ripped off for an hour of mild diversion on crummy rides and junk-food outlets staffed by sallow East Europeans. Unsure where to go next in my hunt, I paused at the entrance to the Gulliver's Kingdom car park. Suddenly, I noticed another car park bang opposite, with the words TREE CATHEDRAL slightly faded but clearly emblazoned on the crossbar of the height barrier. And there it was, less than two hundred yards from the ticket booth of Gulliver's Kingdom. Had the fun-loving staff there just played an elaborate wind-up on me? No offence to them, but they didn't look able or willing. Or were their brains so fried after a day flogging overpriced tat to frenzied kids and angry parents that not one of them had ever noticed what was on the doorstep as they drove out of the car park to return to their brick box in the trees?

They should. Milton Keynes' tree cathedral is an absolute wonder. It is beautiful: quiet, relaxing, uplifting and energising all at once. The nave is a fabulously cool avenue of hornbeam and lime trees, shadowy pines create the exterior walls, statuesque ash make up the choir and gnarly oaks the chancel. In spring and autumn, flowering crocuses nod to the effect of sunlight pouring through stained-glass windows. In fact, the only trees that bring down the whole effect are the four Californian Redwoods put in place in the middle as the four corners of the cathedral's towering spire. They're far from towering, though: rather more stumpy and dusty, with one slowly losing its will to stand. Although the MK tree cathedral is little more than twenty years old, it's a great deal more impressive than the far more celebrated version, planted in the early 1930s, that can be found nearby up on Dunstable Downs. It's just a shame that no one seems to know about it.

If most locals are cheerfully ignorant of the city's supposed pagan design, there are numerous pagan map addicts who have wittered excitedly about the MK alignments on various websites and in Xeroxed magazines called things like *Disciples of Avalon* or *Gaia and Higher*. Never averse to getting the maps and rulers out and proving alignments even when they may not be there, some enthusiasts have detected slight kinks in the three central boulevards, in particular that they are not precisely parallel, and therefore point towards intersections miles away of some significance. Different enthusiasts and different rulers seem to produce different results, however, for no one can quite agree on the location of this supposed point of power somewhere to the west of the city. Any useful feature is seized upon as corroborating evidence for these lines: proximity to a church, a mound or motte, an earthwork, a tumulus, a crossroads, an old inn, a lone tree, an ancient track, a straight track, a ford, just about anything that's older than we are. The urge to believe, to ascribe greater significance, is overwhelming. And it's not just the pagans who so earnestly sign up to such theories: the more psychopathic element of the evangelical Christian movement love this sort of stuff too, all the proof they need of diabolic conspiracy at work. One Christian video from the 1980s warns that the Milton Keynes alignment is an example of 'the Earth Grid and the bizarre lattice patterns of Satan', which makes it sound so enchanting. I hate to disabuse excitable minds on both sides, but from what I could establish in the city archives, there is no cosmic grid or Satanic lattice pattern at work in MK. The alignment came only when one planner had noticed from the map that the three central boulevards pointed north-east; this, he knew, to be the point on the compass where the summer solstice sunrise occurred. It was a useful, and novel, afterthought, rather than anything pre-planned.

I thought about catching the first rays of solstice sunshine beaming down the tree cathedral's nave, but I decided that my best bet for a good view of the phenomenon was from the lofty viewpoint known as the Belvedere, in Campbell Park, to the east of the city centre. Trying to find some people who'd know about the city's mystical alignment, I'd made internet contact with a pagan bikers' group and had met them the previous evening in a village pub about twelve miles out of town.

They were a grand bunch, but no one had much to say on Midsummer Boulevard and its siblings, so I just sank a few beers with them and listened to conversations about classic roads and motorbike parts. The landlord had kindly let me park my camper van in his garden, so it was a 3.30 alarm call the following morning to get me back to MK in time to witness the spectacle. None of the pagan bikers could be persuaded to get up that early (I love fair-weather pagans), but as I walked up the hill towards the Belvedere ten minutes before sunrise, I noticed a couple of figures already there. By the time the sun came up, there were nine of us witnessing it from our vantage point. It was very *not* Stonehenge: there was no chanting or incantation, no robes or hoods. Just nine faintly embarrassed Brits smiling politely at each other, talking about the weather and snapping every ray of the northernmost sunrise of the year with our digital cameras and mobile phones.

The ancients managed their alignments with exquisite precision: the summer sunrise (and winter sunset) at Stonehenge are mathematical in their exactness, as is the midwinter sunrise that, alone of the dawns of the year, penetrates the long chamber of the Newgrange burial mound in Ireland. The planners of Milton Keynes were a little more lackadaisical in their approach, for the sun rises a few degrees to the left (north) of the city's grand axis and then finally hits it square on twenty or so minutes later. In the context of MK, this works all the better, for the first few, low sunbeams would never penetrate the dense lines of trees that stretch the undulating length of Midsummer Boulevard, but by the time the sun is up enough to flood the scene with its rays, it is square on the line. Having been wowed by the sunrise, I raced down to the railway station at the far western end of the axis. Half an hour after dawn, the whole, vast glass frontage was dazzling in reflected sunlight pulsing from its very core. I had expected the whole summer solstice alignment to be a bit of a joke, but it wasn't, and the same feeling applied to the city as a whole. But then, what else would you expect from Satan's very own lattice pattern?

Grope Lane in Shrewsbury – a slightly shorter name than before

7. CARTO EROTICA

> Afterwards as she lay panting on her back, still naked, legs still splayed, she said, 'I want to be fucked everywhere. In every hole. In every position. In every London borough. In every postal district.'
>
> ~ Geoff Nicholson, *Bleeding London*

Comb any map and you will find a host of strange features: odd names, inexplicable and convoluted routes taken by lanes or paths, ghostly remnants of vanished communities, blank spaces where military establishments attempt to hunker down in cartographic secrecy. In only one place, however, can you find a complete set of genitals: Cerne Abbas in mid-Dorset, its infamous chalk giant portrayed on eighteenth-century estate maps in full-frontal splendour. By contrast, the po-faced Ordnance Survey shows him as an outline, but have always coyly emasculated him, even on their largest-scale plans. Not that Cerne is the sole place to hint at the correlation between landscape and the erotic – maps bristle with sexual energy, places that have been known and marked since the earliest times as being laden with libido. Read ex-Teardrop Explodes Julian Cope's *The Modern Antiquarian* and you'll start to see all manner of body parts winking knowingly from the landscape, their names often hinting at their ancient, fecund status.

The Cerne Giant is by far the most celebrated of ancient English chalk-hill figures, and for one reason only. It *is* a very good reason, mind you: a thrusting, rock-hard, thirty-foot-long reason, to be precise. In our phallocentric era, it's no wonder that the Giant has become such a pagan icon for our times, combining, as he does, our twin preoccupations of sex and yesteryear. We want to believe that he represents an age and an attitude before we managed to screw ourselves up so badly about all matters sexual, that his proud, prodigious immodesty pointed straight back to a time when we could rut for England, and with no need for a little blue pill to help us on our way.

Some say, though, that the Cerne Giant points no further back than the seventeenth century. His first mention came in 1694, when the village churchwarden records paying someone three shillings 'for repaireing of ye giant', implying that the figure was at least a few decades old by then. This has led to numerous suggestions that he is little more than a cartoon character, carved in the chalk to lampoon a prominent figure of the day – the suggestion of Oliver Cromwell or Sir Walter Raleigh being particularly popular.

Most of us want to believe that His Perkiness is a great deal older and more venerable, for as archaeologist Rodney Castleden puts it in his book about the Giant, 'absence of evidence is not evidence of absence'. After all, other chalk figures in southern England have been dated back thousands of years: the oldest we can be sure of is the otherworldly Uffington White Horse, alongside the Ridgeway in Oxfordshire. That has been carbon dated to around 1400 BC, from the Bronze Age, and what makes it so exceptional is that it is impossible to get a good view of it from the land: the only way of taking it in properly is from above. How was that achieved three and half thousand years ago? Horses are the most frequent chalk figures in the landscape: the only other ancient human figure is the enigmatic Long Man of Wilmington, exquisitely sited in a bowl on the side of Windover Hill in Sussex. Like the Cerne Giant, many are desperate to believe that his origins date back thousands of years, but there is no empirical evidence from before the turn of the eighteenth century. And there is no truth either in the persistent rumour that, until the prudish Victorians excised them, the Long Man lived up to his name by sporting a set of genitals to outshine his Dorset counterpart.

Despite having seen him in countless photos and postcards or zoomed in on him on Google Earth, your first face-to-face encounter with the Cerne Giant is extraordinary. There he stands, naked, proud and very excited, emblazoned across a baize-green hillside above the sweet Dorset village of Cerne Abbas. Rosy-cheeked little schoolchildren skip around the playground under the arresting sight of a thirty-foot erection on a figure that's nearly two hundred foot high. Not that the Giant has always sported quite such an impressive member (it accounts for some 15 per cent of the body length, which, if translated to a six-foot man, would be something over eleven inches): the earliest drawings, from the eighteenth century, and photos as late as 1902 show that since then the penis has grown upwards and annexed a now-vanished navel, believed to have happened during a 1908 recutting of the figure. At a few stages in history, it disappeared altogether: the Victorians filled in the ditches that made up the outline of his penis and planted shrubs over them. Ironically, that might be why the 1908 recutting got it so wrong and inadvertently created the supersized organ we see today.

We are fortunate that the Giant survived the Victorians at all: they thought nothing, after all, of chiselling suggestive sculptures off medieval churches and castles. Had the mooted railway line ever been built down the sleepy Cerne valley, the Giant would surely have been destroyed. Luckily, plans were shelved and the line was taken up the Frome valley, through nearby Maiden Newton, instead. It's indicative of how far Cerne Abbas's standing had tumbled over the ages, for this had been a major centre of some significance for centuries. The Giant aside, the valley is full of ancient trackways, tumuli and earthworks, and from the tenth century until its dissolution in 1539, Cerne's Benedictine Abbey was one of the wealthiest and most important in southern England.

I finally made it on a long-awaited pilgrimage to Cerne in the spring of 1999, and found a place to camp on the village's outskirts. There was no one else there for a whole four days, and my diary reminds me that it wasn't until the third day that I even started to notice any other, less obvious parts of the Giant – the curious, blank face on his diminutive head, the pronounced nipples, the well-cut six-pack, the club being brandished in his left hand. Until then, it had been his most famous feature that had taken all of my attention; I was utterly hypnotised. But there's more to the hill than just the Giant. Above him is an ancient earthwork, known as the Trendle (aka the Trundle or the Frying Pan), which most historians, pagans and archae-ologists reckon to be the epicentre of the hill's magic and the probable precursor to the Giant itself. This is very much the view of Julian Cope, who writes: 'I'm sure that the crass carving of Mr Big Dick was only done as a last resort when the religion was in such a poor state that they needed a logo, a prehistoric Ronald McDonald to get everyone excited again.'

On May Day morning, when the Giant's penis is said to be precisely angled to the rising sun, the Trendle hosts the first ecstasies of the old festival of Beltane. They used to get a Maypole up there, though now it's left to the Wessex Morris Men to dance in the dawn for an enthusi-astic audience that almost invariably includes the odd bemused foreign TV crew. From my camping vantage point, the whole hill had begun to take on a supremely phallic form, as if this was a giant penis laid out in a far bigger recumbent-body landscape, a sacred form that stretched for five, ten, perhaps more miles across a huge swathe of Dorset. If that were so (and this came to me in such a blinding flash that I'd like to believe there's something in it), then the Trendle would be the glans of the penis. Looking at the 1:25 000 map of the area, the contours of Giant Hill do indeed suggest an appendage of some kind, a high ridge of land jutting far out into the fertile valley that enfolds it. This could explain the slightly odd positioning of Cerne Abbey, and indeed the parish church, both placed below the tip in a perhaps futile attempt to neutralise, Christianise, tame the wild energies that flow from above.

Recumbent landscape figures, of all sizes, have long been one focus of our sacred quest, for they are a natural place to bring the spiritual realm into the physical one, representing nothing less than the figure of God, or the Goddess, on Earth. By definition, such figures make use of hills and mountains for their outline, inherently godly places for their greater proximity to the heavens, their other-worldliness, their extremes of elemental activity, the challenge that they demand of mortals to gain access to them and their long-standing attraction for pilgrims and hermits. Many of our recumbent landscape figures have standing stones aligned to them or forts and temples (latterly abbeys and churches) placed on them in key positions, some are aligned to particular risings and settings of the sun or moon: towering, massive landscapes that combine ceremonial art, astronomy, worship and nature.

They can be seen in all corners of Britain, none better than at the nation's very edge in the Outer Hebrides, where the famous Sleeping Beauty (Cailleach na Mointeach, 'hag of the moors') is a spectacular sight from the standing stones of Callanish. If you're positioned at the top of the main avenue of stones at the time in the 18.6-year cycle of the moon known as lunar standstill (and if you're lucky enough to be blessed with a clear night), a sensational display unfolds. The low full moon rises perfectly over the belly of the figure, before gliding seductively up the length of the body's curves, briefly hiding behind the 'pillow' hill, then reappearing in the very centre of the principal cluster of standing stones, before sinking back below the horizon. While this is undoubtedly Cailleach na Mointeach's finest hour, the recumbent figure is an amazing sight at any time, as are others elsewhere: the Cuillins of Skye, Cumbria's 'pregnant' Black Combe, Wales' Pumlumon, Carn Ingli and Cribarth, Glastonbury and the Golden Cap, the highest cliff on the south coast of England. From a map addict's point of view, the irony is that they are usually impossible to spot on an OS sheet, depending as they do on strange, sometimes fleeting, perspectives and optical illusions played by comparative distance.

According to renowned ley hunter Paul Devereux (in his and Ian Thomson's book *The Ley Guide*), a seven-mile ley line begins at Cerne

Abbas, with St Mary's church, St Augustine's well, the site of the abbey and the Trendle all in a straight line that then proceeds north and slightly eastwards to a tumulus, past a hill fort and, finally, to St Laurence's church and the eponymous holy well at the village of Holwell. It's easily traceable on the map, and goes directly along the length of the ridge line of Giant Hill, the undoubted cock in this magnificently randy landscape. Even a cursory glance at the map shows a wealth of *Carry On* names in the immediate locale: Lawless Coppice, Pound Bottom, Up Sydling, Hog Hill, Plush, Balls Hill, Navvy Shovel, Piddle Wood (and numerous other Piddles), Wancombe, Dickley Hill, High Cank, Smacam Down and, my personal favourite, Aunt Mary's Bottom. There's also a stark warning six miles north-east: the hamlet of Droop.

Despite all this, and despite our national love of a good innuendo, the village of Cerne Abbas itself was a curiously demure little place. The Giant is Dorset's single most visited 'attraction', the area's best-selling postcard and by far the most popular of our chalk-hill figures, and I was expecting the village to be something of a theme park, a Wicked Willy tearoom and a Cock Tails wine bar next to a place selling chocolate and wind-up joke penises, grotesque figurines and cock-swaggering T-shirts. None of it (at least not ten years ago. I see now that the Red Lion pub has renamed itself The Giant, and the website of a village trinket shop boasts of selling 'Cerne Abbas Giant souvenirs, T-shirts, tea towels, aprons, mugs, pens etc.'. Only in true-blue rural England would something so primal be turned into aprons and tea towels). Back at the cusp of the new millennium, there was just one generic postcard in a few shops and, tucked away at the back of the newsagents, a slim volume about the Giant called *The Rude Man of Cerne Abbas*. In the gracious village parish church of St Mary (churchwardens Michael Fulford-Dobson and Clover Hartley-Sharpe), I checked the roll-call of christenings to see if there was any evidence of rampant fertility in the district, but it seemed distinctly lacking (unless, of course, there are loads of heathen nippers rampaging around the lanes, unblemished by a trip to the parish font). The list on the church wall showed that, in the previous ten years, practically every other baby in Cerne had been christened James – including, I suspect, a fair few of the girls.

Next to the official car park and viewing spot for the Giant is a great white gulag of a building staring slap at the chalk figure. Up on the hill itself and peering at it through binoculars, I decided that it was probably an hotel, though it looked rather too brutal even for a Travelodge. Later that night in one of the village's pubs, I asked the gaffer what it was. 'A loony bin,' he answered immediately, before groping unsteadily for more politically sensitive terminology. But that's basically what it is and what it was built for. It's mainly full of elderly people in varying stages of dementia, and every day they sit in worn armchairs and look across the valley at this most exuberant celebration of vitality, tumescence and potency. If they weren't nuts when they went in there, they soon would be: I'd only been looking at him for a couple of days and I was starting to feel distinctly crazy.

You get the unshakeable feeling that Cerne Abbas has a slightly strained, faintly discomfited relationship with its most famous inhabitant. The landlord of the pub I was drinking in told me that he was extending it to include eight tourist bedrooms, which was bringing considerable local opprobrium winging his way. Up till then, there were only six B&B beds in the village, and that was the way people liked to keep it. On Cerne's official website, click on Events and there's no mention whatsoever of the May Day celebrations that bring in thousands of beardy pagans and cider-freaks. Instead, tourists are encouraged to attend Cerne's equestrian endurance ride, the village cricket match, church fête or horticultural show. The official story is all briskly My Little Pony, rather than His Big Penis.

The British Board for Film Classification (BBFC) would perhaps disagree with my assertion that the Cerne Giant is the only set of genitals to be found on a map. In 1992, the BBFC reviewed its guidelines on what could and could not be seen by delicate British eyes. An erect penis was the final taboo, and to quantify their boundary between the acceptably limp and the unacceptably engorged, they came up with the assertion that 'the angle of the penis to the body must not be greater than the angle of the Kintyre peninsula to the west coast of Scotland'. The 'angle of dangle' or 'Mull of Kintyre' rule, as it became known, was rigorously enforced until growing public exposure to the internet made the whole exercise redundant in the tsunami of hardcore that was engulfing a one-handed nation.

This arcane remnant of John Major's Back-to-Basics Britain conjures up some surreal images. I picture a group of BBFC censors sat around and bumping some low-grade porn flick along from frame to frame. An actor starts to get a little excited. 'Where's the map of Scotland?' hollers the chief censor. A flunky rushes to find it. 'Hold it up, Brian, alongside his bits. Ooh, it's almost there. Cut!' Did the BBFC grade all other erections according to a chart of coastal protuberances, like an X-rated version of the Shipping Forecast? Was a Flamborough Head or an Isle of Thanet an absolute no-no, a Llŷn peninsula just a little too risky, a Spurn Head or the Lizard safely within the rules? That said, there is something undeniably penile about Kintyre on the map, and I'm sure it's not just me and the BBFC who have noticed it. The shaft of the peninsula leans lazily out from the coastline, uncircumcised and drooping with just a hint of a bloodrush, before coming to a bulbous conclusion at the glans provided so thoughtfully by Mother Nature. To complete the picture, the neighbouring Isle of Arran makes a particularly convincing ball-bag hanging loose below.

Where nature has failed to provide a sufficiently phallic natural phenomenon, man has never been shy of augmenting it with his own. Many a Neolithic standing stone and monolith is unmistakeably priapic, and placed in its location either as a symbol of aggressive power or as part of a fertility cult: witness the royal Stone of Mannan ('a giant stone penis' – the *Daily Record*) in the main square of Clackmannan; a stone circle of phalli at Aikey Brae near Aberdeen; Samson's

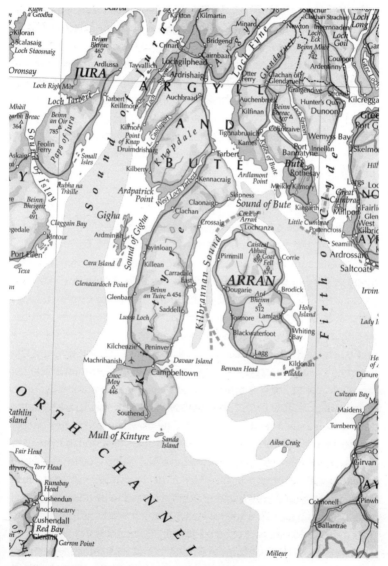

The Scottish solution to the problem of the 'angle of dangle'

Jack on Gower; the Pipers and Mên-an-Tol in west Cornwall; or the massive Obelisk at Avebury, in the process of being destroyed when antiquarian William Stukeley visited and drew it in 1723, placed as it was in a position opposite the 'vulva stone', which thankfully remains with us. That so many standing stones and stone circles had ancient sexual connotations is indicated by their being given Christianised names to do with the devil, or the common myth that they are the bodies of debauched revellers frozen in stone for debasing the Sabbath. Such Puritan overlays tapped into genuine folk memory, passed down through the generations.

Places that exude a female sexuality are, self-evidently, far less overt. Estuaries, fertile plains, river valleys, caves and fogous, barrows, cairns and mother mountains can often be identified on the map by their shape or feminine name; hills such as Mam Tor in the Peak District, Moel Famau ('the rounded hill of the Mothers') in the Clwydian range of north Wales, Mither Tap ('Mother Tit') in the Grampians and the proudly swollen Paps of Jura. More often, though, it's a much more subtle sensuality that marks out a place, something that may only be apparent if you are receptive enough to notice it, or go somewhere often enough to get to know it intricately. A map won't be much help here. There's a fertile little cwm – that Welsh word for a small, sweet, damp cleft in the hillside – near where I live that has whispered vagina energy to me from the day I first moved here. I've walked near and in there with numerous people, and quite a few have picked up exactly the same sensation with no prompting at all from me. I wasn't surprised to learn from a friend who'd grown up here that she used to be taken up to this cwm as a teenager to partake in ancient family witchcraft rituals deep in its mossy folds, as part of an all-female coven of local women.

As the West takes on a more feminist, or at least feminine, agenda, there are many signs that this guile and subtlety of old is changing. Had plans worked out, the Ordnance Survey would now be updating its Newcastle-on-Tyne map to include an explicitly naked female figure, five hundred yards long and with breasts well over a hundred feet high. Unlike the flat chalk outline at Cerne, breast mounds of that size would appear as contours, so there would have been no way the OS could have coyly left off the rude bits in the way that they do with the Giant. The figure, named Coventia, after a Northumbrian water goddess, was planned by architectural sculptor Charles Jencks, designer of the much-lauded Landform installation at the Scottish National Gallery of Modern Art and the delicious Garden of Cosmic Speculation at his own home in Dumfriesshire.

Local Christian groups objected to it – not to the thought of a third-of-a-mile-long naked Amazon reclining in their landscape, but because she was to be named Coventia, which they claimed encouraged paganism. As a result, the lady had her name changed to the revolting municipal fudge of Northumberlandia. Some people objected to the sheer scale of the figure (it was even said that it could endanger pilots landing at nearby Newcastle Airport), so the council ordered that its size be reduced by some 40 per cent. There was a far greater controversy, however, lurking behind the plan, in that it was a sop for a scheme to open a huge opencast coal-mining operation on the site; Northumberlandia was to be a novel use of the slag that would accrue as a result. The headlines almost write themselves. The mining company had cleverly diverted everyone's attention with the giant goddess, and it was left to local councillor Wayne Daley to remind them that 'this is an application for opencast mining, not an application for a woman with 150-foot breasts in South-East Northumberland'. After thousands of complaints, the council finally turned the proposals down, thoroughly annoying both the mining company and the government, who subsequently overturned the decision. Mining has now begun, and the whole Northumberlandia project has been dusted off again as a sweetener – construction is due to begin in 2010, though I would be surprised if she ever feels the north-east breeze billow over her generous contours.

When it comes to an overt sexuality of place, some women happily take men on at their own game. Eve Ensler, the feminist creator of *The Vagina Monologues*, chose New Orleans as the place to hold the tenth-anniversary party of her hit play. And why? Because, of course, she sees it as 'the vagina of America'. 'It is fertile. It's a delta. And everyone wants to party there,' she explained, backing up her theory with a map of the area. One of her *Monologues* actors, Kerry Washington, was initially aghast at the idea, saying: 'When Eve told me New Orleans was the vagina of America, I was like, oh sweet Jesus. Sometimes I think, Eve, do you really want to go there? Really? But now I get it. New Orleans is sexy, everybody loves it – but when it has problems, nobody wants to know.'

The female equivalent of the Kintyre peninsula is most commonly cited to be the island state of Tasmania, off the southern coast of Australia. The shape of the island has long been infused with a certain innuendo, to the point where the phrase 'the map of Tassie' has become regular Aussie slang for a woman's pubic region ('open up the map of Tassie', and so on). While it's not unusual to be able to buy souvenir tea towels and the like emblazoned with a tourist map of Shakespeare Country or Bonnie Scotland, in Tasmania you can purchase not only those, but also pairs of panties with a perfectly placed map of Tassie on the front panel – a memento doubtless bought by far more men than women. A recent Australian TV weather forecast saw the reporter point to the map of Tasmania, and innocently say, 'Looks like it's pretty wet down there,' which sparked off much blokey guffawing in the background of the news studio.

Before street maps became widespread and roads were named in whimsical or Arcadian ways, people had to rely on the literal streetscape of a town to navigate their way around, giving us the legion of Church Lanes, School Roads and High Streets that still form the backbone of our *A–Z*s (High Street being by far the most common road

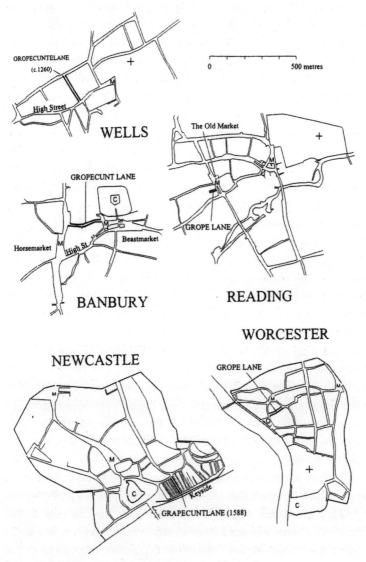

An assortment of medieval Gropecunt Lanes

name in the UK: there are some 5,410 of them). Often, names were culled from trades: Tanners' Row, Smith Street, The Shambles and so on. Where the streets have survived, so have the names, unlike one that said all you need to know about a very popular business; one that, unlike the tanners and smiths, is still with us. Many medieval towns had a Gropecunt Lane, for the c-word wasn't anything like the verbal nuclear warhead that it is today, and streets of this name – mostly putrid alleyways somewhere near the town's main market – were recorded in London, Oxford, York, Norwich, Bristol, Newcastle, Southampton, Hereford, Leeds, Wells, Banbury, Northampton, Peterborough, Reading, Whitby, Worcester, Shrewsbury and Dublin. As the name so precisely implies, these were where any gentleman, landing in a strange town for commerce or a coaching stop, would be guaranteed to find a little action from a range of lead-faced whores. Prostitution was almost as respectable a part of a town's mercantile range as horseshoeing or ale-brewing, so wasn't pushed out of the main drag by squeamish sensibilities. When visiting a new town these days, I apply much the same rule in finding a good breakfast: the area around the market and/or the bus station can normally be relied on to produce the best greasy spoon. Today's stomach-bloater on the site of yesterday's knee-trembler: there's progress.

Unsurprisingly, none of the Gropecunt Lanes have survived the zeal of the censors, although Shrewsbury's is the best extant example. The town is famous for its twisting, medieval passageways, known locally as 'shuts', and there, typically near the site of the old market, is Grope Lane, a narrow defile that zigzags its way down to the main square. According to a directory of the town's street names and an MA thesis, both in the town's archive library, it was named Gropecount Lane in a property deed of 1325, and was still called that as late as 1561. The 530-page thesis, *Shrewsbury: Topography and Domestic Architecture*, was presented to the University of Birmingham in 1953 by one J. T. Smith, although he got his father to do the indexing. Dad, evidently, was either slightly shortsighted or had his prudish hackles raised by the name, for it appears in his index as the far more fragrant Grope Court Lane. The street-name directory goes for the same explanation of Grope Lane's etymology as does the local tourist board these days: trying to conjure up the image of people having to grope their way along its rickety walls in near darkness. It doesn't wash. Everything about the passage reeks of dropped britches and loveless fumbles, even today when the only thing down there that will get your pulse racing is a branch of Costa Coffee.

Oxford's version is the earliest mentioned in documents (as Grope-cunte Lane, c.1237). It is tucked away between the High Street and Merton College, and mutated into Grope Lane, then Grove Street and finally into Magpie Lane, the innocuous moniker by which it is still known (and near where the habitual old groper himself, Bill Clinton, lodged when in the city as a Rhodes Scholar). Grove Lane or Street was the commonest rechristening, although London's famously seedy Grub Street, now Milton Street by the Barbican, and Grape Street in Holborn both possibly hark back to more immodest origins. Certainly, they are located in the right parts of town: just outside the city walls, the hotspot for all of London's seamier doings. Likewise, over the river in South-wark, long the haunt of hookers, actors and cutpurses, there's still a Horselydown Lane almost under Tower Bridge. It may be a corruption of 'Whores Lie Down Lane', though it's more likely to be the lea (meadow) of horses rather than prostitutes prostrating themselves; indeed it's hard to imagine any medieval slapper taking it lying down in the filth of a Southwark alley. There's a popular, internet-fuelled contention that Threadneedle Street in the heart of the City of London also began life in this way, and that its new name is just a euphemism for its old one. While it's sorely tempting to think of the Bank of England as 'the Old Lady of Gropecunt Lane', the road has always surely been too important and too busy for alfresco rutting.

Cast-iron evidence for any of London's Gropecunt Lanes is sparse. There's an *OED* definition from 1230, together with deeds and other legal documents from the thirteenth and fourteenth centuries. From these, we learn that the only definite example in the capital ran from the south of Cheapside to the vicinity of St Pancras church. The church is long gone, but Pancras Lane still exists, one block south of Cheapside. Either side of Gropecunt Lane were Soper Lane (now Queen Street) and Bordhawe Lane, a name that may allude to whores and/or their bordel or bordello (although I rather prefer to think of the eponymous Bored Whore examining her crusty fingernails while some fat punter grunts away at her against the wall). At first glance it seems that Bordhawe Lane has vanished as mysteriously as its neighbour, but maps from the eighteenth to the early twentieth centuries record Bird in Hand Alley and Court, which could be what it became. These are first recorded off 76 Cheapside in 1677, after the whole area was razed to the ground in the Great Fire a decade earlier. The second Great Fire – the Blitz – saw them off for good.

There's much to be said for the literal nomenclature of medieval streetscapes. We could do with a bit more of it today: sweep away the legion of King's Meadows and Willow Heights for the rash of soul-sapping executive developments whose names seem to have been plucked from a focus group random-word generator. On the rare occasions that the names do have any tenuous relevance to their location, it's only to tell us what was once there and has now been forever trashed by the spreading syphilis of brick boxes. Let's see Barratt, McAlpine and the rest inviting us to their show homes at Rabbit Hutch Close or Battery Hen Drive. Eponymous exactitude was a wonderful feature of a medieval town: you'd be in little doubt what to expect in, for instance, London's Hookers Court, Dunghill Lane or the numerous Pissing Alleys and Dirty Lanes. And it wasn't just the odd Gropecunt Lane that could beguile you into its dank environs: politer towns would offer you much the same service in Maiden Lane, a name that has often survived. In the scrofulous slums around Cheapside, for centuries the capital's main commercial thoroughfare, one of the Maiden Lanes sat bang opposite Lad Lane: left for a girl, right for a boy. If you wanted to hedge your bets, the next street up was Love Lane.

The maps have long been excised of their harlots and piss-pots, but there's still plenty enough smut on the OS to satisfy anyone's inner adolescent. A recent Christmas stocking-filler book, *Rude Britain*, became an instant best-seller, filled with photos of signs pointing to the likes of Twatt, Pratt's Bottom, Penistone, Minge Lane, Thong, Brown Willy and Lord Hereford's Knob. Perhaps thanks to the local accent, which can make even a shopping list sound faintly suggestive, the West Midlands seems to be a particularly rich seam of cartographic coarseness. When I lived in Birmingham, I plucked childish delight from taking visitors to one of my favourite Black Country pubs, the Dry Dock at Netherton, probably the only boozer in Britain to contain a narrowboat. To get there from Brum required a drive down a road named Mincing Lane for its first half, and Bell End for the second. This took you into the district of Cock Green, from where a left turn would whisk you to the pub in the area known as Bumble Hole, at the top of Powke Lane. And as if one Bell End wasn't good enough, there's also a nearby hamlet of the same name, just north of Bromsgrove, and only a couple of miles from its natural twin, the village of Lickey End, which comes complete with a road named Twatling Lane. I grew up less than a dozen miles from all of these, which possibly explains quite a lot.

There are occupational hazards to living in a place with a piquant name. Villagers in Fucking, a tiny dab of a place twenty miles north of Salzburg in Austria, became so fed up of carloads of Brits gurning for photos at the village sign that they held a vote in 2004 on changing its name (they decided against). The trend started during the Second World War, when American and British soldiers stationed nearby first noticed the village and came for photos. Now, though, coming away with a picture is nowhere near enough: punters want the sign itself and are arriving after dark with a bag of screwdrivers to get it. In one night in 2003, all four village signs vanished, and replacing them has been a major burden on local taxes. The response to the thieves was to replace the signs with ones bolted and welded to steel posts, embedded into concrete blocks in the ground. The locals are not amused. The police chief stated: 'What is this big Fucking joke? It is puerile.' Tourist guide Andreas Behmüller expanded on our love for his little village: 'The Germans all want to see the Mozart house in Salzburg. Every American seems to care only about *The Sound of Music*. The occasional Japanese wants to see Hitler's birthplace in Braunau. But for the British, it's all about Fucking.' None of them, sadly, explained what residents of the village are known as – nor, indeed, their mothers.

Road-sign larceny is a growing headache for anywhere with a bawdy name or association: those of Llanddewi Brefi, the peaceful Cardiganshire village whose name was plucked off the map and used as the home of Dafydd, 'the only gay in the village' in the *Little Britain* TV show, were, at the height of its success, being half-inched regularly and even ended up for sale on eBay. At the other end of Wales, the two signs pointing towards the village of Sodom rarely survive longer than a month or two before having to be replaced. The village of Lunt, just north of Liverpool, is considering changing its name as folk can barely scrape the paint off the sign before the L is defaced yet again to the inevitable C.

If British censors had to excise a few earthy bodily functions from the map, no surprise that their American counterparts were dealing with a plethora of names that told us all we ever needed to know about that country's troubled history of matters – and manners – both sexual and racial. As the pioneers swept west, features were named and mapped with monotonous inevitability: any hill west of the Appalachians that looked even faintly breast-like would become Squaw's Tit, Squaw's Teat, Squaw's Nipple or some variety thereof. An entire roll-call of playground insults included Dago Gulch (Montana), Nigger Pond and Niggerhead Point (New York), Niggerskull Creek (North Carolina), Jewtown (Georgia and Pennsylvania), Gringo Peak (New Mexico), Jap Bay and the frankly fabulous Jap Gap (Alaska), Dago Joe Spring (Nevada), Gook Creek (Michigan), Chinks Peak (Idaho), plus hundreds and hundreds of other variants. As sensibilities have changed, their gradual renaming has caused endless argument, in State assemblies, local courts, the Federal Board on Geographic Names, even Congress and the Senate. The argument almost always goes the same way: someone will roundly defend the names against the 'political correctness' of their suggested replacements, petitions will be gathered, local radio shock-jocks will shout and holler. Signs get defaced, replaced and stolen, and politicians are left to tiptoe a wary line through the linguistic minefield.

The internet has brought untold erotic possibility into our libidinous little lives, including a phenomenon known as the Sex Map, or Shag Map. It's exactly as you'd expect: a map of places associated with your own sexual history; there are entire websites dedicated to plotting and sharing them. The idea pre-dates the internet, though. Geoff Nicholson's Whitbread-shortlisted novel *Bleeding London* has a character, Judy Tanaka, quoted at the top of this chapter, who wants to be laid in every London postcode district. The wall of her bedsit is covered with a huge street map of the capital, over which she lays different clear plastic sheets. All her visitors get a sheet to themselves and are asked to mark with a cross everywhere they've had sex: 'There were people whose maps centred intensely around Kensington or Belsize Park, others who were concentrated on south London, others who had lived and fucked all over London at every point of the compass.'

This got me thinking. Was there one single existing map that could best encompass my own sexual history? The answer was a blindingly obvious yes. I'd like to claim that it was a plan of the boulevards of Paris, the beaches of Spain, the mountains of Wales or even a corrupted version of the London tube map, a spiced-up game of 'Mornington Crescent', if you like. But it's none of these. It's page 90 of the Birmingham *A–Z*.

I lived and loved on that one page of the second city's street atlas between the ages of twenty-four and thirty-three, and I'm sure I'm not the only one to have found this stretch of south Birmingham an erogenous zone of epic proportions. Page 90 has long been the city's boho quarter, a place for hippies, punks, squatters, junkies, queers, partyheads and polyamorists, sprinkled among the tight terraces of Balsall Heath and the gracious Victorian villas of Moseley. It was a fabulous place to have a second adolescence.

The heady erotica of the Birmingham *A–Z* is just a warm memory these days. Now my thrills have to come from an even less likely cartographic source: the *National Trust Map of Properties*. It was inevitable that someone who started collecting Ordnance Survey maps at the age of seven would end up as a member of the NT. And if you consider that the only other probable outcomes to such a start would have been to end up as a Neighbourhood Watch coordinator or a volunteer on a steam railway, I may well have got away relatively unscathed. There is plenty of time yet, mind.

I love the National Trust. For all their po-faced earnestness and clumsy attempts to repackage themselves in trainers rather than Hush Puppies, they remain one of the finest, quirkiest and most delightful organisations in the land. With a few clear days in a new part of the country, nothing compares to the frisson of anticipation that comes with the first opening of the NT map to see what unexpected treats the area has to offer. I know full well that, a few days and a good few Trust properties later, I will emerge a wiser, happier man for having been allowed to wallow in things of exquisite beauty, exquisitely well presented. I will have had numerous cheery exchanges with other members of the cult, anything from a collaborative smile over a slice of cherry cake in the tea room to a sparky discussion about the eighteenth-century Grand Tour or the Enclosure Acts with one of the erudite volunteer guides sprinkled around each property. I haven't quite yet made the leap into striking up easy conversation with many of my fellow NT members: should that happen, I'm terrified that I'll start buying my clothes from the catalogues that fall out of the *Radio Times*, and end up looking, like rather too many of the male members, the spit of Harold Shipman.

An NT property – especially outwith the school holidays, when it's just me, the Harold Shipmans and their mousy wives visiting – is a failsafe ego boost. In an occurrence that's increasingly rare these days, I'll be well within the bottom ten per cent of the age range, a thrill that makes me positively sashay up to the front door. Not that anyone will notice, as they'll be far too busy adjusting their bifocals, unpacking the thermos and having an argument in tetchy whispers about missing the turning for the B5818 twelve miles back.

The Trust is desperate to modernise, although the irony is that it is its inability to do so that stirs such loyalty in the breasts of the Tupperware generation. There are glimpses that the twenty-first century has arrived, however. I first joined because I felt sorry for the two fragrant ladies on their stall at the National Eisteddfod, the AGM for Welshspeaking Wales. There are hundreds of stalls at the Eisteddfod, though the ones that pull the crowds are those of the publishers, record companies, funky-clothes sellers and protest groups. The NT stand, reeking of lavender and Middle England, had a rather abandoned air, as if no one had been in there for hours. Initially to shelter from the rain, I popped my head around the canvas flap to be greeted by two hugely relieved matronly faces. They were having such a quiet time of it, I felt slightly obliged to join up, and even enrol my partner too, just for the pleasure of seeing their little faces light up at having flogged a joint membership. Her pen poised over the application form, one of the ladies smoothly enquired, 'And Mrs Parker's name is ...?' 'Er, my partner's a man,' I replied. Without missing a beat, she smiled and said, 'How nice ... and his name is?' We were in the club, even if my boyfriend promptly lost his membership card, possibly as a quiet protest.

Membership means that you'll often go to places that you might otherwise not have bothered with (the urge to 'earn' back the cost in offset entrance fees is scarily strong), and stumble accordingly across some real unexpected gems. The delicious irony is that this most buttoned-up of British organisations is the key to some of the country's dirtiest secrets, for no one does depravity quite like the upper classes. Perhaps the Trust's most libidinous landscape is West Wycombe in Buckinghamshire, built and laid out to the very specific tastes of its eighteenth-century owner, the legendary libertine Sir Francis Dashwood, founder of the notorious Hellfire Club. His Palladian mansion is an orgy of marble, statuary and frescoes, much portraying naked nymphs, centaurs, satyrs, cupids, and goddesses with generous curves and golden curls, but it is in the surrounding parkland that he let his fantasies run riot. The centrepiece of the park was a nine-acre lake in the shape of a swan. In his *History of Gardens*, Christopher Thacker, quoting from a volume of *Victoria County History*, describes how Dashwood's lake and gardens were 'laid out by a curious arrangement of streams, bushes and plantation to represent the female form', but one as far from the craggy mountain recumbents of the Hebrides and Wales as could possibly be imagined.

In his book *The Hellfire Club*, American author Daniel P. Mannix is far more explicit. He asserts that two mounds were each topped with a circle of red flowering plants, and that, at a little distance below and between them, was a triangle of dark shrubbery. The effect was particularly startling from the top of West Wycombe Hill, where Sir Francis had lavishly rebuilt the church of St Lawrence. To best enjoy his view, he crowned the church tower with a golden ball, into which he and half a dozen friends could comfortably climb and dine. Mannix states that Sir Francis once took the local priest up the tower to show him the parkland. He asked him, 'What do you think of my gardens?' at which point, by prior arrangement, the fountains started. Two of them spouted a milky-white fluid from the top of each red-flowered mound, while the third gushed from the area of the shrubbery.

As if the landscape needed much more to underscore its theatrical erotica, the parkland was littered with lascivious statuary, temples, grottoes and follies, the least subtle of which is the sole survivor of the recumbent female form, the Temple of Venus. This homage-in-flint to the female genitalia has two curving walls centred on a coy slit that opens into a grotto beneath an earth mound; it reminded me instantly of the many swollen-goddess burial chambers that I've squatted in, such as Belas Knap and Hetty Pegler's Tump in Gloucestershire, Bryn Celli Ddu on Anglesey and the West Kennet barrow in Wiltshire. In Sir Francis's day, an erect flint pillar stood in front of the opening to his temple and dozens of naked statues decorated the scene, including one of Mercury, a wry nod to the liquid metal's status at the time as the only known treatment for syphilis. When Sir Francis's far more strait-laced nephew inherited the estate at the end of the eighteenth century, he wasted no time in destroying the Temple of Venus, the female body alignment and many of the other more suggestive features of the park. It wasn't until 1982 that Sir Francis' namesake, the 11th Baronet, restored a version of the temple that we see today.

That Sir Francis's lake was swan-shaped is thought to have been inspired by the myth of Leda, Queen of the Spartans, who was impregnated by the god Zeus in the shape of a swan, on the same night that she also made love to her husband, Tyndareus. This, together with the pastiche version of female sexuality that the gardens represented, suggest that the entire enterprise was very much the notion – fervent wish, perhaps – of feminine libido as seen through the eyes of men; terminally adolescent men at that. The same could perhaps be said of poor old Northumberlandia, the naughty knickers of Tasmania and maybe even Julian Cope's fervent desire to see a fertile landscape goddess around every corner. Mapping and sex seem to prove that the phrase 'adult male' may well be an oxymoron.

Don't you worry your pretty little head, lady...

8. BOYS' TOYS?

The modern male driver sits behind the wheel, hands his wife
a map and asks her to navigate. With limited spatial ability she
becomes silent and starts turning the map around and feels
incompetent. Then she tries to identify something on the horizon that resembles something on the map. Most men don't
understand that if you don't have specific areas in the brain
for mental map rotation, you'll rotate it in your hands. It
makes perfect sense to a woman to face a map in the direction
she is travelling. For a man to avoid arguments, he should
avoid asking a woman to read a map.

~ Allan and Barbara Pease,
Why Men Don't Listen & Women Can't Read Maps

Go to any map fair, convention or gathering of enthusiasts, and the
first thing that strikes you is the almost complete absence of women.
While hardly hotbeds of testosterone, such occasions only seem to
confirm the prejudice that maps are boys' toys, too technical, too dry
and too rational for the esoteric tastes of the ladies. I've just waded
through the entire membership list of the Charles Close Society, the
fan club for Ordnance Survey maps, to see what the gender split was
there. Out of the six hundred or so members, I could positively identify only twenty-six as female.

'As many as that?' said Charles Close Society founder (and member
number one) Dr Yolande Hodson, when I told her the figure. 'I'm
surprised. I suspect a good many of those twenty-six are map librarians.

They tend to be women, you see. Even so, they're not usually collectors of maps. Many women can't read maps, after all.' I was thunderstruck to hear our most eminent female map addict describe her fellows in such forthright terms. If Dr Hodson is right, she herself is a glorious exception to the rule. Her entire professional career has been in maps, working in the British Library's Map Library, the Military Survey (who are charged with providing the armed services with the best geographic and geodesic information available), and as a historian, curator and author, particularly on matters to do with the Ordnance Survey. Her knowledge of the early years of OS is second to none, and she confessed to me that her ambition in the afterlife is to find OS founding father William Roy, a lifelong bachelor, and marry him. If anyone could tame the old bugger, it's Yolande. She says that although many women are very fond of maps, when it comes to the Charles Close Society and collectors of OS maps, she is usually in a tiny minority. As for most of us, her love of maps ignited at an early age; she says about eight years old. 'If we went on a walk, I'd come back and draw a map of where we'd been. I adored the graphic representation of spatial relationships, and that you could use a map to peel back the various layers of information.'

Yolande Hodson is doubly rare, in that she not only is a map addict (she has three different versions of the entire OS 1:50 000 Landranger series, which is, after all, only a little over thirty years old, and a set of every OS One Inch map of England and Wales published since the beginning of the nineteenth century), but also an avid collector. 'Women,' she said, 'don't tend to have collections in the same way that men do. Not just of maps, but of anything.' She is stout in her defence of the extreme map 'anoraks' (a label she's happy to share) who get, to my eyes, unnecessarily hot and bothered about things like edition numbers and tiny changes in cover illustrations. 'We map historians rely on that level of detailed, obsessive scholarship,' she says. Fair point.

I tell her of a recent Women's Institute meeting at which I was the guest speaker. The branch was in a small Montgomeryshire village, with an attendance of about a dozen ladies and some fabulous sponge cakes. After my spiel, one of the members asked me what I was working on at present. 'A book about maps,' I replied, fully – and condescendingly – expecting the revelation to cause collective eyes to glaze over and precipitate a stampede to the bara brith. Instead, it kickstarted quite a discussion. At least half of the women present were dedicated map enthusiasts, each of them speaking lovingly of the maps that had meant most to them over the years. One lady said, 'It's such a pity that they don't do Bartholomew's maps any more. I always preferred those to the Ordnance Surveys.' Quite a few heads nodded at that one. When I told her this, Yolande laughed. 'Well, of course. Everyone liked Bartholomew maps because they were so beautifully artistic and clear to read. This special appeal helped make them a real threat to the sales of Ordnance Surveys. Don't forget that, at the beginning of the twentieth century, a typical Bartholomew's print run on a map was about ten thousand, against five hundred to a thousand for a comparable OS.'

Among my friends and relatives, many of the good map-readers are women, and I've hardly ever encountered the proverbial hopeless female who looks at an Ordnance Survey as if it is an impenetrable equation in quantum physics. My suspicion is that map-reading is in the same category as driving, an area of life that's perceived to be more masculine, and therefore one in which men cling to the belief that they are better than women, despite overwhelming evidence to the contrary. Just as it is men who you'll find slobbering over all the car magazines in Smith's, having interminable pub conversations about horsepower and torque, or willingly paying twenty quid to hang out in a vast shed on the outskirts of Birmingham just to lust over cars they haven't a hope in hell of ever owning, so it is with the lower-octane cartographic equivalents. Most women, however much they appreciate maps, are not going to bother joining a society to prove it, much less trek halfway across the country to make map-talk with others and browse through a few boxes of musty Geographias. That's what the boys do, and as far as most women are concerned, it's a fine way of keeping them out of trouble. I say 'them'; of course, I mean 'us'.

Allan and Barbara Pease, however, are adamant that women cannot read maps, and that you'd be a fool to ask them to try. According to them, it's all down to factors that haven't changed since we were living in caves, namely very different spatial awareness in the comparative brains of men and women, together with different fields of vision. The left-right split in the brain is less pronounced in women, thanks to a thicker nerve tube (the corpus callosum) connecting the two sides. This gives women greater intuitive powers and a superior ability to multi-task. Men, by comparison, with their spindly little corpora callosa, can only concentrate on or do one thing at a time. However, when that one thing is reading a map and navigating, they do it well. Likewise, with regards to what we see and how we see it, the Peases state that men, true to our hunter-gatherer origins, tend towards tunnel vision or extreme focusing on one thing, while a woman has far wider peripheral vision, 'so that she could monitor any predators sneaking up on the nest'.

Like most clichés, the one about women having to turn the map upside down if they're travelling south has some considerable truth to it. It's something I've witnessed on a few occasions – and, if I'm honest, slightly sniggered at – but never particularly thought it to be of any great significance. After all, turning the map to fit the direction in which you're travelling has been recommended by every British Army map-reading manual since 1906, and as long as a navigator can get you to your destination, who cares how they do it? But this is a subject that gets people very excited indeed. In 1997, young Derby inventor Ashley Sims had the idea for an upside-down map of Britain, not as a *Scotland For Ever!* piece of bravado, but as a pure navigational aid. He produced a prototype: on one side, the country was mapped in the familiar way, with north at the top, and, on the other, it was inverted, with south uppermost. On both sides, names of towns and villages and road numbers were the right way up, so that, whether you were heading north or south, you had an easily legible map going in the same direction that needed no huffing, puffing and turning around.

Ashley took his idea to W. H. Smith and Waterstone's, but neither was interested. In fact, both were loftily dismissive of it as little more than a one-minute gimmick, a cutesy joke in a section of their retail empires not much accustomed to humour. But, in both cases, it was only male executives that he saw. After his double rejection, Ashley was contacted by a female executive from W. H. Smith, who hadn't been present at the meeting. She'd heard the idea from one of her colleagues and had got it immediately. Under her tutelage, Smith's took on the project, and the *Upside Down Map* (and then *Upside Down Road Atlas*) of Great Britain were born. They received massive publicity: a few 'and finally ...' TV news pieces and similarly wry press coverage. The *Daily Mail* ran a story about the map and offered a free copy to the first hundred people to write in. They had fifteen thousand requests – all but a tiny handful from women. Ashley went on to publish upside-down maps of other places; the series sold over 300,000 copies before his Dutch publisher went bust and took the series with them.

Ironically, the muse for Ashley's map was a man: his father John, a trucker. Returning from Scotland to Derby one day, his dad grew furious with trying to work out the route home. 'If you turn the map upside down, the place names are unreadable and if you read the map backwards in the direction you are driving, right-hand turns and places are on the left and vice versa. Travelling north I had no problems. But I found the long journey back with the same map very difficult. I couldn't understand why anybody hadn't printed a map the other way round to eliminate the problem.' So Ashley did. The experience set him up with a hunger for some other cracking ideas; since the upside-down maps (a concept that he thinks is now redundant, thanks to the ubiquitous satnav), he's gone on to invent Jellyatrics (jelly babies in the shape of pensioners, to celebrate the popular sweet's eightieth birthday), Proofers (paper tabs that can be placed in drinks to test for the presence of date-rape drugs) and make films about the peregrine falcons of Derby Cathedral and the bikers of Matlock Bath. That's what you call a proper bloke's progression through life: get madly absorbed in one thing for a while, then wear it out before galloping off to the next. It's one of the things I always loved my dad for, the swift succession of hobbies that he hurled himself into with such gusto: the town fête, the church youth club, home-brewed beer, grape-growing for Château Kidderminster wine, the twin-town association, camera club, gardening club, Man in the Kitchen classes at the local FE college, coaching paralympians, tracing the family tree. Some of his crazes have had more effect on the family than others. The stench of boiling hops clung to us all during his home-brew phase, though that was nothing compared with the disruption that came from his sudden dedication to the local brass band. He'd never played any instrument before, and, not one to duck a challenge, took up with a tuba as his debut. If I read a passage from any of the books that I studied for A level, I can still hear the booming, tuneless fart of tuba scales in the kitchen below me and feel the floorboards shake in consternation. Unlike my dad, I've not been much of a serial hobbyist, unless you count the maps, of course. That's never been a red-hot fling, though; always the steady relationship, with its many ups and downs, but long settled into companionable quiet.

Women (and only women) swivelling maps round to face the direction in which they are travelling has become the most regular comedy leitmotif for men who are convinced that they have the monopoly on cartographic savvy. In 2007, the psychology department at the University of Warwick published an analysis of the findings from a huge BBC online poll, in which 198,121 people participated (109,612 men and 88,509 women). The principal thrust of the study was to see how ageing affects cognitive and spatial awareness, but you'd never have known that from the resulting media coverage. That focused instead on the very unsurprising finding that 'men outperformed women on tests of mental rotation and line angle judgment, whereas women outperformed men on tests of category fluency and object location memory'. Or, as the papers and virtually all of the male blogosphere had it: 'Women can't read maps, but at least they'll be able to find the car keys.'

The headlines were further sensationalised by the inclusion within the test, not just of gender, but of sexual identity too. That produced the result that when it came to the mental rotation of cuboid objects that look like overgrown Tetris blocks, there was a definite hierarchy of ability: heterosexual men first, then bisexual men, gay men, lesbians, bisexual women and, lastly, heterosexual women. The red-blooded papers loved that, and cheered it to the rafters like a drunken rugby team: the *Daily Telegraph* headlined their story about the report 'Needing Directions? Men, Stay Straight'. Of all the tests, this was the one that was most identified with the ability to read a map, for that demands the skill of being able to translate an image from two dimensions into a mental picture of it in three, which can then be rotated and turned in the brain. Having tried the test, much to my horror – and despite my earlier lie that I don't think people who have to twirl the map around are second-class citizens – I scored abysmally on this skill, lower than the average woman's score and much lower than the average man's. The concluding report of my test suggested that I was the kind of person who'd have trouble reading maps, especially if I was going in a different direction to that of the plan. How very dare it.

In a 2008 BBC documentary *Born That Way?*, actor John Barrowman undertook a variety of quasi-scientific tests to establish whether his being gay was a matter of nature, nurture or a juvenile overdose on show tunes. In one sequence, Barrowman was seen in a car, navigating between appointments, turning the map round in all directions to match the bearings of the route they were taking. 'Aha!' seized the psychoanalyst watching the footage. 'He reads maps just like a woman.' This was, we were reliably informed, yet another piece of evidence that gay men were hard-wired in a more feminine way than our heterosexual brethren. My boyfriend had to stop me hurling a chair through the television at this point.

I'm sure we weren't the only gay household erupting in fury at such meaningless analysis. Come to that, I would think that there were a fair few women viewers aiming their own missiles at the screen. Many gay men, and many women of all sexualities and none, are quite brilliant with maps, whether they turn them to suit the direction in which they're travelling regularly, occasionally or not at all. In fact, from a completely unscientific survey of all the people I've ever either been navigated by or discussed maps with, I'd go so far as to say that map addiction is a *very* common trait amongst many gay men, not perhaps the ones of the John Barrowman stereotype, but the rest of us who, thankfully, make up the vast majority of the gay male spectrum. I'm an occasional user of an online social networking site used predominantly by gay men, and set up a group within it solely to talk about maps. The plug for my group says simply, 'For those who can read a map like others read *Heat* or *Hello!*, and who aren't ashamed to say so'. There are nearly a hundred members and regular discussions on everything from the favourite features on the London *A–Z* to the best internet resources for historical mapping. And I don't think anyone has to turn their computer screen upside down to join in.

The big question behind all of these studies is that old chestnut of nature versus nurture. At risk of sounding like one of those flip sentences you see Carrie Bradshaw elegantly tap into her laptop on *Sex and the City*:

> … is it just self-fulfilling prophecy that women are crap at maps?

Have they been told this so often, and so vehemently, that they've disengaged from maps without quite bothering to see if there is any truth in it or not? Fran Loots certainly believes that to be the case. She is the director of Breathing Space Outdoors, a Perthshire-based training organisation that offers numerous courses in outdoor skills. One of the most successful has been her two-day course, unambiguously titled 'Women CAN Read Maps'. She came up with the idea having reached that thirtysomething stage of life where a good few of her friends were disentangling themselves from dead relationships that they'd been in since their late teenage years. Out and about in the Scottish mountains with these friends, it soon became apparent to Fran that map-reading was an unexpected casualty of these break-ups: the women had become so used to ceding all navigational responsibility to their ex-partners, it had left them scared of a map and its mysteries, and lacking in the confidence to do very much about it. The course was born.

Fran likens map-reading to riding a bike, in that it takes good instruction and regular practice. For the Women CAN Read Maps course, the students gather and their first session has them sharing their stories and phobias around maps. The terror of looking daft underpins so many of these; Fran tells me that this falls away, usually in great gusts of knowing laughter, as each woman confesses her bad map moments – anything from getting confused about symbols to the soul-crushing times when an impatient boyfriend snatched the map out of her hands and muttered that she'd best leave it to him.

Over the two days of the course, Fran takes the women out into woods and hills, encouraging them to use all of their senses and try different vantage points in working out how to position themselves. They learn to judge distances, use compasses and grid references, what the various symbols and different scales of an OS mean and how contours work, all backed up with practical examples on the ground. Symbolically, the course finishes at a fabulous viewpoint where the participants can quite literally see how far they've come. And there is no snobbery here about rotating the map to fit the view – it is, as Fran puts it, 'The simplest way to eliminate any margin of error. After all, you don't have to read a map as if it's a book, and it's a lot easier to move the map than move a mountain.'

The course has been phenomenally successful, and it's evidently one than Fran herself enjoys hugely. 'I love the camaraderie and the fact that, in just two short days, you can see what a huge difference it's made to the participants. It's been like that every single time; no one has ended the course without having improved their map-reading massively.' On the surface, this might just be about maps, but – as so often – there are far bigger, meatier issues lurking beneath: rebuilding the sometimes fragile confidence of women trying to overcome an all-too-symbolic block in their minds, a block that was once almost imperceptible, but which has since been built up into the size and shape of a massive brick wall by others. Most importantly, perhaps, demystifying the map also demystifies the landscape, helping re-root people in the countryside and wildernesses that make them sing. It's strong, yet subtle stuff, a magical alchemy with life-changing effect.

Another Scot, former World Champion rally driver Louise Aitken-Walker, echoes Fran's points. 'Women only get lost because they've got their husbands screaming at them,' she says, adding that some of the world's top male rally drivers choose to have female co-drivers because they are superior navigators. Someone had better tell Allan and Barbara Pease in their cave.

That so many women feel excluded by maps comes as no great surprise, however. Until only very recently, modern cartography has almost always been a resolutely conservative area, reinforcing every assumption that maps are for men, and ladies really shouldn't bother their pretty little heads about them. Throughout the twentieth century, this can be seen quite dramatically, sometimes hilariously, in the design of the maps, especially the cover images used to catch the eye of a potential punter. American oil-company maps, distributed free through the network of service stations, were the mainstay of popular mapping from the 1920s until the '70s: their covers speak volumes. Interestingly, in the early years of motoring, women shared centre stage with the men: the advent of the motor car meant independence for all, whether brilliantined chaps or their uniformly gorgeous gals. Shell maps of the mid-1930s even showed women at the wheel, firmly in control.

After the Second World War, however, the covers had all changed: a woman was only glimpsed through the window of a car, usually wiping the snotty noses of her offspring or looking vacantly into space, while the husband filled up, posed questions to the attendants, pored over maps and checked oil levels. British maps of the same era had even less of a female presence: as we saw in Chapter 3, of the few Ordnance Surveys that showed people rather than winsome landscapes or overgrown royal crests, the vast majority were men only, whether they were driving, hiking, cycling or just pausing mid-ramble to fill their pipes with a fistful of Ready Rubbed. Ladies were permitted only on tourist maps, most famously on the 1932 OS of the Chilterns, where a modern young couple stride out along a hillside together. As can be seen in the colour section, it's a gorgeous fantasy of a picture: a church and a few rustic cottages poke their heads above the lush parapet of greenery, the corn-cloaked hills seem to smile with benign charm. Most fantastical of all, the couple are walking abreast, rather than the more common reality of him marching ahead as he consults the map, while she trots along obediently in his wake, soaking in her usual view of the back of his head.

Lloyd A. Brown's classic book *The Story of Maps*, originally published in 1949, begins with the words: 'This is the story of maps: the men who made them and the methods they employed.' He's only being slightly sexist, for the list of women cartographers is surprisingly skimpy. Although this was obviously a matter of lack of opportunity, rather than lack of ability, it is hard to pinpoint a specifically feminine, or even feminist, school of map-making, at least until very recent times. Women were often put to work on maps, as embroiderers, engravers, artists, colourists or sewers and stitchers, but this was usually to help their father, husband or brother in his trade, or as lowly employees in the firm. In the eighteenth century, there was a short-lived craze among some gentlewomen for mapping; the finest product from that age came from the eminent French astronomer Nicole-Reine Étable de la Brière Lepaute (1723–88), who, together with two noble lady friends, calculated the precise timings and orbit of the forthcoming 1764 solar eclipse and produced a quite gorgeous map of its trajectory. She also correctly predicted the return of Halley's Comet in 1759.

War brought women into cartography, just as it brought them into many other traditionally masculine areas of work. During the Second World War, thousands of women were enthusiastically drafted into the mapping divisions of the American military: Millie the Mapper became a lesser-known compatriot of the iconic Rosie the Riveter, whose Rockwell-designed poster, rolling her sleeves up to the slogan 'We Can Do It!', inspired millions of women into war-work. In Britain, where the need was just as acute, the response was no less hearty, although orchestrated in a rather more mealy-mouthed way by the authorities. Many new women geographers and cartographers were drafted into the Ordnance Survey and the Hydrographic Office of the Admiralty, but only as an emergency – and temporary – measure. The OS, in particular, found the adjustment a little hard to take; an internal memorandum states baldly that 'it would be desirable that the whole recruitment should *not* be from women'. Neither were they paid anything like their male colleagues, as an instruction from the Treasury made starchily clear:

> ... the sort of work which you expect from these women draughts-
> men (who it seems to us hardly merit the title in the full sense)
> appears to be on rather a lower scale than that of the Office of

Works employees; in fact we are inclined to think that the suggested title [Mapping Assistant] should be changed to that of Learner Tracers (below age 18) and Tracers (from age 18 and after completion of the probationary period).

Ironically, by the outbreak of the Second World War, the most famous product of a female cartographer in British history had already been published: the London *A–Z*. The story of its creator, Phyllis Pearsall (1906–96), is one of map-making's most celebrated, and with good cause: it's a blockbuster movie-in-waiting, albeit with a wildly embellished script. Ever tuned to its marketing potential, Phyllis spun her own tale for all that she could, and others have pitched in subsequently to enrich it with even more lavish quantities of sugar and spice. The popular version, repeated ad nauseam through the press, across the internet and forming the basis of Sarah Hartley's saccharine biography, *Mrs P's Journey*, is that Phyllis came up with the idea for the London *A–Z* one night in 1935, after getting lost and soaked in a downpour on the way to a party. The very next day, she sprang out of bed at 5.00 a.m., and set to walking and cataloguing every one of the 23,000 streets of the capital, a task that took the best part of the year, with Phyllis tramping the streets each day from five in the morning until nigh on midnight. The only other maps available were hideously out-of-date large-scale Ordnance Surveys that hadn't been updated since the First World War. Single-handedly, Phyllis found a draughtsman, and between the two of them, they researched, drew, wrote, indexed and had printed the first copies of the *A–Z*, which Phyllis then took around all of the booksellers, most of whom dismissed her without a second glance. After a week of trying to be seen by the chief buyer for W. H. Smith, he finally took her into his office and ordered a raft of her maps, which were an instant best-seller. To cope with the demand, the tiny Phyllis had to cart copies all over London in a borrowed wheelbarrow. It's a lovely story, but it doesn't entirely coincide with the truth.

That Phyllis Pearsall was an indomitable woman is not in question. Indeed, she was possibly even more spirited and determined than the overly winsome account of the *A–Z* would have us believe. Phyllis (née Gross) was the daughter of two theatrically extravagant characters, her Hungarian-Jewish father Alexander Gross (formerly 'Grosz'), and her Irish-Italian-English mother Bella Crowley, a suffragette playwright. You'd struggle to find two more insufferably selfish, highly strung people: Phyllis's childhood was a minefield of constant relocation, divorce, abandonment and abuse, all caked in wildly fluctuating wealth. The money came from her father's Geographia Map Company, which had done spectacularly well out of the First World War, by providing millions of much-sought-after war maps to the general public through the newspapers. Despite that, the company, and her father, went bankrupt in 1920, he being ousted by an internal putsch orchestrated by his estranged wife's brother, Frank Crowley. Geographia passed into new hands, and Alexander Gross limped over to New York, where he set up another map-making business with the same name. In Alexander's absence (and to his inevitable fury, though he soon came on board), Frank Crowley wormed his way into Phyllis's affections and got her to join him in his own map-selling concerns. To Phyllis, this was a way of both rehabilitating her father's reputation in London and making some money to support her career as an artist. The two of them, together with a small team of draughtsmen and printers, produced extravagant wall maps of the world, and then one of England and Wales. In her autobiography, *From Bedsitter to Household Name*, Phyllis states that the idea of a London street atlas came from her draughtsman, Mr Fountain, in conjunction with her father, still busily controlling events, even from New York. There is no mention of a wet dinner party. Neither was the idea launched in the complete vacuum that the romantics would have us believe: there already existed a slew of London street maps and atlases, published by, among others, Bacon, Philip's, Bartholomew and her father's old company, Geographia. Phyllis's unique contributions to the genre were to be comprehensive, including every last mews and alley for the very first time, to be bang up to date, to include information such as bus routes and selected house numbers along main roads, and to produce it as a cheap, cheerful, portable option, for most of the rivals were ostentatiously classy and far too large to be popped into a coat pocket or handbag.

None of this is to decry or denigrate the achievements of the amazing Mrs Pearsall. Her gritty determination to honour her family and power her way through almost insurmountable problems is a major inspiration. The company that she founded, Geographers', which changed its name to the Geographers' A–Z Map Company in 1972 in recognition of the universal knowledge of the A–Z brand, has been a pillar of steadiness and good practice in the often cut-throat world of map publishing. This was entirely thanks to Phyllis herself, particularly her decision in 1966 to put all her shares in the company into a trust that would secure the set-up from potential hostile bids, takeovers or mergers in the event of her death. As it was, she lived for a further thirty years, dying just a month before her ninetieth birthday, and still working as the managing director and chairman of the company. Staff of Geographers' A–Z are notoriously loyal, long-serving and very well looked after: 'A family business indeed,' are the concluding words of her eccentric autobiography, 'but the family not by inheritance, but by worth. May God bless the ship and all who sail in her!' Hers *was* a decidedly feminine way of running a map-making business, but spare us the extraneous fluff and schmaltz that has clung to her reputation ever since.

The *A–Z* is the Cinderella of British mapping, a fact that infuriated Phyllis Pearsall throughout her long life. It's hard to see quite why. Perhaps it is down to the unorthodox origins of the company. Perhaps it is thanks to the indomitable, sometimes bizarre, characters of both Phyllis and her father, neither of whom were ever granted access to the British establishment, in cartography or anything else (although the

Royal Geographical Society, from which Alexander had been expelled on his first bankruptcy, finally recognised the family's achievements with an exhibition in 1986 to mark Geographers' half-century). Perhaps it is because the *A–Z* is such a functional map, one to stuff in your back pocket rather than be taken out and admired in company or mounted beautifully on a wall. Despite its ubiquity in the corner shops and bedsits of London, the *A–Z* and Phyllis Pearsall barely ever scrape a mention in academic studies of urban British mapping.

While cartographic snobbery – not a force to be underestimated – undoubtedly plays a part in this, there *is* something curiously lowly about the *A–Z*, especially before it became full colour in the 1990s. Looking at my 1985 copy now, the one I bought on arriving in London for university, the cover has long since detached itself, its monochrome pages have yellowed, a few have fallen out, the corners have turned up, coffee-cup stains pepper the indigestibly packed streets of Archway and Bethnal Green, ancient biro notes, arrows, rendezvous and phone numbers are scribbled throughout like arcane graffiti. I'd sooner mark my own skin than deface an Ordnance Survey map, but the cheap paper and graceless bulk of the *A–Z* seem almost to demand it. It is, to be honest, a bit of a mess: not just the jumbled remnants of my student social life, but the maps themselves. Too busy, too packed, too difficult to read; at eighteen, I loved the chaos of it and hurtled around the city streets like a pinball. At forty-two, it overwhelms me, hurts my eyes and makes me want a lie-down. Of course, I could get the supersized version of the *A–Z*, but that removes the point of having it in the first place, namely its portability and concision. These days, when I go to London, I use a rival street atlas (the AA's) that is far calmer on the eyes and soul. This it achieves by not packing in half as much detail as the *A–Z*: I'd be lost trying to find, for instance, the neighbouring Canning Town streets, so comprehensively labelled by the *A–Z* as Woodstock St, Sabbarton St, Willan Wall and Nelson St, for these appear in the AA atlas as W S, S S, Wl W and Nl St respectively. Many streets are indexed and then given an asterisk to indicate that, 'due to scale restrictions', they're not named on the maps at all. No such infuriating selectivity in the *A–Z*, which manages to squeeze absolutely everything into a book considerably smaller, and about half the weight, of the AA equivalent.

Is there anything identifiably feminine about the cartography of the *A–Z*? Hard to say, especially when you consider its long association with that most blokeish of groups, London's black-cab drivers. If there is, it's in the more nebulous qualities of the atlases, their sheer democracy and classlessness, their refusal to pander to the snobbery and pomposity of the mapping grandees. To that end, the inclusion, for the first time, of bus information and house numbers on long main roads, to stop people getting off the bus at number 40 and finding it's still a mile walk to number 512, could be said to be a female touch, the triumph of common-or-garden practicality over the fancy flourishes for the cognoscenti that were the mainstay of earlier mapping.

There are some maps that could *only* have been designed and executed by women; the finest example I've ever encountered presented itself at the end of a month-long holiday in Thailand a couple of years ago. On our return to Bangkok, we gladly ditched the *Lonely Planet*, which had only taken us to bars and restaurants full of other people frantically combing the same guide. I'd heard of the Nancy Chandler map of the city, which sounded intriguing, and sought one out. Nancy came to Bangkok in 1969, a freewheeling San Fran hippy chick and artist. In the 1970s, she drew and published her first map of the city, to immediate success. Over thirty years later, it's still going strong and has bred numerous imitators, though none with the panache of the original.

As can be seen in the colour section, Nancy's map is phenomenal. It was a whole new way of looking at the city, any city, and it bears all the hallmarks of being dreamed up and drawn by women. Most shockingly to a male map addict, there are seven different maps spread over both sides of a near A1 sheet, and *none of them has a scale*. In terms of area of coverage, the maps range from a plan of Greater Bangkok to a close-up of the Chatuchak weekend market, and you swiftly work out the relative scale of them automatically. Instead of trying to plot your way according to how far in miles or metres one thing is to the next, scale is wholly secondary to landmarks (from major temples to minor cafés) and the relative distance between them. Fantastic, oddball, sometimes funny textual hints and notes plaster the plan, many utterly intriguing and none of them superfluous. Until 2008, all of this was handwritten by Nancy, although it's now done in a computer font that keeps that casual feel. Unusual recommendations, for food, shops and sights, come thick and fast. It works – really works – on an intuitive level, which, in a city as vast and dizzying as Bangkok, is way more useful than any plod-along scale map. I have to admit that my first reaction to it was shock; like the city itself, it is colourful and chaotic, a riot of pink, purple, blue, yellow and green. My partner took to it immediately. When we visit a new city, I'll be struggling with the map, searching for street names in a strange tongue, even a strange alphabet, and getting hopelessly lost, while he quietly plots his way around instinctively and spatially. He has all the natural sense of direction that I lack and it's always him that will find our way back to the car or the station, not me, the *soi-disant* travel writer.

Enthralled by this map that turned pretty much every cartographic convention on its head, yet worked so brilliantly, I contacted Nancy and her daughter, Nima, who now runs the company. Nancy stressed that she had no cartographic training, and that she'd approached the maps more as an artist. But, like Phyllis Pearsall, forty years and six thousand miles away, the main way to plot the city was to walk it, and this she did, as even the maps held in the Bangkok City Map Department were less than wholly accurate. How had the map changed over the three decades? Nima: 'When I started working with my mother on the map, we introduced an index, not only so I could figure out what was on the map (there was, and still is, so very much on it), but also to enable those using it to more easily find what they might be interested in. Of course, I wanted grid lines introduced, but Nancy The Artist insisted they would ruin the artistic appeal of the map, so we compromised by using fold lines as grids. That does make it harder to find things as a single grid may cover a lot of territory, but as Nancy says, "Maybe while looking for one thing, a person will discover something else nearby of interest." It's true. And very much like what happens when exploring cities like Bangkok and Chiang Mai. You can be wandering down a side street, using it as a short cut to somewhere else, when you come across an amazing little antique shop or a quiet peaceful Chinese temple that draws you in.'

I had a hunch that their maps (they also do one of Thailand's second city, Chiang Mai) would appeal to women more than men, and wondered if their sales showed this. 'Yes,' Nima replied. She said that their international distributor once told her that 80 per cent of maps are bought by men, but that 80 per cent of their early customers were women and that, today, their website sales indicate that the figure's still at least 60 per cent. She continued: 'We believe the reason we attract more interest from women is because of the way women think in terms of landmarks and points of interest. Women do have a different way of looking at a city, which is much more landmark oriented than street straight, so to speak. Most men want driving maps (perhaps because they are so hesitant to ask for directions). Men prefer maps with everything perfectly to scale, in colours they are accustomed to, and with only the details they are interested in. Women, however, in our belief, are interested in everything out there, from the little ladies who do "invisible mending" on the sidewalk to where they can take the kids for a fun day out to great little boutiques, cafés and such. There are those who are at first taken aback by the colourful, initially chaotic nature of our maps. Given ten or twenty minutes with one of them, however, and you can see their faces light up as they figure out how it works. Time and time again, especially with men who prefer more plain-colour, street-oriented maps, I've seen them become "true believers"!'

The Chandlers can count me among their true believers. Their map made the massive, sprawling, confusing and occasionally scary city of Bangkok manageable, friendly even. It demystified the chaos, whereas the angular blocks of text, interminable listings and chilly maps of the *Lonely Planet* only exacerbated it. I wasn't in the slightest bit surprised when Nima told me: 'To our amazement, we get five to ten emails or letters a week thanking us for the maps. Who ever would have thought of writing a thank-you letter to a map-maker?' Women, that's who. And very polite gay men.

The image of Nancy Chandler or Phyllis Pearsall pounding the chaotic streets of their respective cities is fabulously inspiring. Although Phyllis's tale has taken on the air of a game of Chinese Whispers, where the eventual story is miles from the original, her early days of mapping London came at a crucial point in her life. She'd just walked out – literally, left him fast asleep in Venice – on her husband of eight years, and she was still only twenty-nine. All her life, she'd been on the move, and was unable, or unwilling, to stop. Walking attentively through the streets of London was perpetual motion for sure, but on a very different scale. Used to big, full-screen images glimpsed at speed, Phyllis was now observing all the minutiae of life in one of the world's truly great cities. She would have seen dockers at dawn, City gents in the rush hour, ladies lunching, kids hurtling through school gates, the drunkards and detritus of the night, obscene poverty and wealth alike, all flashing past as she briskly strode through. The discipline and rhythm of hitting the city streets at five o'clock in the morning and walking, walking, walking well beyond nightfall, seeing the daily billow and sag of a vast metropolis, gave the task a near-spiritual hue. The job was an extended linear meditation.

These days, city walking is a big literary business. I suspect that Phyllis Pearsall, armed with her notebooks, pencils and unwavering discipline to getting a very specific job done, would be bemused to find that her paths have been followed by so many 'gentleman strollers of the city streets' (Baudelaire), the idle *flâneurs* who publish their verbal, sometimes verbose, maps and are hailed as geniuses of psycho-geography. Of course, we have learned much from some of the great exponents of the art, especially in London from the likes of Peter Ackroyd, Iain Sinclair, Will Self and Nick Papadimitriou. At its best, their work riffs off far earlier visionary and occult writing, born in an age when London was ballooning in size and status, casually, some-times cruelly, dominating the nation, an empire and the world. To walk the city, even from the cosy surrounds of the fireside, in the company of Ackroyd or Sinclair is to revel in the connections made, the eye for the rusty and rotting, the sometimes haughty disregard for the over-hyped landmarks, the comprehensive sweep that fuses politics, history and topography through observation and trenchant supposition. The role of the stroller is crucial to all of this, not only because walking is the perfect method of inquisitive locomotion, but also as a way of reclaiming urban spaces, from where the pedestrian was so brutally edged out and marginalised in the immediate post-war years.

Nowhere is it decreed (for it doesn't need to be), but psycho-geography is a something of a boy's sport – or, rather more accurately, a middle-aged man's. There he goes, bustling by in a cloud of Ralgex and stewed tea, armed with a map or two, a bus pass, a waterproof, a camera, a notebook and a rekindled sense of adventure last felt when playing Cowboys and Indians. He knows that, ultimately, his work is ephemeral and unlikely to save or change lives, but still, beneath the jowly surface and air of gruffness, there's the unmistakeable strut of a man on a mission. He layers his investigations with fancy names – deep mapping, deep topography, the *dérive* – as a smokescreen for their inherent ordinariness, for what could be more common sense than a good walk and an enthusiasm for local history, gilded by the chance to be highly opinionated about it?

Is there much difference between the psychogeographer and the stalwart of the local history society? They'd both like to think so: the literary *flâneur* has no time for the pernickety obsessions of those who worry like terriers over the puny bones of their half-dozen streets, while the local historians, as Will Self put it, 'view us as insufferably bogus and travelling – if anywhere at all – right up ourselves'. From an outsider's perspective, however, there are very many cross-overs, not least in the fact that both groups largely comprise men of a certain age. Men of my age, I realise, with a faint shudder.

Either way, psychogeographic wanderings and becoming chairman of the Hither Green History Society *are* mutually dependable occupations, both terribly male and terribly British (yes, I know the French have an illustrious track record in psychogeography, not least having defined it in the first place, and the Americans are getting quite obsessed by it these days, but there is a peculiarly British strain to it that occupies me the most). And both love, collect and spend many long hours with their maps. The greatest difference is humour: a deep map of anywhere needs irony, poetry and a sharp sense of both the ridiculous and the sublime, not qualities generally found among the serried ranks of bank managers in the average local history society. If that sounds harsh, I say it with some considerable, and rather bitter, experience. Having written and presented dozens of 'sense of place' television programmes all around Wales, I soon learned that it wasn't often the best idea to interview in any given location the retired gentleman who'd written the exhaustive book about the village or town we were in, for, whatever the question, he could only regurgitate vast chunks of his bone-dry text, which made for tricky editing and stodgy viewing.

Worse, occasional appearance on the box has meant that I've been buttonholed too many times by men who want to talk to me – no, talk *at* me – for hours about their unbounded enthusiasm for steam trains, steam engines, vintage cars, telegraph poles, village water pumps, milestones, road signs, army bases or phone boxes. One recent experience nearly tipped me over the edge. I was staying the night in a border town, during its annual festival. I'd clocked a poster for a comedy gig, featuring an old mate of mine from my stand-up days of a decade earlier, and thought it would be good to catch up with him again. It was. The gig was great fun, it was a joy to see him and we caught up over a couple of pints in the bar afterwards. He was with the other performers, and, before long, a bevy of young beauties had latched on to us, giggling and fluttering at every utterance from the comedians they'd just been applauding, even according the same flattery to me by dint of association. I'd forgotten that flirty, ego-stiffening aspect to the stand-up gig, surely one of the main reasons so many young men go in for it in the first place.

Out of the corner of my eye, I noticed a man, aged about sixty and dressed entirely in varying shades of beige, bearing down on me. 'You're the telly bloke, aren't you, does them programmes about local history?' 'Er, sort of,' I demurred. He ploughed on regardless. 'You know much about the old mines? I've been down every old mine shaft in this county. There's waterwheels and everything down there. Where were you last week on your programme? Ceredigion? You been to the lead mines in Cwmystwyth?' And on. And on. As it was quite noisy, he leant into me and blasted me with a deadly cocktail of tedium and halitosis about all the old mine shafts he'd ever explored. There was absolutely no escape; he was practically pinning me to the bar. I looked up to see my comedian mate give me a thumbs up and a wink as he prepared to leave with his gaggle of groupies, and watched as my carefree old life trilled and tittered its way out of the door, before wrenching myself back to my new life, which was still delivering a monologue about the joys of old mine shafts some six inches from my face. Perhaps he's fallen down one by now; you can but hope.

One of the most inventive of psychogeographers is anarchic polymath Bill Drummond. It is, seemingly, the law of the land to follow up any mention of him with the description 'the man who burned a million quid', referring to that famously cupid stunt that saw him and Jimmy Cauty incinerate a large chunk of the money that had been culled from their short, but glorious, career as the KLF. Drummond's speciality is drawing shapes or words on maps, and then walking them. As manager of Echo and the Bunnymen, he sent the band off on a tour of remote outposts, such as the Outer Hebrides and Iceland. 'It's not random,' he explained. 'If you look at a map of the world, the whole tour's in the shape of a rabbit's ears.' He employed the same idea for the 1984 Bunnymen-themed day of activity in Liverpool that Channel 4 filmed for a special of *The Tube*. Hundreds of Bunnymen fans were packed off on a bike ride, again following the shape of a rabbit that Drummond had drawn on a city map. A manhole cover at the bottom of Mathew Street, home of the Cavern Club, served as the rabbit's navel, the omphalos of the city's grandiloquent rock 'n' roll myth-making. Best, and blokiest, of all have been his cartographic equivalents of pissing in the snow: writing his name, BILL, in big letters across various maps and then walking them out on the ground. The rock-star ego collides with the quiet conjuring of the urban witch. I haven't yet tried it with MIKE, but I know that one day I will.

It's something of a relief to find that there is a cross-over, however apparently slight, between map addiction and the scuzzy excesses of rock 'n' roll. Maps may well be imbued with the spirit of 'Enid Blyton, Radio 4 and the National Trust', as the Product Manager from the Ordnance Survey had so elegantly put it, but they can tickle our primal urges too if we let them. There are many punks, rockers and rappers whose art is imbued with a map sensibility; who have employed real and fictional maps as cover imagery, talked about them directly in their lyrics and titles, or used them to demonstrate a profound sense of place. Mirroring my terror that map adoration may mean a swift descent into bombast and bigotry goes the worry that, in music-meets-maps terms, the ground would largely be occupied by prog-rock dinosaurs who fried their tiny minds over King Arthur and Stonehenge in the 1970s, leaving only enough brain cells to become celebrity spokesmen for UKIP. You just know that their home studio walls are adorned with a few first-edition antique maps, probably with the exorbitant price tag still prominently attached. Thankfully, they're far from the only ones on the hallowed turf. If those grizzly old Spinal Tappers are the ten-thousand-quid showboat maps, then legends like Bill Drummond, his arch-nemesis Julian Cope, Andy Partridge, Nick Drake and Robert Plant are battered, much-used Ordnance Surveys, Neil Hannon of The Divine Comedy, Damon Albarn and Luke Haines (particularly in his Black Box Recorder days) are leather-bound road atlases with a golden silk bookmark, while Ray Davies, Morrissey, Mike Skinner of The Streets and Jarvis Cocker are A–Zs of London, Manchester (De-Luxe Edition), Birmingham and Sheffield respectively.

Anarchy meets pedantry in music, in maps and in any other pursuit that gets gentlemen a little sweaty and excited. It's all part of our faintly autistic desire to structure the world around us so that it fits, to collect, order, categorise and alphabetise our chosen obsessions. This is why the happiest men are those that can make their living out of their favourite hobbies, for that gives them carte blanche to be as picky and pernickety as they like: it's all research, it's all useful, it's all tax deductible and it's all good for business. At least, that's what they tell their wives and partners as they vanish into some obscure corner of cyberspace to nail down a rarity or plunge into a three-hour geekfest discussion. Women, I think, appreciate maps just as much as men. Many are just as good at reading them as we are. They see them as a practical, useful tool with only an occasional patina of aesthetic or emotional appeal. We love them like our brothers; rather more, in fact. *Vive la différence.*

A recent sign demanding that you ignore your satnav. My sentiments entirely

9. PRATNAV

The Doncaster man who slavishly followed his satnav to the edge of a West Yorkshire cliff has been fined nearly £1000 for driving without due care and attention.

Robert Jones, who drives for a living, said: 'It kept insisting the path was a road even as it was getting narrower and steeper so I just trusted it. You don't expect to be taken nearly over a cliff.'

One local witness commented: 'It's like something from *The Italian Job*, but what a waste of police time. It's all very well and good trusting your satnav, but how about trusting your eyes?'

~ *Daily Express* (September 2009)

A damp, dreary day in Merthyr Tydfil. There aren't many other kinds of day in Merthyr, especially in October. I'm sat in my camper van in the world's most unprepossessing lay-by, just off a busy, noisy junction of the A470. It's not the sort of lay-by that inspires cracking open a beer and a pork pie as you soak in the view; it rather more suggests killing someone, quite possibly yourself. As ever, I'm waiting for the walkie-talkie to burst into life – *We're ready!* – to tell me that the camera crew are in position to film me lumbering past, just one more drive-by shot in the 500-piece jigsaw of shots that we must finish in three short days to produce another episode of my round-Wales-with-my-dog-in-a-camper-van TV series. I'd wanted to call the series *Camper Cymru* (pun fully intended). That was disallowed, not because of the weak double entendre, but because the word *Cymru* might put viewers off, make them think that the series was in the Welsh language, despite being on ITV, just after *Emmerdale*. So I've been saddled with *Great Welsh Roads* as a title. This is not one of them.

The minutes drag by. The walkie-talkie remains stubbornly silent. Surely to God, they haven't got lost again? It's something of a hindrance trying to film travelogues with colleagues who, for all their many fabulous and redeeming qualities, have neither any sense of direction nor ability to read a map. Every time I wave them off to set up somewhere for a shot of me trundling towards or away from them, I get a sinking feeling in my guts that I might not see them again for hours. Usually, they get most spectacularly lost just at the point where the walkie-talkie range has vanished, along with the signal on everybody's mobiles. At least – and this is pretty much the sole advantage of being on the outskirts of Merthyr – there's a steady five bars on my phone.

A flash sports car pulls up alongside. From within, a man and a woman stare at me with a slightly scary ferocity. What do they want? Is it a drive-by shooting? Aggressively proactive dogging? They signal me to wind my window down, which I do, reluctantly. The dog starts to growl behind me.

''Ere, mate,' says the man, in pure Estuary, as he cranes over the woman in the passenger seat. 'Which bit o' Cardiff is this?'

'It's not Cardiff,' I reply. 'It's Merthyr. Merthyr Tydfil.'

'Nah, mate, it's Cardiff. Satnav says so. Which way's the centre?'

'Honest, it's not Cardiff. This is Merthyr. Cardiff's twenty-five miles down the road. That way.' I point vaguely and, I hope, helpfully.

'That's bollocks!' he explodes. She nods. 'It's all the same down 'ere anyway, innit? This is Cardiff, innit? Satnav says so.'

'Well ask your bloody satnav then.' I gracelessly wind the window back up and realise that they are now glaring very hard. Oh shit. I really don't fancy being the first statistic of Satnav Rage.

The walkie-talkie erupts into life – *OK Mike, we're ready for you.* Thank God for that. I kangaroo hop out of the lay-by and leave them in a cloud of blue diesel smoke.

⚠

I despise satnavs. I tried hard not to, because I didn't want to mark myself quite so obviously as a crusty old Luddite, but my God, they really are a loathsome invention. When I go in friends' cars, and they reach to turn on the satnav, it takes every shred of self-control not to rip the thing out of their hands and beat them to a bloody pulp with a road atlas. When these devices first appeared on the scene, I started with a fairly open mind, intrigued by the idea of a moving map on your dashboard and all of the possibilities that could entail. A neighbour, always keen on the latest gadget, had invested in one and proudly showed it off to me one evening. We walked it around the village, and the little screen kept changing, an arrow flashing on our exact position. I was quietly impressed, and even thinking of getting one.

Then I saw them in action, and the admiration quickly turned to loathing. As an experiment, I borrowed my neighbour's device one day when I had to go and meet someone about forty miles away, on the other side of Montgomeryshire. I left the map at home, and entrusted myself instead to the monotone instructions. Of course, I had a vague idea in my head as to which route I'd take, but before long Sally, the satnav voice, had veered from that and ordered me down a side road. OK, I thought, this is an alternative route; could be interesting. Suspend all critical thinking – a seemingly automatic process for satnav users – and let Sally do the work. We burrowed further into high-hedged country lanes, through villages I'd never heard of and in what I felt sure was the wrong direction. Sally smoothly assured me otherwise, and, more fool me, I believed her. We reached a bridge over a tiny stream, and she let out a contented sigh: 'You have arrived at your destination.' 'No, I bloody haven't!' I shouted back at her. 'We're in the middle of sodding nowhere!' Sally, not used to being talked to like that, gave me the silent treatment.

Because I'd been idiot enough not to bring the map with me, I had absolutely no clue as to where she'd dumped me. Remembering a farmhouse about half a mile back down the lane, I executed an awkward seven-point turn and headed there. It felt like the beginning of a particularly poor horror movie to knock on a remote farm door and blurt out: 'Sorry, but could you tell me where I am?' as the opening gambit. Luckily, the farmer thought it was hilarious and soon put me on the right road (not, incidentally, the one grumpy Sally was taking me down). I was a full six miles from where I was supposed to be, and arrived for my rendezvous very late and fuming. Back in my village, the satnav's owner shook his head in wonder when I returned it and told him the story. 'Never given me any trouble,' he said. One wet night a few months later, Sally told him to turn right somewhere near Warrington. He obeyed and then found himself going south on the northbound carriageway of a – thankfully fairly quiet – motorway. Swiftly realising the mistake, he tugged the car on to the hard shoulder and sat there panting for a few heart-stopping moments, the headlights of the oncoming cars screaming past just inches away. Dazzled and dazed, he didn't notice the coloured flashing lights that were also bearing down on him at speed, and suddenly found a police vehicle had pulled up behind him. He got an enormous bollocking, a fine, three points and a whole load of new grey hairs. And he's *still* seeing her.

Over the next couple of years, my hatred of satnavs congealed like sour milk. With only one exception that I can remember, every time I've been in a vehicle under their control, something has gone wrong. And every day seemed to bring yet another of those stories about ambulances going hundreds of miles out of their way, or lorries getting wedged in farm tracks, stuck under bridges or teetering on cliff edges, all thanks to the blind adherence of drivers to an electronic brain, instead of giving their own a bit of a polish. Obviously, I giggled like a schoolgirl at every one of these stories, none more so than the one, in March 2007, of the posh bird who drove her £96,000 Mercedes into a swollen Leicestershire river, because 'Satnav said so'. She was rescued in the nick of time, and driven by a villager to a nearby motorway service station, where a chauffer-driven Bentley arrived to speed her on her way. The Merc sat in the river for a week, before being towed out and written off. The reason that this story, above the countless others, is worthy of being carved in stone is simple. It is the most poetic satnav mishap yet, for the river was called the Sense, and the village Sheepy Magna. I'm guessing that that's Latin for 'big, dull sheep that follows without questioning'.

Satnavs are one more gadget to disempower us, to turn us into mindless jelly brains that cannot take any responsibility for ourselves, and don't see why we should have to. It's one more nagging computerised voice humming like a hornet in our ears, one more screen in lives that are already dominated by them at home, at work, in the pub, in the street, by the bed, in shops and stations, on buses and trains, for business, for leisure and for love. And if they seem prone to nagging on the occasional car journey, I can't imagine how anyone who drives for a living copes with them. It's much worse for them, as the nag in the cab is also having a good snoop; tracking technology is used on most professional drivers these days, as they hurtle around trying to keep to an impossible timetable. Every satnav-accompanied journey I've been on has massively underestimated the time it takes to get anywhere. Have twenty even slight underestimations in one day, and things will start to unravel, your sanity first. Perhaps the only way to keep to their unrealistic timetable is to drive like a maniac, tailgate everyone in front of you and do some spectacularly dangerous overtaking. For there always seems to be the latest, top-of-the-range satnav on the dashboard of anyone I ever see driving like that.

And what are they doing to our spatial awareness and sense of geography? A satnav only ever shows you the next short stretch of road;

plenty of people admit that they've no idea of where their journey has actually taken them – if you asked them to show you on the map, they'd shrug and look away. Bridgewater could be next to Bradford, King's Lynn a suburb of Liverpool, for all they know. And, worse, for all they care. In fairness, the country that satnavs steer them through isn't really worth knowing anyway, for it's just the next mile of roads and junctions, traffic lights, speed cameras, petrol stations and contraflow systems that make an appearance: the nation boiled down to its least uplifting features. Not that satnavs can entirely be blamed for that, as they are merely the latest in a long continuum of maps that denude our geography of its blips and bumps, its warts of history and character. This is a process that has been going on apace ever since road atlases made their first appearance, and has accelerated through the last fifty years of obsession with motorways as the only way to travel. The satnav and the motorway are perfect companions, promoting driving not travelling, anger and frustration instead of wonder and excitement. It's no coincidence that the first midwives of the motorway were Hitler and Mussolini.

⚠

In 2008, the British Cartographic Society (BCS) launched a surprise counter-attack with their pronouncement that the relentless march of online maps and satnavs was rendering historical landmarks invisible: features such as churches, ancient woodlands and old buildings that help us understand a landscape. The then BCS president, Mary Spence, found herself whisked between various TV studios to make her case, which also contained dark warnings that the teaching of map-reading was disappearing from schools, and that 'the consequence will be long-term damage to future generations of map-readers'.

She continued, saying how 'corporate cartographers are demolishing thousands of years of history – not to mention Britain's remarkable geography – at a stroke, by not including them on maps', particularly singling out the ubiquitous Google maps for criticism. Using Tewkesbury in Gloucestershire as an example, she compared the Ordnance Survey's portrait of the town with Google's version. On the OS 1:50 000, features include the lovely Norman abbey, the site of a 1471 battle, a prehistoric mound called Margaret's Camp, two museums, the River Swilgate, a tourist office, various churches, the hospital, the council offices, a weir, some mills and marinas, an assortment of footpaths, a school, the cemetery, a disused railway, a golf course, two campsites and a picnic area. If you print off the Google map, even at the highest resolution, the only feature marked aside from road names is the Tewkesbury Park Hotel Golf and Country Club. 'There is just a hole where the abbey is,' said Ms Spence. 'This is tragic. They call this a map but it is so inadequate. It has not been interpreted in any way. It has no landmarks on it.' The previous morning, she said, she had walked to the Royal Geographical Society in South Kensington along Exhibition Road, home to the Natural History Museum, the Science Museum and the V&A; none were shown on the Google map of the area.

She was supported as a prophet and pilloried as a throwback in almost equal measure. The BBC ran one of their online 'Have Your Say' debates in response to the BCS complaints, and it was as full of illumination and wisdom as ever. I have to confess to a slight addiction to 'Have Your Say' (HYS to the cognoscenti); not as a contributor, but as a wide-eyed reader of the venom and warped logic that it so magnificently showcases every day. Of course, this is the same for any internet forum, each one a watering hole for all the braggarts, bullies and bullshitters of our world to parade their flimsy knowledge of any given topic, but the BBC version seems to be a magnet for some of the finest of the breed. When I'm working at home and the pace flags or ennui descends, ten minutes in the wacky world of HYS almost always does the trick in restoring my bounce. And the 'maps versus satnav' debate was every bit as hilarious as I could have hoped.

There are often thousands of contributions, so the best way to see where the wind is blowing is by ordering them according to which ones have received the greatest number of Readers' Recommendations. Of the top five most recommended, two ploughed a much-grooved HYS furrow:

How long will it be before the location of every Mosque in England is included on maps? boomed a regular klaxon of the boards, always able to twist any debate into a fulsome rant against Islam. This was the second most recommended contribution from among the thousands. Another poster (nom de plume 'angry man', in case you were in any doubt) disappeared up the same mental cul-de-sac with a contribution that attracted hundreds of recommendations: *Has anyone ever produced a map with 'old building' being depicted? Buildings are like ladies (an endangered species in this day and age). So one should not speak openly of their age, simply muse and wonder. This is like saying philatelist's* [sic] *weep every time I post a letter of complaint about the taste of the glue on stamps these days. It may have escaped the British Cartographic Society attention but there appears to be Holy war on the go. So it maybe just prudent not to list Churches on maps.*

It's not just the Islamaphobes spewing their spleen on to their keyboards; on absolutely any given topic, there's a queue of myopic malcontents determined to yoke their particular obsession to the debate. That catch-all Political Correctness *Gone Mad!* is always a dependable one:

I'd be more concerned about Political Correctness destroying our history and culture than a certain type of map. Plus the appalingly [sic] *bad quality of TV programming that fills peoples* [more sic] *heads.* Thank you, Mr D of Woking, and the couple of dozen people who voted for the sagacity of your contribution. Worryingly, even more thought this dribbling hooey worthy of a thumbs up: *The people wiping out history of PC idealists who decide that teaching kids about British chrisitan* [sic] *history may offend minority religious groups, or British military history will offend foreigners, or things like the industrial revolution will offend socialists and marxists.*

Even among those who managed to remember what the topic in hand actually was, one of the most popular declarations came from 'a serving Rayal [sic] Navy officer': *Sat navs are for people who are being dumbed down by the chav culture.* Attracting far fewer votes but voicing rather greater wisdom, Jonathan Fox of Manchester: *I don't see what the problem is? I can download points of interest to my Sat Nav. I can view the location I am interested in from any perspective and in 3 dimensions. I can get additional data of a location with the use of wikipedia markers on the map and there are often accompanying photos. This is far superior to maps of old. OS and the British Cartographic Society restricted the use of their maps by the use of copyright. They should innovate instead of complaining. Tough Luck!*

Good points all by Mr Fox, but entirely dependent on that old maxim – the downfall of many of us – that any piece of technology is only as good as the idiot operating it. Mary Spence's warning was about the disappearance of fundamental data from the base line of our most generally used cartography. Yes, you *could* overlay your satnav or your online map with the most phenomenal level of detail, be it fifteenth-century, and *only* fifteenth-century, churches, stone circles or Conservative Clubs. But only if you knew how, had sourced the information online and actively bothered to call the information up. The chance encounter with something remarkable is the casualty of such bespoke choice, and that is to lose one of a map's greatest qualities.

Mary Spence's comparison of the difference in detail between the OS and Google maps of Tewkesbury highlights this point to perfection, although you'll find much the same yawning gap anywhere. Ed Parsons, geospatial technologist at Google, retorts: 'These traditional landmarks are still on the map but people need to search for them. Interactive maps will display precisely the information people want, when they want it. You couldn't possibly have everything already pinpointed.' But you will, of course, have the Tewkesbury Park Hotel Golf and Country Club flagged large, whether you called it up or not. That's what makes me feel quite queasy about this new generation of mapping; its relentless tilt towards what Mary Spence calls 'corporate blankwash', the emphasis of the bland and businesslike over anything else.

We can be too shrill about this, for sure. There are millions of people who never look at maps other than the ones on their mobile, computer screen or satnav, but then they wouldn't have been poring over Ordnance Surveys twenty years ago either. They'd have been using a three-quid road atlas and studiously ignoring all the marked abbeys, museums and other things that get the rest of us a little hot under our Barbour collars. Google maps may be filleted of all the things that, to us, make life interesting, but they're not really pretending to do anything else. And they do have a quite significant ace up their sleeve, in that just one click of the mouse will give you the most stunning aerial views of pretty much anywhere on Earth, plus a basic road map to go with it. In any case, we are only in the very early stages of the digital-map revolution. They will continue to innovate and improve, as must we all. One day, I hope to be able to customise an online map with layers showing pubs from the CAMRA guide, second-hand book-shops, Indian restaurants, National Trust properties, lakes you can swim in, a majority of Welsh speakers, optimum sunshine hours and nudist beaches. If anywhere combines the lot, I'm moving there.

⚠

While it's going to take a knock on the head for me to love satnavs, especially as they're predicted to be programmed with even greater amounts of busybody nagging, when it comes to maps on the internet I need no such persuasion: the possibilities are endless and terrifically exciting. When I feel myself getting grumpy about the soulless, corpo-rate maps online, or the internet sucking the surprise out of so many areas of life, I picture myself as a seven-year-old, craning his neck up to the delicious rows of Ordnance Surveys in the local library, and wonder what he would have made of it all. Or my grandfather, a mathematician and irascible polymath, who had his first go on a computer – my hulking tank of a thing, a glorified typewriter with a disk drive that took two people to lift – only a week before he died, and dissolved into wide-eyed, almost giggly wonder at its potential.

As with all things computer-related, there is an inevitable amount of the Emperor's new clothes about online mapping. Applications are given fancy names and sexy descriptions, which then transpire to be little more than the cyberspace version of colouring in a map with a set of felt-tip pens. At least I had the decency to keep the ones I did as a map brat to myself. 'Mashups' is the big new word in web-based mapping: stick your data on to a Google map, jiggle it around a bit, dapple it with a few colours and pop-up text boxes or pictures before hyping it into cyberspace as something new and funky. Some really are: fascinating and imaginative ways of processing information, they bring an idea or story to life far quicker – and so much more beautifully – than any other. All too often, though, mashups are just like the rest of the internet, in that they're all mouth and no trousers, incontinent egomania, electronic autism or vigilante paranoia.

There is – and this is something facing many of us – all too great a danger that our sworn affection for the paper map may become an unhealthy inability to cope with anything that has a plug on the end of it. That cannot be good. As many of these chapters have led me to conclude, there exists a strain of map addiction that starts to tip over into something quite alarming, be it obsessive pettiness and pedantry, a glowering suburban fascism, an all-consuming nostalgia for unspecific 'old days' or, quite likely, a rancid mixture of them all.

Take, for example, a publishing company that specialises in books on local and railway history, churning out dozens of worthy tomes that can doubtless be found on many the same bookshelf as a well-worn

OS collection. Its big boast is that it has never yet used digital technology in any way, and has no intention of doing so in the future, as if to do so was somehow to climb into bed with the devil himself. Even to make an issue out of it, as this company does, suggests that it's some kind of badge of pride (homemade, of course, probably with one of those kits from the 1970s that gives you a badge that's ugly, badly cut out and the size of a saucer). Digital technology and desk-top publishing in books! Whatever next?

What map addict could possibly fail to be enthralled by the access we now have to most of the world's great map libraries, these days just a click or two away? Or the ability to look in detail at every kind of mapping product – paper sheets included – on the exhaustive websites of the many different cartographic companies in just about every country on the planet? Or the scores of tantalising blogs and fan sites that bring absolutely every kind of map, from political to joke, from two hours or five hundred years ago, to our attention? In researching this book, I've been lucky enough to talk with dozens of fascinating map experts and addicts, some in person, some on the phone, some via email. The fact that I've been able to find them so easily has all been thanks to the internet; it is helping forge a far more democratic community of cartographers and map enthusiasts than the elitist conservatism of only thirty years ago. It's the long-awaited, slow-burning victory of the amateur geek.

⚠

Just as the second-most-bullied kid in the playground is likely to be the one most fiercely kicking the crap out of the only one beneath him in the pecking order, so I joined in with the sneering at a former colleague who, when he got a little tiddly at someone's leaving party, invited us all to challenge him on his knowledge of British postcodes. We could give him a town, and he would fire back with its first few postcode digits. Alternatively, we could throw him a TD12, a PO8 or a B91 and he would instantly come back with its location (Coldstream,

Waterlooville and Solihull, in case you're interested, and I suspect you might be). This was twenty years ago, before such things could be found instantly on a million websites, so we could only draw the conclusion that he spent long winter evenings with the Royal Mail postcode directory as his sole companion.

I was, of course, sneakily very impressed, and would sidle quietly up to him in the office kitchen for months afterwards, trying in vain to catch him out with an obscure Scottish postcode, but I don't remember him ever failing in the task. Had he been around a hundred years earlier, he would have been cheered to the rafters in numerous variety theatres ('The Great Postcodio'), sandwiched between a sword swallower and a Pearly Queen, but the modern age condemned him only to audiences of disdainful, drunken workmates. Duncan, I'm sorry. You are a hero.

Since they were first introduced in a trial scheme in Norwich in 1959, postcodes have quietly wormed into every area of our lives. After we've pressed 2, 6, 1, the hash button and 2 again, and waited thirteen minutes while we're told how important our call is, details of our post-code is one of the first things any call centre will want to know. We're telling them more than we perhaps realise. A year or so ago, I caught a fascinating programme on Radio 4 about the humble postcode's ubiquity, and how it was increasingly used to define our perceived needs, shopping habits, government services and profile. In order to target sales, marketing companies split us all into eleven groups, further divided into sixty-one categories, according to our code. 'Motorway Magnets' go to garden centres, read the *Daily Mail* and are likely to say 'junction 7 of the M4' when they're asked where they live; 'City Adventurers', in their converted inner-city loft apartments, have stripped wooden floors and the latest KitchenAid Artisan food mixer; 'Global Connectors' are largely foreign, live in Chelsea or Kensington, read the *FT* and have yachts; 'British-born Asian Entrepreneurs' live in Tudorbethan houses in a doughnut around London, particularly to the north and east. On the radio programme, I was mildly alarmed to hear my postcode area mentioned in the context that we're all written off as 'Rural Isolationists'. What do we get? Gun catalogues and promotional offers on Kenny Rogers CDs?

By the early 1990s, Britain was thoroughly used to its postcodes – gone were the days I remember in the 1970s when elderly relatives would scratch it on to an envelope with as much concentration as if they were copying out the Chinese alphabet. A whole generation had grown up with postcodes as second nature, an integral part of their identity even, and the High Street started to reflect that. I remember first noticing the trend in Liverpool in about 1992, although with the local phone code, rather than postcode: T-shirts emblazoned with a huge 051. Clever, I thought. As with most smart ideas, it was quickly done to death, with phone codes plastering clothes and even as a name for bars, shops and things like taxi services. But then in 1995, British Telecom decided to slide a 1 in after the initial 0, and 0121 or 0141 didn't look quite as cool or classy. The postcode's moment had arrived: aspirational bars and meat-market nightclubs sprang up everywhere, from NW3 to BT1. Sporting your postcode as a name only really works in either a main post town that can use xx1, or a specific city code with some cachet (such as M20 for Didsbury in Manchester or W11 for Notting Hill). On that basis, and on very many others, the DY10 night-club in Kidderminster, so proud of being in the tenth division of the Dudley postcode, doesn't quite make the grade.

⚠

While we go drinking in our local postcode, wear it on our chests and tap it into our satnavs to get anywhere, our neighbours in the Republic of Ireland miss out on all the fun. Ireland and Albania are the only countries in Europe without postcodes. In fact, Ireland's address system is enough to make a British über-nostalgist weep, for not only are there no codes, they've not changed their thirty-two counties since 1606. Until the early 2000s, lacking a postcode was something of which people in Ireland were generally quietly proud, and boasted how they weren't bombarded so easily by junk mail as us on this side of the water. It also helped cement Ireland's self-image and reputation as a place that took life at a rather more leisurely pace; the communications equivalent of letting your Guinness settle properly.

Such old-fashioned values won't work on your satnav or online map, however: punching in a road name, when the road can be at least a couple of miles long, renders electronic mapping almost redundant. While this was annoying enough for individual users, it was causing massive problems for delivery and despatch companies, whose vans, on the strictest of schedules, could be seen lost in the lanes of rural Ireland on a daily basis. With the sharp rise in online shopping, this was fast becoming a major headache. Worse, ambulances and fire engines were vanishing into the ether too. The problem was only exacerbated by the use of traditional townland names in Irish addresses: these sometimes cover a vast area and can have many duplicate addresses under the one umbrella. That works just fine when the only person having to navigate their way through the minefield is the postman who knows every scattered customer on his round, but for anyone else, it's impossible.

In 2005, disquiet had swelled to such a level that the government had little choice but to announce their intention of creating a national postcode system, promising to bring it in by 2008. Reviews and reports were commissioned, experts consulted, while the press and internet boards speculated as to what sort of system might be brought in. Then silence, the whole thing quietly shelved. The main obstacles seem to have come from the state's postal agency, An Post, well aware that the EU is demanding the opening up of government agencies to private competition by 2010; An Post's greatest commercial asset is its intimate knowledge of the idiosyncratic Irish system and it simply did not want to hand too much useful ammunition to potential rivals. Also helping to scupper the plans were disagreements over what kind of postcode system was needed, the fear of losing the traditional town-land names, and the global credit crisis, which has left the Irish government coffers in a perilous state.

'An Irish solution to an Irish problem' is something of a well-worn maxim, but it's ridden to the rescue yet again. Frustrated with the delays, one man decided to create his own postcode system for the whole country. With a background in marine and satellite navigation, Gary Delaney worked out a system based on geographical coordinates that gives every property a unique code, specific to within six metres – unlike the British postcode, which can group a dozen or more addresses together, sometimes significant distances apart. In June 2008, he launched the project online to considerable acclaim and has struck a deal with a satnav company to include his data in their systems. The alphanumeric Position Orientated Navigation Codes (or PONC, pronounced 'punk' and the Irish word for 'point') have been taken up with huge enthusiasm by mapping websites, couriers and many individual users. There's the distinct possibility that the government may well adopt Gary's system as the official one, as it will save it a vast amount of time, trouble and expense. For politicians, it's a guaranteed win-win: they get a ready-made system at a knock-down price, and if anyone doesn't like it (and you can guarantee that there will be plenty), then it wasn't their doing.

⚠

People complained when maps started to get too technical and topographic, rather than expressive and essentially subjective. They grumbled at the imposition of contours, then grid lines, at the loss of antiquarian data, boundaries and isobaths, at new names, old names, different typefaces, too much detail, too little detail, colour shading and cover shots. Now that cartography is poised on the cusp of its greatest revolution for five hundred years, the voices of doom have swollen to deafening proportions, and their biggest terror is that we are breeding a generation who will not get the same chance that we had to become map addicts, that we are the last of a dying breed. Could that terror be masking the real fear – that those following us are going to be so much better equipped than we've ever been to make maps do what they want and need? That actually, it's we, not they, who are going to be the poorer in the equation?

I can't begin to imagine how exciting most schools would be these days for an aspiring map addict. Good teaching using the best of new, and old, technology would be absolute dynamite in a receptive young mind, and the extra stuff you could find out for yourself would take it to levels of excitement and enthusiasm that we couldn't have dreamed of. According to Jonathan Breckon, spokesman for the Royal Geographical Society, schoolchildren are still taught map-reading (they've got their free OS to play with, for starters), but also get introduced to data presented digitally – and they love it, and have minds that are sufficiently elastic to take it all. 'Geographic Information Systems [GIS] have revolutionised geography in schools,' he says. 'Teachers have found that they bring the classroom alive. Maps can be beautiful in a way that information on a screen can never be, but there is no question that technology has the wow factor. When we do courses on Google Earth, they sell out completely. One of the advantages is the sheer quantity of information you can show on screen, and the fact that you can zoom in at different levels. You can track panthers in Africa using satellite navigation.'

He does sound a warning note, however, that will keep on board the addicts of paper maps (or 'dead-tree maps' as the cyber-evangelists disparage them on numerous breathless blogs). 'You'd be bonkers to rely on Global Positioning Systems completely. Power fails, technology fails, and it's controlled by the US military.' It's not an either/or, an artificial scrap between the paper maps and their electronic upstart siblings. In the glorious world of map addiction, whether we're fifteen or fifty, we *can* have it all. Though I'll still pass on the satnav, thank you.

Llyn Cau, Cadair Idris

10. GOING OFF-MAP

> For weeks, I had studied maps, large-scale and small, but maps are not reality at all – they can be tyrants. I know people who are so immersed in road maps that they never see the countryside they pass through, and others who, having traced a route, are held to it as though held by flanged wheels to rails.
> ~ John Steinbeck, *Travels with Charley*

At the beginning of Chapter 1, I wrote about the gulf between the British way of interaction with its landscape, and that of the Americans and the Australians. They have their wild west, their outback, their boondocks, their deserts: places vast and unknowable that demand lengthy pilgrimages and absolute respect. We, on the other hand, have signposted nature trails and the Ramblers, national parks and the National Trust, Sunday outings and Millets waterproofs. Our landscape, like our maps, is tidy, parcelled, thorough. We don't do wilderness.

Since writing that, I've read Robert Macfarlane's magisterial odyssey *The Wild Places*, where the disgustingly young and talented author treks around these islands ('the archipelago' as he likes to call them) in search of the truly wild. He finds plenty of it, and not always in the obvious places. On every page, Macfarlane is clambering up trees, slipping shamanically into lochs in the dead of winter and rolling out his bivouac bag for a night's kip on top of a Scottish mountain or in a Cumbrian snowdrift. The lightness of his touch on the landscape is perfectly mirrored in the light, luminous prose with which he tells us of his travels. As I read, I couldn't quite decide whether to love him or loathe him (the dust-jacket photo persuaded me towards the former).

I've travelled many of the same roads and tracks as Robert Macfarlane, criss-crossed the archipelago dozens of times for scores of reasons. Yet his instinctive, elemental interaction with the landscape is an ideal that I fall far short of, and the question wouldn't leave me as I read: *Was it because I was just too much of a map addict?* Macfarlane discusses maps on many occasions in *The Wild Places*; he is evidently as dotty about them as any of us, but they are to him mere bit players in his adventures. The splendours of deep nature always come first. I began to marvel at the menageries of wild creatures that seemed to cosy up to Macfarlane at every stage of his odyssey. Hares and hawks – his totem animals – are forever peering around rocks, hopping through heather or soaring overhead and serenading him. Where were they on my many walks, I wondered, a little sorely. I see the odd hare, have had a few intoxicating one-to-ones with wild deer and was once sung to by a red kite (it has a strangely squeaky sound that belies its savage bulk and vicious talons; it reminded me of Julie Burchill), but that's about it. Then it hit me. A husk of snow-white hares could be doing a conga through the bracken right in front of me, and I probably wouldn't notice, as chances are I'll either be hidden behind the map or furiously consulting the internal one, like the screen on the back of an aeroplane seat, that shows my current position. I'm too blinded by the fake representation of the world to see the real thing properly.

Has map addiction skewed my view of the countryside? I'm afraid it probably has. Maps are methodical little worlds, the rough and ragged landscape tidied up into blocks of uniform colour and sweetly functional symbols. They breathe rules and order in an inherently disorderly world. I guiltily recalled the hundreds of walks that I've spoiled for myself and others by getting in a complete fluster over the map, because we've gone slightly out of our way, or reached an unexpected impasse. The map tells me where the permitted routes are, and if I fall off them, I feel as nervous as a child waiting to be shouted at. My temples throb, sweat begins to drip, flies swarm over me, my coordination goes and the whole supposedly relaxing experience begins to take on a nightmarish tinge – especially for those poor buggers accompanying me. I can't imagine Robert bloody Macfarlane ever acting like such a prize idiot. He glides through the landscape like a sinewy ghost, while I puff and pant, red-faced, through it, terrified that I might be going the wrong way. Wrong? Is the word even in Macfarlane's strapping great vocabulary?

The most Macfarlanesque thing I've ever done is spend a night alone with my dog on the summit of Cadair Idris. That took more puffing, panting and throbbing temples than even I thought I was capable of. It was one of those ideas that comes out of nowhere to whisper in your ear, and once the whisper is heard, there is no getting out of it, however much you wriggle. The whisper came a month or two before I was to move into the house in which I still live; my perhaps overdue, and rather precarious, launch on to the property ladder. It felt like a commitment in a way that renting somewhere new never had; I was acting on pure instinct and I desperately wanted it to work.

The house is in a small village that lies immediately south of the massif of Cadair Idris; the mountain commands the valley, dictates our weather, light and mood. It is the guv'nor. As with all mountains, and especially Welsh mountains, there are innumerable legends and lore associated with Cadair, but the most enduring is that if you spend a night on the summit (some versions have specific nights, in others it doesn't seem to matter), you will either go mad or become a poet. Some versions add death as a third option, and in my head I pictured the odds like a curious board game – three equal wedges of colour making up a circle, and a pointer in the middle to spin and decide my fate. Even with only a third of the circle promising something desirable (although who can slide a cigarette paper between poetry and madness?), the whisper told me very clearly that I needed to go and pay my respects to the guv'nor, overnight, before moving into my new home. Contracts would be exchanged in early November, so, said the whisper, Hallowe'en is your night. Hallowe'en, Samhain, Calan Gaeaf, the night in which the veils between the worlds briefly thin or part and the spirits of the dead travel freely: just the night to spend alone on top of a three-thousand-foot mountain. And – ooh, look – it'll be a full moon to boot. The whisper became a roar, and try as I might, it wasn't shifting.

I'd climbed Cadair before, so decided to minimise the potential map fluster by going up the same route, from Minffordd, below the mountain's southern flank. It's a glorious ascent, which bounds up rough stone steps for the first seven hundred feet, through an oak forest tucked into the banks of a peaty river that hurtles down the mountain in great gallops and falls. This brings you to the icy corrie lake of Llyn Cau beneath the eponymous *cadair*, the chair. Flustering badly, I'd left it too late leaving home, and the light was already fading by the time I reached the lake, with more than a thousand feet still to go. I'd passed the last of that day's walkers returning to their cars a while back. There was nobody left on the mountain, except me. I was overwhelmed by the realisation, looked around in vain for any token of human life and felt such a profound stab of loneliness that I struggled for breath. A sugary cup of tea from my thermos brought me back, but not that far. I lunged for my mobile phone, entertaining skittish thoughts that I could ring my pagan guru, with whom I'd talked about the plan, and draw warm words of balm and absolution from her. 'You don't have to go on, Mike. You've done very well,' was what I wanted to hear her saying. No chance. No signal. Without the amnesty I needed, I had to go on, and wearily began to climb the path up the side of the great chair.

Once you reach the top of the chair, it's a climactic spot and a brilliant view, but the mountain has a nasty sting in its tail still to come. From there to the summit, Pen-y-gadair, you have to descend a couple of hundred feet, painfully aware that what goes down will have to go up again, before the final six-hundred-foot ascent. On this section, there's no real path, for the top of Cadair Idris is a mass of loose boulders scattered in all directions, through which you must gingerly pick your own way. From the top of the chair I looked west to the sea and the thinning line of orange glow still left in the aftermath of sunset. Stars were glittering in the gaps between the clouds. I felt absolutely terrified of the last haul to come, scrambling up those unforgiving boulders in pitch darkness and a growing wind. The poor dog clung to my feet, as nervous and wretched as I was.

It was horrible. As we limped higher, the thought that I was stuck here for at least the next fourteen hours of darkness clamped my heart and sent spasms of panic through me. Finally, we hauled ourselves over the last few boulders to the summit. The full moon hung low to the east, casting silver shadows down the Mawddach estuary. A few pin-pricks of orange light – Barmouth and a corner of Dolgellau – only underlined how very far we were from anything comfortable, and how very long that was going to remain the case. Tears prickled my eyes, and not entirely due to the westerly wind whipping across the barren peak. And then my guts gave way.

I'd hoped that I could contain any need for a bowel evacuation until getting down off the mountain the next morning, but this three-second warning told me otherwise. Trousers ripped down, I squatted over a moonlit hollow in the ground and the world exploded out of my innards. At exactly the same moment, a stream of burning vomit rose up into my throat and shot like alien ectoplasm across the rocks in front of me. More followed, at both ends; much, much more. I clung to the rocks at my side and prayed that I wouldn't fall over, for it felt as if I'd never get up again if I did. For the first time, I began to ponder the possibility that the pointer on my own particular board game might land on something other than a golden lifetime of poetry.

After a minute or so of violent, simultaneous expulsion, I was wrung out and empty, cold and shaking. But a peace descended on me that I hadn't experienced all day. I was purged, of what I didn't know, but I felt light, giddy and strangely calm. I sprang up, trying to avoid treading in anything nasty, and looked at my surroundings anew as they shone in the moonlight. How different a landscape looks at night. The shadows are so much deeper, your perspective alters completely, sounds become magnified, distances shrunk and views distorted. I was suddenly awestruck to be there, and charged around with the dog, clapping and whooping in joy. The noise whipped away into the black.

There's a tiny stone bothy on Cadair's summit, to shelter its many bedraggled visitors, and I was keen to get in there, light a few candles, have some food and a whisky and try to sleep a while. By now, the wind was bellowing and the silver-tinged clouds stormed by just overhead. Occasional downpours crashed out of nowhere, swirling around in all directions so that it even rained upwards. Never has a stone hut looked so cosy. In *The Wild Places*, Robert Macfarlane stumbles across a walkers' bothy in the far north-west of Scotland, an area that makes Cadair Idris look as remote as Widnes. It is deep winter, a storm is raging outside, and the bothy contains candles and a stacked pile of dried peat next to a well-used fireplace. Macfarlane lights the fire, and settles down to read the notes about the place that have been left on the mantelpiece. The storm continues to howl and rattle outside. So far, so lovely. And then, just as the thin winter light starts to die out for the night, what does he do? He decides to forsake a dreamy doze by a peat fire for the joys of slogging back two miles to the beach, wading through a swollen, freezing river, with the storm still blowing, in gathering darkness. And all because he fancied sleeping in a sand dune. I was destined never to be Robert Macfarlane, and if clinging too closely to the maps and their rules had stopped that, then that was fine by me. He is quite, quite brilliant at what he does, but thank God he does it so that the rest of us don't have to. I bet he's never simultaneously puked and shat himself in sheer terror on top of a mountain. And if he has, I hope his congregation of totem animals made it out of the way in time.

So, the question remains, can you be too much of a map addict? I'd say so. Getting lost occasionally is essential for the soul, but we mappies are not very good at it. To us, being lost is synonymous with failure, not adventure. Being unable to give a precise grid reference for our location at any point in time makes us prone to panic, with all of the unpleasant side effects – not least to those around us – that that suggests. It's only in recent years that I've begun to go anywhere without a map. Occasionally, I forget to take one and then experience that hot spasm of horror when I remember, the kind that normal people only feel on realising that they've lost their wallet. Sometimes, I force myself not to take a map with me on a walk or a journey, an experience that can be anything from liberating to terrifying.

When I moved to where I now live seven years ago, I tried to wean myself off taking the Explorer map out on every single local walk, figuring that it would sometimes be better just to walk with no real sense of where or why, to create a mental map of my *milltir sgwar* (square mile) that wasn't just a replica of the Ordnance Survey version. It worked: having spent decades combing Wales, England, Ireland and Scotland like a hyperactive toddler, an armful of maps careering me up hills, through woods, into remote country churches and along lanes deserted except for a few wheel-snapping sheepdogs, suddenly I wanted to stop and dig down instead, to find roots where there had only previously been the tiniest of tendrils. Instead of the big views and guide-book sights, it was time to get intimate with individual rocks, trees, ferns, pools, mosses, streams: to be intoxicated by the anticipation of where the snowdrops, bluebells, wild garlic, hedgerow raspberries, whinberries and mushrooms would soon be sprouting; to trek to favourite swimming pools in the river at the end of a summer's day; to half dread, half thrill at the day in mid-November when the sun disappears behind the mountain, ushering in a three-month break of log fires and early nights. None of this needed a map; in fact, it actively needed *not* to be accompanied by frantic map-checking. Of course, on the occasions when I did spend a happy few hours, or even a full day, roaming the hills, rivers and forests of my neighbourhood without a map, almost the first thing I'd do on coming home was gallop to the map shelves in my den and painstakingly retrace my tracks across the contours.

While I can now just about comb my local patch without the map, the idea of doing it in an area I don't know very well remains terrifying. I've managed it occasionally, and always feel clammily proud of the achievement, but it doesn't feel right; indeed, it feels as if I am denying myself one of the main joys of walking in the first place, namely to compare the route on the map with the reality around me. I like to stop at the high points, check the map and see the names of the peaks, lakes and villages spread out below. And as for the idea of a map-free road journey, that was blown out of the water by a recent trip down to Cardiff, when an accident had closed the main road, and I was forced, without so much as a garage road atlas for company, into a bewildering knot of Breconshire lanes that took over an hour to extricate myself from, not helped by the fact that years of over-reliance on maps have dulled any innate sense of direction.

The psychology of collecting has spawned much recent study. Some focuses on the passion involved, some the harmless enjoyment, but rather more chooses to tar avid collectors with obsessive, compulsive, even neurotic and fetishistic tendencies, of making up for empty childhoods and fighting off existential meaningless. Such analyses pinpoint the thrill of the hunt as the driving motivation in collecting anything, and talk of the rapid falling-off of pleasure once the rare collectible has finally been snared.

This was very much the conclusion of Werner Muensterberger, German psychoanalyst and ethnographer, author of *Collecting: An Unruly Passion*. He compares obsessive collecting with gambling addiction, and states that it is just as destructive to one's health, finances, personal relationships, work, responsibilities and sense of self as extreme gambling, or any other more louche addiction. In *The Island of Lost Maps*, a highly entertaining examination of the strange career of American map thief Gilbert Bland, author Miles Harvey goes to visit Muensterberger to probe him on the psychology of the cartomaniac. The veteran psychoanalyst declares that map addicts he has encountered all tended to have fragmented childhoods in some way; that either their parents had split up, they'd moved house a great deal, or both. Harvey talks to another psychologist, Harriette Kaley, and she agrees: 'For each of us, our early life seems like the distant past, and in that sense it's like an ancient land – far off, foreign, and unknown. It occurred to me that it's not unlike the way fairy tales begin: "Once upon a time in a faraway place." And I think there must be something in map collecting that taps into that. In some sense, old maps reach back into a part of life that you can't quite grasp, and give you a sense of where you've come from. They give you a feeling of being rooted.'

Reading this startled me. Yes, my parents had split up when I was four years old, we had moved around a fair bit, largely due to the tectonic plates of family life shifting so massively in those early years, but could all this really be connected with my love of maps? I decided not, absolutely not; after all, Miles Harvey had been writing about a man addicted to pilfering antique maps from some of the great North American map libraries. I quite like antique maps, but I'm much more excited by comparatively modern ones, those that are far more topographically accurate. Being fond of Ordnance Survey maps hardly put me in the same category, surely. I re-read the interview with Muensterberger, where he talked of the collecting addiction (neurosis, fetish) and how, even in the most sober and upright of souls, it can lead to a skewed sense of right and wrong, as well as danger, meaning that theft can be so easily justified in the addicted brain. My mind floated back to those sessions in the far upstairs corner of the Midland Educational Bookshop in Worcester, when I'd go in, a teenager driven, to steal four or five OS maps at a time. It hadn't felt like stealing, though; I *deserved* those maps, they were rightfully mine. The techno thump of my heart-beat, the terror and the thrill, the sweat, the almost erotic charge of the heist, the flood of subsequent relief on a successful outcome all came roaring back to me. Who was I kidding? I was a textbook case.

The antique-map proviso doesn't wash either. In fact, it's far easier to see that someone is hankering back to a past that's only just out of reach, before the ruptures of family life tore the sanctuary apart, by obsessing over maps from their childhood, than it is to see the same drive in lusting after maps that are centuries old. I look at an OS map of 1960s Worcestershire, the kind you could find in a car-boot sale for fifty pence, and it can almost make me cry, so poignant and innocent does it look. I admire a 1610 John Speed original of my home county, which could go for a four-figure sum at auction, and nothing much stirs, save for a quiet admiration of the mellow valleys and tiny towns. I'd have the OS sheet every time.

I thought of my unswerving *Desert Island Discs* choices: the two gazetteers of Britain from the time I was born, and my overwhelmingly sentimental attachment to them, and the country they portray. I recalled a conversation with OS map dealer David Archer, who told me that by far the most avidly collected of all the series that he sells is the one-inch Seventh Series, the last of what had been the OS's flagship collection since its inception in the eighteenth century, and the one that was finally wiped out in 1974 by metrication. Not only were his sales reflecting a nostalgia for the final hurrah of the Imperial OS, they were boosted by the simple fact that most map collectors are blokes in their fifties and sixties, and that those were the first maps they fell in love with as boys. David told me that there is a 5–10-year delay in his business, that when any new map series emerges, the cartophilic collectors shun and slag them off for the first few years, before even-tually taking to them only when they become sufficiently long in the tooth to have gained a certain dust-covered antiquity. I remembered my favourite map museum, in the Romanian capital Bucharest, a bequest to the nation of his personal collection by former prime minister Adrian Nastase. Knowing nothing about him when I went there, I imagined him to be a warm, cultured man with a philanthropic bent. I soon discovered that his career had gone from Ceausescu lickspittle (when he authored a book called *Human Rights – A Retrogade Concept*) to a thin veneer of democracy that had covered allegations of electoral fraud, corruption and nepotism, all garnished with an addiction to boar-hunting that, in January 2005, saw him shoot and kill twenty-three on one trip. Staying in Bucharest, Ceausescu's love of cartography is evident in the stylised maps of his monster palace scribed on its floor tiles. Quite honestly, we're nuts.

Nastase's collection points to another danger area for the map addict: the cold certainty that the map market, particularly in antiques, has gone the same way as vintage cars, period properties and art, namely rife with brash one-upmanship from people who are only collecting as either an investment or a status symbol. The antique-map market has been helped in that regard by the fact that it is zero-rated for VAT, so provides an even more attractive proposition for the greedy and acquisitive. These *nouveau mappies* are hated by real enthusiasts, who have watched prices soar out of their range as a whole load of parvenus, who wouldn't know their Ogilby from their Oxfordshire, have brazened their way into the auction rooms and specialist dealerships. Nuts, and raging snobs to boot: it's a winning combination.

Nearly twenty years of writing guide books has left me thoroughly disabused as to their value. As a writer, you love to imagine that your words are carefully weighed by readers of impeccable discernment, and that if they have a bone to pick, it will be a fine piece of constructive criticism from which everyone will emerge smiling. Writing guide books, stuck in a rigid formula, soon rids you of that fanciful notion. The vast majority of their readers couldn't give a toss who has written the words that are steering them mechanically around their holiday destination. They'll never write to say if they enjoyed the book, but they sure as hell will put pen to paper (or digit to keyboard) to moan like stuck pigs if the meal you mentioned wasn't on the menu any longer, if the hotel was more expensive than you'd said, if the museum wasn't actually open on a Monday or if the pub you'd loved had overcharged them twenty pence for two halves of Double Dragon shandy. Someone once wrote me a letter of complaint about a farmhouse B&B I'd heartily recommended in the *Rough Guide to Wales*, because they were served a fried egg with a hard yolk for their breakfast, and what was I going to do about it?

When, in 2008, a media row erupted after erstwhile Lonely Planet author Thomas Kohnstamm revealed that he had made up whole accounts in his contributions to various South American guides, most of us who had ever seen our work published in a guide book breathed a small sigh of relief that the secret was finally out, and that it wasn't us that had got nobbled in the process (although secretly, we were ragingly jealous of just how much coverage he'd levered out of his confession). Even if the author of your guide book is the most scrupulous fact-checker, who trots obediently around every recommended B&B and bounces up and down on each and every one of their bedsprings, the text will still be riddled with inaccuracies, supposition and personal prejudice. If you've got a week to cover twenty towns, fourteen castles, eighty-three hotels, eighteen campsites, ninety eateries plus an assortment of museums, views, beaches, country parks, bus stations, walks, internet cafés, bookshops, craft shops, tourist railways and bars, then somewhere is going to get a bum deal: perhaps the place where it was raining when you arrived or which was closed for essential maintenance, where someone was less than enthusiastic to see you or where you stepped in some dog shit and then hit your head on the way in. By the time you're repeating the process on your sixth or eighth week, it's all starting to blur.

Writing guide books for a living was most definitely an extension of my map addiction. The dogmatic certainties of a map are writ large in the ethos of a guide book, especially the breed (Lonely Planet, the Rough Guides, Footprint, Bradt and so on) that like to think they cover every aspect of your trip: they get you there, get you around, find you places to stay, eat and get drunk, tell you what to order and how to pronounce it (though you'll still just jab at the menu and say everything slowly in English), steer you clear of places that they've decided to write off, give you just enough history and cultural context to look smug in a museum and unerringly point you towards all the places where you'll meet people *just like you*. Plus maps. What's not to love?

Plenty is the answer. Guide books are tyrannous in the wrong hands, and by the wrong hands, I mean any that cling to them like a shipwreck survivor to a raft. Sit in any café or bar in some tourist hotspot and just watch your fellow imbibers poring joylessly over their guide books, always looking for the next hit as decreed by the gods of LP or RG. The guide is yet another screen, a buffer between you and place you're supposed to be experiencing. I was sick of them.

So it was that when my boyfriend and I recently InterRailed from Paris to Montenegro and thence into Albania and Corfu, snaking our way through northern and then Eastern Europe, I wanted to do it without a guide book. At first, it felt like diving without oxygen: what brilliant places were passing us by, spectacular sights, fabulous hostels and warm bars full of cheery fellow travellers and clinking glasses? Gradually, though, we learned to trust our instincts instead. It's not difficult. Place full equals probably good, place empty save for a surly waiter or two, probably not. We shopped around, asked local people for personal recommendations, which were invariably informed and bang up to date, rather than three years old and written by a misanthropic shag monster on his gap year (or worse – and far more likely in those guides founded in youthful 1980s rebellion, but which have become the very establishment they set out to scorch – by a misanthropic middle-aged grump, bitterly past it as a shag monster, and who's more likely to be found slumped in his hotel in front of CNN than checking out the coolest bars in town, which, in any case, give him a headache and a vague dose of existential angst these days).

The guide-book-free trip was a liberation. Not only was my rucksack unencumbered with a weighty paper brick, neither was my head. Seeing fellow travellers clambering aboard the train clutching their Lonely Planet as if it were a set of rosary beads had me chuckling into my chest with glee. Every new place was a blank canvas, rather than a paint-by-numbers portrait of venues that had had to make little effort since being so heartily recommended in every guide book for the past few years, decades in some cases. We even ended up in towns and cities that barely scraped any mention in the guides, and they were some of the best of all.

Almost true. I did cave in as the InterRailing part of our trip came to a close in Montenegro. We were planning on spending at least a week there, get a car and get off the beaten track a little. I was also keen to read up on the history and politics of Europe's newest independent nation-state (unless you count Kosovo, which I'm not sure that I do yet), so I hunted around a couple of the very fine bookshops of Belgrade for an English-language guide to Montenegro. There was a grand choice of one, the Bradt guide, so I bought it. Of course, there are upsides to guide books, and this one reminded me of that. If there's a strong authorial voice, and it's a voice that you largely agree with, it is like travelling with a knowledgeable and enthusiastic friend. The *Bradt Guide to Montenegro* didn't quite fall into that category, but we did come to love its author, a motherly character who'd spent twenty-five years travelling the world as a diplomat's wife, before settling back into life in London where, according to her biography, 'she turned her hand to journalism, writing in a freelance capacity for magazines about travel and food'. Her utterances on this little country perfectly accorded with such a background, filtered as they were through a very British, slightly colonial sensibility where everything could be sorted out with a stiff gin. She did help lead us to a few lovely spots, but far more than that, she gave us a many a good belly laugh.

Travelling without a guide book is one thing; travelling without a map – well, that's just a step too far. That's diving without oxygen, legs strapped together and blindfold. But I did my best to rein myself in. If I go for a night in, say, Snowdonia, all of an hour away, I'll generally take the entire oeuvre of OS maps that cover every inch of the way between here and there, and in both medium and large scale. That's despite having lived in this area for a decade and knowing my way around pretty well. For a European journey that eventually took in sixteen countries in nearly six weeks, it was patently impossible to cover all bases, especially when everything had to be carried on my back, so I had to content myself with the legendary *Thomas Cook Rail Map of Europe* (consulted almost hourly), augmented by detailed maps that I picked up along the way of places where we were spending a bit of time and wanted to mooch around. It was just about enough for my extreme needs.

There's no guide book that could have prepared me for the shock of coming home. We'd only been able to get a flight that bundled us into Gatwick at sometime after midnight, so that it took four times as long, at four times the cost, to travel the last two hundred and fifty miles as it had done the previous twelve hundred. Trying to get across Britain on public transport in the dead of night is a dispiriting experience, especially when it conspires to dump you, hollow-eyed and sleepless, in the middle of the Birmingham morning rush hour.

The rot had already begun to set in when we disembarked from the boat that had brought us over from Sarande to Corfu. Albania and Greece are just ten miles apart at this point: it must have been agony for the Albanians, under the despotic regime of Enver Hoxha, to be within touching distance of a world that was physically, culturally and economically fenced off. Still is, to a large extent: travel is chronically difficult and prohibitively expensive on an Albanian passport, private boats are few and the hatred towards Albanians in neighbouring countries – and beyond – is staggering. For us, though, it was easy. Just a quick hop across the bay and, after a month of the rawness and brawn of Eastern Europe, we found ourselves somewhere that was so comfortably padded and primed to our Anglo-American sensibilities. Stopping just long enough to buy that day's copy of *The Times*, we ran straight into a bar for mojitos and club sandwiches to celebrate, but it was a curiously bittersweet celebration. For the first time in weeks, we could hear all around us accents from Glasgow, Manchester and London. After a month of listening to voices brimful of spark and enthusiasm, eager to chew over world politics or history, to swap cultural insights and ribald jokes, the British voices grated. They were whining and moaning, threatening and complaining, shouting drunkenly from bars or boorishly from the windows of speeding hire cars and mopeds. So were the ones in the newspaper. It felt like we'd been listening to adults for weeks, and now suddenly we'd been dropped into a vat of whinging toddlers in the big pool of coloured balls at the Ikea crèche.

Trekking across Britain on public transport two days later, the sensation only deepened. Having travelled through so many other European countries, the level of public infantilisation here was truly shocking, and the causes so horribly obvious. Nagging announcements and nagging signs everywhere: one in Birmingham New Street was even addressed to 'Parents or Guardians of Children with Balloons', warning them not to let said balloons drift up into the station ceiling, alongside the usual finger-wagging riot of no eating, drinking, smoking, music, access, littering, loitering, ball games, suspicious packages, funny looks, swearing at staff, touching this or that, using mobile phones, wearing bike helmets, leaving baggage unattended, running, jumping, dive-bombing or heavy petting. Barely a minute went by, both on the platforms and the trains, without a robotic tannoy announcement, often telling us nothing more than to remember to listen to the announcements. Everyone looked hypnotised. It was the only way to cope with the white noise.

Despite the constant backdrop of whining and hectoring, Britain looked quite wonderful that night. A coach from Gatwick landed us in Oxford at 3.00 a.m. First train anywhere useful was the 6.30 to Birmingham, so we searched for a hedge in which to stash our backpacks before wandering into the city. Thankfully, we remembered just in time that we were back in Britain, thus needing a hedge out of sight of a CCTV camera, lest we return to find our bags detonated in a controlled explosion, half of Oxford closed off and the Sky Newscopter hovering eagerly overhead. It was early June, the birds chirruped excitedly at the prospect of sunrise, students in dicky bows and ball gowns reeled out of various clubs or lay shouting and prone on the pavement ('Facking hell, Toby, I'm sooooo faaaacking pissed'). We slid past our leaders of tomorrow entirely unnoticed, as did the watchful few black and brown faces making their way back from working in late-night burger bars or on their way to clean offices and streets. Everyone was having their own bespoke nocturnal experience of the dreaming spires.

Through Carfax, the sky was brightening into dawn over Broad Street, touching the immortal gables and chimneys of Balliol and Trinity. I ambled over to a large tourist map of the city centre and drank in its ancient shapes and names, a silent roll-call of the famous and the infamous who had padded these streets before us. It was so English, a familiar map of a familiar place, and my heart ached with gratitude that this hotch-potch of history and hysteria was my country, this was where I called home, and that it looked so wonderful. My boyfriend, who'd spent his only year of living outside Wales lodging in Oxford a decade earlier, gave me a whirlwind tour of hand-picked sights, interspersing them with half-remembered parties, favourite coffee shops or pubs and old friends. By now, most of the carousing students had either copped off or passed out; there was barely anyone else around. To stroll about the honeyed streets and cloak-and-dagger alleys of Oxford at sunrise on a fine midsummer morning, before the tourniquet of traffic chokes it to near death, is the purest of ecstasies. We had the Radcliffe Camera to ourselves, walked undisturbed down the middle of the High Street, St Giles' and St Aldate's and could see not one punter to please in Magpie, née Gropecunt, Lane.

We ambled back towards the station through the bright, silent streets of Jericho, and then along the misty banks of the Oxford Canal. Herons eyed us warily as we passed the dozens of houseboats decorated with flowers and mail boxes, bicycles and coal scuttles. Of course, all this is threatened by developers, but I couldn't bear to think about that just then. It was too magical to contemplate anything other than that moment in time, the lazy splash of a few early birds, the barges slumbering in their vapours and the bright new leaves on the willows, ashes and oaks leaning towards the water.

A couple of hours later, we surfaced again like moles in the middle of Birmingham. Yes, we'd been nagged and grumped at to get there, and yes, there was a distinctly haunted look to the thousands of people pouring in and out of New Street station, but it still looked amazing to my bloodshot eyes. The pavements crackled with an efficient energy that blazed all those people, cars, buses, trains and goods every day through this seething mass of all kinds of everyone. My biggest fear about being a map addict is that it's a one-way ticket to becoming the worst kind of Little Englander, for too many of my fellows seem to have gone that way. To them, the Birmingham rush hour must be a vision of hell itself, the million shades of skin, the hollow-eyed waifs, the punks, poofs and junkies, the leisure wear, the jewellery, the noise, the sheer bloody chaos, the youthful arrogance of it all. But I loved it, and miss it terribly. There was a surge of something in those pavements that I hadn't felt for months. It was the surge, the spark of diversity, our historic defining feature and single biggest asset as a country – and the one that we are most in danger of trying to abandon.

On our trip, it had become increasingly obvious that there were some dreadful levels of racism in the newly splintered Eastern Europe, parts of which are galloping into monocultural paranoia. We barely saw a non-white face between leaving Berlin and docking in Corfu, ten countries later. And, although I'd far rather deal with naked, naive prejudice than the slippery circumlocution of the Western mainstream, some of the stuff we heard made my eyes water. I'd struck up a conversation with the lady who ran the tourist office in an idyllic Slovakian mountain village. She, like very many people we met, was nostalgic for the Communist times, and mourned the demise of Czechoslovakia, just as people we'd met had mourned the collapse of Yugoslavia and even East Germany. During the Czechoslovakia days, she'd been an eminent scientist and had travelled the world to attend conferences, something that doubtless was a great deal more fulfilling, and lucrative, than dealing with a few uppity German and Polish tourists. I asked her where she'd been. 'Oh, America, a few times, the Far East, all over Europe, Australia once.' 'Never Africa?' I asked. She wrinkled her nose. 'No. I never go to Africa. I not like black people.' I spluttered, but she ploughed on. 'Black people no good. They smell like WC.' I tried to picture some poor black German, Italian or Brit pitching up in her tourist office, asking where to stay, and felt faintly sick. The next day, we got the train out of the town in the valley below. On the platform was a plaque, written in Slovakian and English:

> *On this site stood the railway station*
> *From which, on March 25th, 1942,*
> *The first transport left for the Auschwitz Death camp,*
> *Carrying a thousand Slovak Jewish girls.*
> *To honour generations past,*
> *To remind generations to come.*
> 2002

Standing outside Birmingham New Street station, soaking in the fizz of the rush hour, my eyes were drawn to a wall-mounted city-centre bus map. It looked so soothingly familiar: names and shapes that had played their part in every stage of my life. Then I started to notice that there was also much on it that made me feel like a complete stranger. Since leaving Brum only eight years earlier, whole streets had disappeared or been re-routed, new ones had sprung up. Walkways, bus stops, shopping centres and open spaces were not the ones that I'd known. The new Bullring is the major culprit, and I get lost within it every time I go there, unable to stop recalling the landmarks that it has so thoroughly supplanted in the city's latest wholesale sweep-out of its centre. For that's Birmingham, a perpetual skyline of cranes and scaffolding, the restless cycle of constant reinvention, of knocking it all down and building it up again: repeat until the end of time.

There was one more map, and one more journey, to get us home. We slunk out of the motley hubbub of Birmingham city centre and on to the little train that bumps its way every couple of hours out west to the Welsh coast. I gazed affectionately at the earthy names on the Arriva Trains Wales network map on the carriage's wall: the full-throated song of Llwyngwril, Ystrad Mynach, Dyffryn Ardudwy, Llanwrda, each the cause in England of equal parts terror and haughty condescension ('It sounds like spitting, and there's *no vowels*'). The map's sleek and straight lines attempted to ape the smooth functionality of Harry Beck's tube map, but Llandanwg is no Ladbroke Grove. It might work stylistically, but it conjures up all the wrong associations: vitality and velocity, rather than the more glorious truth of single tracks unhurriedly snaking through mountain passes, stone villages, impossibly green fields and above wind-battered beaches.

One of the reasons that I'd wanted to do the trip we were just finishing was to look at these newly independent countries of Eastern Europe through Welsh eyes. Although every fibre of my physical body is rooted in the English Midlands, and that won't – can't – ever change, nearly a decade since moving from there, I have found myself thinking more and more as a Welshman. It is a truly special culture, and one that I feel hugely privileged to have been given such access to. The trip was to test whether those commitments to diversity and to Wales – Welsh-speaking Wales in particular – were compatible. They are. *Cymru Cymraeg*, Welsh-speaking Wales, is one of the most unexpectedly diverse and quietly tolerant societies I've ever encountered. Not in that bullet-point, tick-box fashion so beloved of New Labour's New Britain, but in ways that are rooted deep in rock and soul, the ways that matter.

I've often been accused of staking a chameleon claim to come from anywhere and everywhere. There's considerable truth in the charge: I've written and broadcast of my sense of home in Birmingham, in the Black Country, in Kidderminster, in wider Worcestershire, in the reviled Hereford and Worcester, in London and throughout Wales. I feel of them all, yet none of them, and I'm sure that part of that comes from my love of maps. My great heroine, Jan Morris, speaks of her taking ownership of a place by writing a book about it. For me, my map collection gives me that same sense of belonging to as many places as I can handle. Of course, a life of such gadfly inconstancy will never root me as deeply as those who can trace their lineage back hundreds of years in one parish and who stay put for their duration; as the product of nomadic families, I'd come to terms with that long ago. I'll never, for instance, quite get that intense rivalry that pitches village against village, valley against valley, city against city, country against country – the ubiquitous human need to define ourselves by constant comparison, and competition, with our nearest neighbours.

For now, though, my perspective felt ever more Welsh as we clattered through the countryside among growing hills and gloomier crags. The view was right up there with all the train journeys of the previous six weeks, as good as anything the Transylvanian Alps, the Slovakian

Tatra mountains or the valleys of the Rhine and Danube had thrown our way. Lambs and calves bobbed around the fields, arthritic hawthorns frothed with blossom, sessile oaks were budding on the banks of rushing streams, beech trees shimmered in a haze of luminous lime green. My nose pressed to the window, I think I was beginning to dribble when my boyfriend snapped me out of my distraction by asking, 'So, how many countries did we do, then?' Well, that depends. Could we include Bosnia-Herzegovina, despite seeing only a few miles of it from the train window as we creaked our way from Serbia to Montenegro? Yes, we decided we could. And were we counting England and Wales as separate countries? Oh, yes.

It is perfectly possible to love both England and Wales, Scotland too, and yet, on balance, want to see the end of the British nation-state. Too often, the enthusiasm for separation in any of the countries is presented only in oppositional terms, of provoking a fight with the neighbours where there is no need of one. Our trip had shown that separation is difficult and fraught, but that it can also be hugely rewarding and liberating. It had also shown me that countries with far, far fewer substantive and historic advantages than Wales, England or Scotland were firmly on their own journey, and that the inherent distinctiveness of our three countries was considerably greater than in many places now separated by international borders. Just as people should not be imprisoned unnecessarily, neither should natural nations. And since leaving Gatwick hours earlier, we had most definitely crossed two different nations. I adore them both, will collect maps of them both until the day I drop and will use those maps to explore as many corners of them as I can.

I pledge also to leave the maps behind more often. After eighteen months of travelling, researching and writing this book, I dreamed last night that I was physically stuck in a map. It was a very beautiful map: a large, coloured street plan of Georgian London, full of grand streets named in hand-carved fonts. There was no other life in there except for me, and I thrashed and flailed my way through the empty streets searching for the way out, while simultaneously loving the unique tour that only I was party to. My last memory in the dream was admiring some tiny, hand-painted trees in the middle of Hanover Square, before waking up, slightly smothered under the duvet and gasping for air.

It's definitely time to go off-map for a while.

BIBLIOGRAPHY

Peter Ackroyd, *Albion: The Origins of the English Imagination*, Nan A. Talese, 2003

— *London: The Biography*, Anchor, 2003

— *Thames: Sacred River*, Chatto, Bodley Head & Cape, 2007

'Aleph' (William Harvey), *Geographical Fun: being humourous outlines of various countries*, Hodder & Stoughton, 1869

Gabriel Alington and Gabriel Hogg, *The Hereford Mappa Mundi*, Gracewing, 1996

John Ayto and Ian Crofton, *Brewer's Britain and Ireland: The History, Culture, Folklore and Etymology of 7500 Places in These Islands*, Weidenfeld & Nicolson, 2006

Geoffrey Spink Bagley, *A Pictorial Guide to Romney Marsh*, Rye Museum Association, 1986

Peter Barber (ed.), *The Map Book*, Weidenfeld & Nicolson, 2005

Ashley Baynton-Williams, *Town and City Maps of the British Isles 1800–1855*, Dolphin Publications, 1993

Rex Beddis, *A New Geography of Britain*, Oxford University Press, 1985

Terence Bendixson and John Platt, *Milton Keynes: Image and Reality*, Granta Editions, 1991

Lynne Bevan (ed.), *Indecent Exposure: Sexuality, Society and the Archaeological Record*, Cruithne Press, 2001

Jeremy Black, *Maps and Politics*, Reaktion Books, 2000

Jorge Luis Borges, 'On Exactitude in Science', *The Aleph*, Penguin, 2004

David Brandon, *Rutland & Stamford Curiosities*, Dovecote Press, 2003

Peter Bridgewater, *An Eccentric Tour of Sussex*, Snake River Press, 2007

Lloyd A. Brown, *The Story of Maps*, Dover Publications, 1980

John Paddy Browne, *Map Cover Art*, Ordnance Survey, 1991

Bill Bryson, *Notes from a Small Island*, Harper Perennial, 2001

David Buisseret (ed.), *Monarchs, Ministers and Maps: Emergence of Cartography as a Tool of Government in Early Modern Europe*, University of Chicago Press, 1992

Lewis Carroll, *Sylvie and Bruno*, Bastian Books, 2008

Rodney Castleden, *The Cerne Giant*, Dorset Publishing Company, 1998

Julian Cope, *The Modern Antiquarian*, Thorsons, 1998

Merlin Coverley, *Psychogeography*, Pocket Essentials, 2007

Paul Devereux and Ian Thomson, *The Ley Guide*, Empress, 1988

Bill Drummond, *45*, Abacus, 2001

Tim Dunn, *Bekonscot: Historic Model Village*, Jarrold, 2004

Gwynfor Evans and Marian Delyth, *Cymru o Hud*, Y Lolfa, 2004

Fergus Fleming, *Barrow's Boys*, Granta Books, 2001

Brian Friel, *Translations*, Longman, 2000

Leslie Gardiner, *Bartholomew, 150 Years*, Bartholomew, 1976

Bamber Gascoigne, *Encyclopedia of Britain: The A–Z of Britain's Past and Present*, 1994

Nigel Gilbert, *A History of Kidderminster*, Phillimore & Co., 1994

Fay Godwin, *Our Forbidden Land*, Jonathan Cape, 1990

Russell Grant, *The Real Counties of Britain*, Virgin Books, 1996

J. B. Harley, *Ordnance Survey Maps: A Descriptive Manual*, Ordnance Survey, 1976

Katharine Harmon, *You Are Here: Personal Geographies and Other Maps of the Imagination*, Princeton Architectural Press, 2003

David Hart (ed.), *Border Country: Poems in Process*, Wood Wind Publications, 1991

Sarah Hartley, *Mrs P's Journey: The Remarkable Story of the Woman Who Created the A–Z Map*, Pocket Books, 2002

Miles Harvey, *The Island of Lost Maps: A True Story of Cartographic Crime*, Phoenix, 2002

Benedict le Vay, *Eccentric Britain*, Bradt Travel Guides, 2005

David N. Livingstone, *The Geographical Tradition*, Blackwell, 1992

C. B. Muriel Lock, *Modern Maps and Atlases: An Outline Guide to 20th Century Literature*, Clive Bingley, 1969

Robert Macfarlane, *The Wild Places*, Granta Books, 2008

Daniel P. Mannix, *The Hellfire Club*, ibooks Inc., 2001

Mark Monmonier, *From Squaw Tit to Whorehouse Meadow: How Maps Name, Claim and Inflame*, University of Chicago Press, 1997

— *How to Lie with Maps*, University of Chicago Press, 1991

Jan Morris, *Conundrum*, Faber & Faber, 2002

— *Trieste, and the Meaning of Nowhere*, Faber & Faber, 2002

— *Wales*, Oxford University Press, 1982

Thomas Moule, *The County Maps of Old England*, Dolphin, 1993

Werner Muensterberger, *Collecting: An Unruly Passion*, Princeton University Press, 1993

Agim Neza, *Welcome to Albania*, Ilar Publishing House, 2008

Geoff Nicholson, *Bleeding London*, Orion, 1999

Yolande O'Donoghue, *William Roy 1726–1790: Pioneer of the Ordnance Survey*, British Library Publishing Division, 1977

Richard Oliver, *Ordnance Survey Maps: A Concise Guide for Historians*, Charles Close Society for the Study of Ordnance Survey Maps, 2005

Tim Owen and Elaine Pilbeam, *Ordnance Survey: Map-makers to Britain Since 1791*, Ordnance Survey, 1992

Phyllis Pearsall, *From Bedsitter to Household Name: The Personal Story of A–Z Maps*, Geographers' A–Z Map Co., 1990

Allan and Barbara Pease, *Why Men Don't Listen & Women Can't Read Maps*, Broadway Books, 2001

Nigel Pennick, *Celtic Sacred Landscapes*, Thames & Hudson, 2000

Oliver Rackham, *The Illustrated History of the Countryside*, Weidenfeld & Nicolson, 2003

Arthur Ransome, *Swallows and Amazons*, Red Fox, 2001

Trevor Rowley, *The English Landscape in the Twentieth Century*, Hambledon Continuum, 2006

Major-General William Roy, *An Account of the Measurement of a Base on Hounslow Heath*, Royal Society, 1785

Lorna Sage, *Bad Blood*, HarperPerennial, 2007

Malcolm Saville, *The Gay Dolphin*, Girls Gone By, 2007

— *Wings Over Witchend*, John Goodchild Publishers, 1984

Iain Sinclair, *London Orbital*, Penguin, 2003

Will Self, *Psychogeography,* Bloomsbury, 2007

Mick Sharp, *The Way and the Light: Saints and Pilgrims in Celtic and Medieval Britain*, Aurum Press, 2000

J. T. Smith, *Topography and Domestic Architecture in Shrewsbury Down to 1700*, MA thesis, University of Birmingham, 1953

Rebecca Solnit, *A Field Guide to Getting Lost*, Penguin, 2006

John Speed, *The Counties of Britain: A Tudor Atlas*, Pavilion Books, 1995

— *Imperii Magnæ Britanniæ* ('Theatre of the Empire of Great Britain'), Jonathan Potter in association with Drayton Manor Publishing, 1991

John Steinbeck, *Travels with Charley: In Search of America*, Penguin, 2005

Danny Sullivan, *Ley Lines*, Green Magic, 2004

Homer Sykes, *Mysterious Britain*, Weidenfeld & Nicolson, 2001

Christopher Thacker, *History of Gardens*, University of California Press, 1992

Colm Tóibín, *Bad Blood: A Walk along the Irish Border*, Picador, 2001

Catherine Tuck, *Landscapes and Desire*, History Press, 2003

Alfred Wainwright, *Memoirs of a Fellwanderer*, Frances Lincoln, 2003

Bryan Waites, *Remember Rutland!*, Spiegl Press, 1984

Alfred Watkins, *The Old Straight Track*, Abacus, 1994

Simon Winchester, *The Map that Changed the World*, Penguin, 2002

WEBSITES

MAP LIBRARIES AND RESOURCES

www.bl.uk/reshelp/findhelprestype/maps/ – details of British Library map collections and online resources www.bodley.ox.ac.uk/guides/maps/linkfrme.htm – Bodleian Library (Oxford) Map Room, with a phenomenal international directory of map resources, libraries and specialist websites

www.cartography.org.uk – British Cartography Society

www.charlesclosesociety.org – website of Ordnance Survey's very own 'fan club'

www.david-archer-maps.co.uk/content/ – most comprehensive second-hand OS map seller on the internet

www.geograph.org.uk – fascinating project to photograph every one of the 331,000 kilometre grid squares on the OS network, plus a fair bit of discussion and diversion

www.llgc.org.uk/index.php?id=73 – National Library of Wales map collection

www.maphistory.info/ – huge resource site and links collection

ni.chol.as/media/sillytube.html *and* www.geofftech.co.uk – home of the daft tube maps and variations on the theme

www.nls.uk/maps/ – National Library of Scotland

www.openstreetmap.org/ – a Wiki map of the whole world, free to all

www.ordnancesurvey.co.uk/oswebsite/ – briskly authoritative, with the superb Get-a-Map feature which enables you to look at anywhere on the latest OS at either 1:50 000 or 1:25 000

www.rgs.org/HomePage.htm – Royal Geographical Society

www.sasi.group.shef.ac.uk/worldmapper/index.html – wide variety of facts and figures interpreted through morphed world maps

www.secret-bases.co.uk – gateway for Alan Turnbull's astonishing collection of information about military and government sites that were kept from the maps until satellite technology made such rulings redundant

www.topsoc.org – London Topographical Society, a great jumping-off point for historical mapping of the capital

wheresthepath.googlepages.com – split screen and full interactivity gives you the chance to compare like for like, with OS map on one side, the landscape as captured by Google Earth on the other

BLOGS AND DISCUSSION

cartophilia.com/blog/ – great blog, newsy and always thoughtful

www.cartotalk.com – mainly American mapping, but useful and interesting

www.cbrd.co.uk – site of CBRD (Chris's British Road Directory); astonishing stuff about, well, UK roads

www.gearthblog.com – the very latest Google Earth and Street View

googlesightseeing.com – blogs, posts and trivia about Google Earth

mapscroll.blogspot.com – feisty new map blog

www.mcwetboy.net/maproom/ – one of the finest map blogs on the internet, and a good hopping-off point to others; updates daily

www.sabre-roads.org.uk – comprehensive directory and information about UK roads, including lively forums

strangemaps.wordpress.com – the Strange Maps blog is every cartophile's favourite; maps showing all manner of historical, cultural and social patterns are paraded, and written about with wit and knowledge

PICTURE CREDITS

All images by Mike Parker except the following pages: 10, The Estate of Malcolm Saville; 35, *The AA Illustrated Road Book of England and Wales*; 42, National Portrait Gallery; 59, Pete Reed; 74, The Ordnance Survey; 117, John Paddy Browne, *Map Cover Art*; 130, WikiCommons (http://en.wikipedia.org/wiki/File:Baarle-Nassau_fronti%C3%A8re_caf% C3%A9.jpg); 138, Heiko Burkhardt; 148, National Library of Scotland; 151, The Ordnance Survey; 166, Kyle Fletcher; 174, Mercator Projection Map © Collins Bartholomew Ltd. 2009; 174, Oxford Cartographers; 200, Hereford Cathedral; 207, British Library; 235, *Times Comprehensive Atlas of the World*, 12th edition (www.timesatlas.com); 239, Nick Baker and Richard Holt, *Indecent Exposure: Sexuality, Society and the Archaeological Record*; 250, Mapsofpa.com; 276, Wales News Service.

Plate section credits: 1, extract from *Bartholemew Half Inch Map Series, Sheet 50, Arisaig and Lochaber*, 1972; 4, Nancy Chandler's Map of Bangkok (www.nancychandler.net); 7, GeoMap (top) © GeoEye satellite image, London Underground map (bottom) © TfL from the London Transport Museum collection; 8, extract from *Institut Géographique National 1/25 000: 0821 OT* (bottom) © IGN 2010. **Ordnance Survey maps:** 2, extracts from *One-inch Map of Great Britain, Sheet 168, Winchester*, 1959 (top), *OS Landranger 1:50 000, Sheet 185, Winchester and Basingstoke*, 2005 (bottom) 3, extracts from *OS Landranger 1:50 000, Sheet 151, Stratford-upon-Avon*, 1979 (top) and 2008 (bottom); 5, front cover of *Ordnance Survey "One-inch" Map of the Chilterns*; 6, front covers of *Ordnance Survey Tourist Map of the Lake District* (foreground), *Ordnance Survey Tourist Map of Loch Lomond and the Trossachs* (background); 8, extract from *OS Explorer Map, Sheet 23, Cadair Idris and Llyn Tegid*, 2008. All reproduced by permission of Ordnance Survey on behalf of HMSO © crown copyright.

ACKNOWLEDGEMENTS

Map Addict has been a long time in the making. Thanks to my family for the initial indulgence and inspiration, especially my late grandparents, Dick and Nancy Theakston, and my mum, Jane Parker; also my dad and stepmum, David and Anne, fellow Parker Up Club members Sue and Andy, plus Helen, Julia, Alison and Grant.

So many people have shared with me their enthusiasm for maps and the places they portray: a by-no-means exhaustive list includes Chris Fleet and Laragh Quinney at the National Library of Scotland in Edinburgh, Dr Yolande Hodson, Richard Oliver, Ashley Sims, Fran Loots, Nancy and Nima Chandler, Bryn Jones, Paula Good, the staff of Ordnance Survey, Terry Jones, Alan Ereira, Ali Kedge, Dr Hilary L. Turner, Sam Taylor, Gary Delaney, Jim Coe, Jenny McLellan at the Milton Keynes City Discovery Centre, David Archer, Jan Morris, Paul Woodland, Lou Hart, Linda Brown, Julieann Heskin, Caz Ward, John Hefin, Bruce at the Rutland Museum in Oakham, Russell Grant, Helen Williams-Ellis, Jon Woolcott, Gordon and Vicky Peters, Alan Parkinson, Scott Willison, Julie Schofield, Dr Laura Vaughan, Audrey Christie, Matthew Gidley, Anne-Marie Carty, Dafydd Prys, François Turlure, Rev. John Davies, Tim Dunn, Jim Perrin, Rodney Leary, David Bannister, Pete Telfer, Swsi Kemp, Helen Sandler, Jane Hoy, Noel Dunne, Nick Fenwick, Ifor ap Glyn, Damian Walford Davies, Emyr Jenkins, Paul Whitfield, Tristan Hughes, Susan Blakiston at Anelog, and members of both the Glantwymyn Women's Institute and the Cernunnos Pagan Bikers' Group! Many thanks to my agent, Rebecca Winfield, who knuckledusted me and the script into submission, to editor Denise Bates and all of those at Collins, especially their cartographic crew in Glasgow – Mick Ashworth, David Jamieson, Jethro Lennox, David Mumford and Roger Pountain.

Huge appreciation to Yr Academi Gymreig, the Welsh Academy, for their bursary award that helped buy some time to travel and write this book.

Sôn arbennig i Preds: diolch, cariad, am bopeth.

Mike Parker's career path has been a scenic B-road rather than a speedy motorway: spells as a stand-up comedian, tour guide, TV travelogue presenter, columnist and guide book author have all depended on his lifelong love of maps and acute sense of place. Much as he enjoys travelling abroad, Mike passionately believes that British maps are the best in the world, and that the landscape they portray is right up there too.

mapaddict@btinternet.com

INDEX